REALTY CHECK

Real Estate Secrets
for First-Time Canadian Home Buyers

D1073285

REALTY CHECK

Real Estate Secrets
for First-Time Canadian Home Buyers

Sandra Rinomato

WILEY
John Wiley & Sons Canada, Ltd.

Library and Archives Canada Cataloguing in Publication

Rinomato, Sandra
    Realty check : the real scoop on real estate for first-time Canadian home buyers / Sandra Rinomato.

ISBN 978-0-470-15760-2

    1. House buying--Canada. I. Title.
HD1379.R53 2008   643'.120971   C2008-905704-X

Production Credits
Cover design: Ian Koo
Interior text design: Adrian So
Typesetter: Pat Loi
Printer: Friesens

John Wiley & Sons Canada, Ltd.
6045 Freemont Blvd.
Mississauga, Ontario
L5R 4J3

Printed in Canada

1 2 3 4 5 FP 12 11 10 09 08

Table of Contents

EPISODE 7: Big, Bad Realtor ··· 135

In which Sandra takes the once-bitten, twice-shy Jill and Henry beyond their suspicions and fears about realtors—and walks them right through the front door of their new townhouse

EPISODE 8: "You Like It? I Own It" ··· 157

In which Sandra and Mr. Daniels shine a light on the shady dealings of mortgage fraudsters

EPISODE 9: A Time To Sell ··· 173

In which Katie and Bill look beyond "fluffing" and start seeing the flesh and bones of what's for sale, and in which Sandra shows readers how to sell that house when the time comes

Preface

To buy or not to buy? That is *not* the question! Of course you should buy. But what, when, where, why and how? Those are the important questions that you need to ask yourself, and they are the same ones I've set out to answer in this book.

As host of HGTV's popular *Property Virgins*, and as an experienced realtor who specializes in dealing with first-time homebuyers, I'm here to guide you through the complicated process of buying your first home. From the moment you begin your search until you cross the threshold of your newly purchased house, I'll be there with you.

I'll share my first-hand insights and hard-won professional knowledge as I take you on a unique journey that separates fact from fiction in the world of real estate. I'll take you to the inside track, into some of the lesser-known areas of real estate—such as the importance of pre-approved financing, the complexities of mortgage loan options, the basics of condominium status certificates, and the reality of closing costs, to name a few. I'll reveal some helpful tips and money-saving strategies that I've learned through the years as a highly successful realtor—tips and strategies that can empower you, as a first-time homebuyer, to conquer the fear and uncertainty usually associated with your first property purchase.

Along the way, I'll share some intimate autobiographical revelations—as well as a lot of insights and laughs. There's no shortage of those in my life as I attempt to surmount the daily challenges and diverse responsibilities of being a businesswoman and stepmother!

Making a first-time property purchase can be both fun and profitable. In fact, it should be. I encourage you to jump on board and find out how you can gain by losing your virginity!

Acknowledgements

When I was a child, I wrote a story. My sister ripped it out of my hands and read it while I sobbed in the corner, feeling vulnerable and exposed. She was just a kid herself and meant no harm but all these years later I still remember that moment. I had written from my soul and was not prepared for anyone to look deep into the machinations of my mind. I wasn't sure if I was brilliant or a freak, but the latter seemed most likely.

Being on TV brings much the same feeling, but with somewhat less sobbing. By agreeing to do the show I opened myself up to criticism, judgement and misinterpretation, but for some reason I didn't mind. I think it was because I was doing what I love best, helping people, which is far more important than my egotism.

There are many people to thank and I must begin with Shelby Taylor for picking my reel out of the garbage after so many months and so many realtors had auditioned, and for convincing Simon Lloyd and Phil Whelan to put their faith in me. Thank you, gentlemen, for taking a big chance on an untrained personality. I mean, seriously, who would have thought that at my age I would begin a career in television! Simon, you created the show and I hope that I have done you proud. Many thanks to HGTV for its support.

Thanks to one of my first directors, Karen Yarosky, and first director of photography, Jen Polo, for making it easy for me to be on camera that first year. You kept it real by being the professional and kind women you are. Your input and ideas were always spot on. I would know it was gold when I would see Karen frantically chewing her gum and twirling her curls. Jen, you always had a great line for me when I needed it. I am especially grateful to you both for never, ever showing me the monitor, as I would surely have headed for the hills! Peter Joseph, Host Whisperer, thanks for giving me confidence and guidance and for "not changing me." Catherine Hughes and Kuba, you two made me laugh and made me comfortable and I still miss you both, along with the illustrious Giselle Rabba whose dedication went unnoticed by most but certainly not by me. You all made it possible for me to be myself and focus on what I do best.

Sid Goldberg, director, a calming presence on set, an entertaining storyteller, a good friend and colleague, I thank you for being a confidant, and for sharing your veteran insights with me, without lording your two Emmy Awards over my head. Ryan Coxworthy, director of photography, my friend, my saviour at times (I daresay too often), I could not make it through another season without you. Your love of the show is evident as you dedicate yourself to making it the best it can be. You are always ready to sacrifice yourself for me and the good of the show, and you always go that extra mile to make me look less repulsive, even when I say, "Let's just go!" Sid and Ryan, you two have become my friends and my knights, and I hope we continue this great working relationship triangle.

Joe Queenan, exuberant gentleman, shake and bake, my favourite South African, I miss you and all the great things you did for me, and wish you great success. Marnie Brooks, you crazy wonderful talented make-up artist, you never complain about how hideous I look at 7 a.m., and how tough I make your job, always making me feel good even when you don't. You persevered through a hurricane and a faulty itinerary to make a very important day so special. I love working with you. Thanks for making the days go by faster.

All the folks behind the scenes who help make the show a success, I appreciate what you do and know that it is you who deserve the credit. It's because of the good people at HGTV, Cineflix/Nextfilm, and the success of the show *Property Virgins*, that I was able to entertain the thought of publishing some stories of successful first-time homebuyers in order to help people traverse the minefield of home buying.

Without all of you, Don Loney, my editor, would never have made the call to say he was interested in reading my manuscript. Don has been an intriguing and lovely person to work with and get to know. I'm sure dealing with a loud, strong-willed woman with no writing experience has presented some challenges and a few giggles. I am grateful that you allowed my personality to shine, or glare, good or bad. Nicole Langlois, substantive and copy editor, thank you for your hard work and tolerance. You are a strong, intelligent woman and I have learned much from you, and have enjoyed your feedback and great ideas. My sincere thanks to John Wiley & Sons for publishing this work, and for allowing me so much influence.

To my eclectic friends who have all at one time or another helped me with your generosity and kindness—and, above all, your acceptance. You've made this wacky journey of life a bit more navigable, and I promise to keep my seat belt on for the remainder of the ride in order to make it easier on all of you. Thanks for being there in bad times and in good. My family, you crazy bunch, thanks for giving me my sense of humour, my strength, your support—and for not having me locked up when I went against the grain. To my gorgeous stepson, thank you for your uninhibited love and for never complaining about my two or three (or four) careers that take me away. My favourite days are those we spend in the pool together, walking on our hands and doing flips and I only wish every day were like that.

John Lagakos, real estate partner extraordinaire, your many talents and knowledge are so valued and important to me, and our friendship is one that will endure. Little did we know just how well the three of us would complement each other's strengths and weaknesses, creating the perfect triumvirate. A stroke of brilliance on Gary's part, one that he never lets us forget.

I would be remiss if I didn't mention the amazing doctors and nurses at Toronto General Hospital and the Canadian health care system for making my risky surgery a possibility and a success. My gratitude is unbounded and I will continue to show it through fundraising.

Thank you to all the viewers and fans of *Property Virgins* for your tremendous support. The show is nothing without you. The best part of being on a TV show and having a book published is that I have the opportunity to help so many people. I love to receive e-mails from people that I've unknowingly helped in some way, either by giving information that was useful to them during their home hunt and purchase, or by bringing down a brick wall of fear and uncertainty thus enabling them to take the steps to home ownership. Knowing that I reach so many of you is incredibly rewarding and makes me happy that I chanced vulnerability and put myself out there. Your kindness is warming and I thank you all.

To my husband, my biggest fan, who had faith in me long before I did, for putting up with the new life and challenges that this cresting wave has brought and for encouraging me in everything I do. You saved my life and now I dedicate it to you.

The author is grateful to Doug Gray, author of *Making Money in Real Estate*, for his kind permission to reprint checklists and charts found in the Appendix. For more information about Doug Gray's books, seminars and articles, please visit his website www.homebuyer.ca.

E P I S O D E

Knowing What You Want

In which Sandra wins at Monopoly and finds the joy of real estate, and in which Ray and Yvonne find the starter home they never knew they wanted

"I won!" I screamed, and jumped up from the kitchen table.

"Congratulations, Sandra, you're so smart," said my mom. She beamed proudly as she reached over to give me a hug and a big, warm kiss on the cheek.

My Aunt Grace's shocking and spiteful words cut through the air. "Of course she won. It's because she cheated. I know she cheated."

My smile froze instantly, then evaporated completely. My body trembled as tears started to sting my eyes.

Well, if looks could kill! My mom just stared at my aunt and said, "What are you talking about, Gracie? Sandra won fair and square. She doesn't cheat."

"A child cannot beat adults at Monopoly and you know it," said Aunt Gracie. "It's impossible. I'm telling you, she cheated. I saw her do it."

Very slowly, in a stern, measured tone of voice, my mom replied, "Sour grapes. That's all. I watched Sandra play too and she won fair and square. Now don't be such a sore loser, Gracie."

Then my mom turned my skinny 10-year-old body toward her, gazed directly into my eyes and said, "Congratulations, Sandra, I sure wish I could be as good as you are at this darn game." She laughed as she continued, "I certainly don't know where you get it from, but I know it's not from this side of the family." She glanced warningly in her younger sister's direction.

My aunt was relentless in her personal attack on me. "Sandra, you should be ashamed of yourself. Nobody likes a cheater," she huffed.

But I didn't feel ashamed—not at all. In fact what I felt instead was pride because I knew that I had not cheated. And then it happened. Lightning struck! At least I think it did. Or was I suddenly just appearing in my very own movie? I could hear a beautiful orchestral arrangement on a soundtrack and I could see the clouds part as two blond angels blew their trumpets heralding an important proclamation. At that precise moment, on that exact spot, I proudly shouted to one and all: "I have decided to become some one who sells for a living." Yes indeed, I had decided that I would trade in selling the "little pretend houses" from the Monopoly board game, and instead I'd sell the "big real houses" that people wanted to buy and live in forever. Hallelujah!

Mmm . . . sorry. Let's rewind! I know—and let's face it, so did you—that I can't credit that long ago game of Monopoly as the decisive factor in my becoming a realtor. Nope, not by a long shot! The clouds didn't part, the trumpets didn't blare, and sadly enough there weren't any blond angels, either. But since life's mysteries are complicated to say the least, even I have to admit that I was mildly surprised when many years later I actually did find myself selling my very first "big real house" to a family that wanted to buy it and live in it forever. I'll never forget the satisfaction that I felt after successfully completing that initial transaction and acquiring my first SOLD sign. I recall that

I took a step back while saying a silent "wow" to myself, because I really loved the sense of accomplishment from knowing that I had been an integral team member throughout that family's first-time home-buying process.

But after all the hard work that had been involved, I also savoured a secret sense of relief when that transaction was finalized. Because whoever said that selling real estate was easy? The truth is, there is plenty more to this business than readily meets the eye. I'll get to more of those gory details later, but let's for the moment accentuate the positive. The most positive memory from that first sale, one that I still cherish, is the look of genuine happiness and joy that those first-time homebuyers showed when they took possession of the key to the front door of their dream house. Their pride of ownership was contagious. And luckily I even had a few tissues in my purse to help that excited woman deal with her tears! It was her tears of joy that told me what an impact I'd had. Yep, I felt like I was walking 10 feet off the ground— and I couldn't wait to do it all over again!

WHAT *EVERY* BUYER NEEDS

It was a long road between my mother's kitchen table and my first client's front door. But now that I'm a seasoned, respected professional realtor, this book is all about how I can help you make a wise real estate purchase. All first-time homebuyers want their experience to be fun and exciting and their investment financially sound, and a good realtor also wants these for his or her clients. So this is my first piece of advice for you: *it all starts with the realtor.*

There are some qualities that any realtor should have if you're going to work with him or her. Honesty is the first quality. I want to say "thank you" to my bitter aunt for her personal attack on me all those years ago because it was on that memorable night that I learned an invaluable lesson about myself: honesty really is the best policy, and I knew that I had played honestly. I also learned that I needed the confidence to stand my ground and speak up for myself because it's important not to be bullied. Now, I'm not a saint, nor do I pretend to be. But I do respect and practise the life lessons that I've learned and am therefore able to bring the components of trustworthiness and personal confidence, along with the practical real estate knowledge I've acquired, to the table during all my business dealings. Those qualities are what every nervous first-time homebuyer needs in a realtor.

You see, as a first-timer, you are probably about to make the single largest and most expensive purchase of your life. It won't be accomplished by a snap decision, nor will you make that decision entirely by yourself, since many professionals—such as mortgage brokers, bank personnel, real estate lawyers and home inspectors—will be involved in the process. Who you choose as your realtor is the first decision that will start the ball rolling on a series of decisions and ultimately a deal in which a lot of money will be spent. Do I need to remind you that that money is yours? No, I didn't think so. Do I need to remind you that you aren't in Las Vegas rolling the dice on a game of chance and praying for blind luck to strike? No, I didn't think so.

The realtor you choose becomes your front line of defence, the person who guides you expertly through a convoluted maze of important decisions to the final goal of buying your home. If you make a good choice, you'll have a trustworthy realtor by your side from beginning to end of what can be a complicated, sometimes intimidating and even potentially hazardous process. Your realtor needs the ability to steer you away from possible pitfalls—pitfalls that you may not even be aware of.

A realtor's reputation within the real estate industry is a crucial factor for you to be aware of as you make your choice. It will tell you a lot about the way that realtor operates, and whether other people see him or her as credible, trustworthy and reliable. So, lesson number two: *do your homework before you let a realtor work with you.*

BUT DO YOU REALLY NEED A REALTOR? WHAT CAN A REALTOR DO FOR YOU?

One of the first tasks for the realtor is to help educate you, the buyer, about the home-buying process, and about the state of the market you're about to jump into. There is a great deal of "accepted wisdom" constantly making the rounds in improperly researched newspaper and magazine articles, at cocktail parties and around the office water cooler. Unfortunately, many so-called facts turn out to be misinformation, or a manipulation or misrepresentation of the truth.

This is why I caution all my clients to enter into this potential minefield of uncertainty with their eyes wide open. I ask them to start their journey by reading my free "Buyer's Package," which is a comprehensive and informative booklet that outlines for them the giant step they are about to take and what they can expect to encounter along the way. I invariably find that leading my clients through that Buyer's Package at the beginning of our professional relationship is extremely helpful. And because the re-sale housing market is constantly shifting, I diligently keep the essential information within that booklet refined and updated every six months.

An experienced realtor will possess the intimate knowledge, or have the industry connections, to locate any number of hard facts for their clients on such diverse topics as social demographics (age groups and lifestyle choices), local school data, taxation authorities, municipal bylaws and suggestions about safe areas that the buyer can investigate on their own. If I don't know the answer to a buyer's question, I never make excuses. Instead, I'll give the buyer a realistic timeline and then get back to them within that time period.

A good realtor is there for a buyer—every step of the way. A competent and committed realtor will be ready to assist his or her clients in any number of ways before and after the closing, and will not leave them like a pair of sitting ducks when they could be facing an unforeseen homeowner's crisis. I prefer to nurture my relationships with previous homebuyers by dropping in to say hello about six months after their closing date. It's always nice to see them within their new environment. I am also quick to offer to help out if they feel that some small detail has been overlooked. I've noticed that being attentive to the small details and making a commitment to sustained service has often been the catalyst for a future referral.

The realtor you ultimately choose to work with should be equally willing and able to help you understand what the process is all about, and should help you to separate the fact from the fiction that's out there about real estate. If a prospective realtor can't answer your questions to your satisfaction, or isn't willing to try, you probably need to keep looking.

REALTOR—OR FORTUNE TELLER? WHAT A REALTOR *CAN'T* DO FOR YOU

I've learned the hard way, during more than 12 years' worth of experience, that the satisfaction of a successfully completed transaction and the realization of a first-time homebuyer's dreams do not come easily. At times I must wear many hats at the same time if I'm going to warn my clients of any potentially dangerous missteps before they take them.

Some of those roles that I assume to varying degrees are financial advisor, accountant, computer whiz, marriage counsellor, psychiatrist, receptionist, detective, business consultant, home inspector, home decorator and psychic. Okay, okay—psychic sounds a bit extreme! But it is true that almost every first-time homebuyer's initial question is about my ability to foresee the future and make a prediction about which way the market is headed. The next question is how that information would affect them if they were to complete a purchase at that very moment. So I make it clear that although I can supply market statistics and provide an analysis of those statistics, and even offer an educated opinion, I cannot and will not make predictions! That will likely be true for any realtor you work with.

We are all aware that the housing market fluctuates due to a number of variables such as interest rates, time of year, long-term market cycles and so on. So is there ever a perfect time to make your purchase? Well, yes and no. Certainly when interest rates are low, or if the number of homes for sale exceeds the demand (a buyer's market, as it's called), then obviously that would be a very beneficial time to be a buyer; you'd probably want to strike while the iron is hot. But when the opposite conditions are in place, for instance when there are more buyers than homes available for sale (a seller's market), it's a more advantageous time to be a seller than a buyer. If you're able to make your purchase during a time of balance, when the playing field is level for both buyers and sellers, then the likelihood of being squeezed or overpaying is lessened.

Having said that, if you buy in a seller's market, you could easily turn a quick profit if you plan and buy well, by selling within a reasonable time frame. Many have made hundreds of thousands of dollars by buying and selling in just such conditions. Likewise, buying in a buyer's market, holding the property for a while, and then selling when conditions change to a more favourable environment for sellers is another great way to make money in real estate. Have I confused you? Good, because ultimately, if the time is right for you to buy real estate, my advice is this: buy real estate!

People also worry about the long-term trends in the housing market. They want to know if a hot market is going to suddenly cool off—right after they've purchased! That would have the effect of making their home's value drop quickly, which wouldn't matter too much if they were planning to stay in that home for a number of years because over time that dip in the market would even itself out and values would come up again. But it could mean a disastrous loss of equity if they had to sell again fairly soon (in a year or two, let's say) during that much cooler market. And they certainly wouldn't have much equity to borrow against for a while.

Well, it's true that such things have happened. The last time in Canada was in the recession of the late 1980s and early 1990s, when a major market "correction" took the wind out of many homeowners' sails. A lot of people had to sit tight on their houses while they waited for housing prices to slowly climb back up to where they'd been only a few years—or even months—prior to when they'd bought. Some people took advantage of lower prices and moved up into larger homes, offsetting the loss on the lower-priced home they were leaving by saving a lot of money on the larger home they were moving to. Could a market correction happen again? Sure it could. Just remember, though, that an investment in real estate has historically proven to be one of the safest investments you can make, with very healthy returns. Never believe that the housing market has reached its highest level: prices do trend upwards over time, even if it seems impossible. And that means you'll still be making a good investment.

The bottom line is this: *you need to buy when the time is right for you.*

So, let me repeat: the real estate market fluctuates and I do not make predictions. However, with all my clients I try to be the "head" while they are the "heart." In other words, the buyer will most likely get carried away with the emotions of the purchase, and I will always be looking out for the business or investment side of things. I will always let clients know what areas or what type of house may be stigmatized and difficult to sell in a soft market, like a lot that backs onto a dump, has hydro wires overhead. The buyer makes the ultimate decision, but my job is to inform them so they can make a considered choice.

And though I say I don't make predictions, I will make this one. Almost every family has what I call a "Chicken Little" type, a negative know-it-all who will gladly tell you, "Wait . . . don't buy now . . . the market is headed for a downturn . . . it's going to crash!" Who needs that? Certainly not you. If you want to feel a sense of security about where the market is right now, consult with your realtor and study the current buying and selling trends. I also recommend that you direct your inquiries to the Canada Mortgage and Housing Corporation, which is an excellent source of information for learning about the current housing market. The CMHC's Market Analysis Centre assists homebuyers in understanding what the heck is going on so that you will feel confident and able to make your own informed decisions.

HOW DO YOU FIND A GOOD REALTOR?

You can find one at an open house, at a fundraiser or even at the realty office. Check out who has a lot of For Sale signs or ads in the area, and ask your friends for references if they've used a realtor they can recommend for honesty, efficiency, knowledge and thoroughness. If you've met a realtor you think you might like to work with, get references from that person and then follow up. Pay attention to your gut feelings about any realtor you meet, but also ask the hard questions about their track record and their reputation. Just think of it like dating: if you find someone who has the same moral fabric as you do, or perhaps has shared interests or whatever it is that clicks, it could be a good fit. On the other hand, the guy with a lot of signs may be too busy to give you the time and hand-holding you need. I recommend finding an agent who has some sort of "buyer's package" of info—like I do—because that will demonstrate that they are used to working with first-timers. Many agents are not, and it can be an unpleasant experience for everyone!

Once you've found an agent who feels right to you, try them on for size. I ask for the Buyer Representation Agreement only to be signed for a short period at first, so both parties can find out if the arrangement works. If I don't live up to my promises, my client can walk. Likewise, if I don't think my clients are being truthful or upfront, or do not show a reasonable amount of respect for me and my team (for instance, if they fail to show up on time, or at all for a meeting), then we lose them. Communicate your expectations to your realtor, and ask the realtor to let you know their expectations as well. In my real estate team, we don't expect our clients to sign anything we wouldn't sign.

There are real benefits to signing a Buyer Representation Agreement. In my opinion, the single most important factor is that your realtor is able and obliged to give you his real estate opinion. Really, why hire a realtor except to benefit from his or her knowledge and expertise? I recently bought property well beyond my home turf and I insisted on a Buyer Representation Agreement. Even though I am a realtor, I am the first to admit that I could benefit from another realtor's knowledge of the area in which I wanted to buy. The laws and bylaws, the land and issues peculiar to that terrain, and the "do's and don'ts" are all very different from where I practise real estate, and I wanted to be certain that I was getting all the info I needed to make a well-considered choice. Does that surprise you? It shouldn't! I always preach about how important it is to hire a realtor. And baby, I walk the talk.

A Buyer Representation Agreement is also important because of the level of accountability that your realtor owes you once you've signed with him or her. A realtor always owes you honesty and fairness regardless of a contract, but in simple terms, with a Buyer Representation Agreement in place the realtor will provide *all* the information you need to know regarding issues that may affect the value of the property you are interested in. The realtor will answer questions you may not even *know* are questions to ask. With the agreement in place your realtor is bound to you with "fiduciary duties" (loyalty; obedience; full disclosure; duty to use skill, care and diligence; duty to account for all monies) and protects your information—your motivation for buying, your willingness to pay a premium for certain features, etc. In other words, what you tell your realtor stays with your realtor, unless you direct him or her to share this information with the other side—that is, the seller.

IT'S A ROLLER COASTER, THAT'S FOR CERTAIN

Even when you do find just the right realtor to work with you, it's almost certainly true that you will also suffer a certain level of frustration, stress and anxiety during the emotional roller coaster ride of your home-buying experience. But who ever said that *buying* real estate was easy? You will probably become the class champ at second-guessing yourself, as your emotions constantly push and pull you in conflicting directions.

Then, even after the buying process itself is completed, there's still the possibility of "buyer's remorse" setting in. It's that insidious form of self-doubt and insecurity that raises its ugly head to keep you awake at night sweating and wondering if you actually did make the right decisions after all. Well, just so you know, those "what ifs?" and "if onlys" are a frequent phenomenon among homebuyers (first-timers as well as the more experienced), so it's best to make yourself aware of it and be ready to let it go. Remember that although you are taking a financial risk, the lending institution that has provided you with a mortgage has a great deal more at stake—and, believe me, lenders do not stay in business by losing money, so they must have loaned you that money for a good reason. Remind yourself that you qualified for your mortgage and, as long as you were honest with the bank and yourself, you can trust your lender's judgement and faith in your ability to handle the financials. Canadian lenders are quite conservative, much more so than our friends to the south. With more restrictive requirements by Canadian lenders, neither borrowers nor banks have been affected the way that Americans were in 2007 and 2008. Our situation is very different, primarily because our lenders are far more strict when it comes to their requirements (they insist on certain gross debt service ratios *and* total debt service ratios). Some people complain, the way a teenager complains about their curfew, but in the long run it is for their own good—and yours.

As you start out, remember that the search for a good buyer-realtor relationship is a two-way street: you've got a job to do too. Just as you expect certain qualities and traits in a realtor, I expect certain things from my clients. I expect them to stay alert, to ask questions, to take notes, to keep organized and to seek knowledge. In return, I am happy to become a temporary mentor to them, to offer counsel and advice, and to answer their real estate questions. This will be true of any good buyer-realtor relationship.

Here's a basic rule in life: let yourself learn from what other people have gone through before you. Throughout this book, I'm going to tell you some real-life stories of clients I've worked with (all names changed to protect the innocent, of course!). Maybe you'll see yourself in their stories, and just maybe there will be something that can make it easier for you to be a first-time buyer. In this chapter, I'll introduce you to a young couple who started the home-buying process without being really sure what they wanted—but who got what they needed (and wanted) in the end!

MEET RAY AND YVONNE

I remember so clearly the day I received a call from Ray telling me that he and his wife, Yvonne, were ready to buy their first home. The excitement in his voice came through loud and clear. But I also thought that I could hear a touch of urgency, so I shuffled some other appointments to accommodate his request to meet later that same day. The couple arrived promptly two hours later.

I liked Ray and Yvonne from the moment I met them. They were very open with me as we discussed their strong desire to become first-time homebuyers. They both smiled a lot and were extremely enthusiastic, so those friendly qualities made it easy for me to bond with them. Yvonne told me that since neither of them knew much when it came to real estate, she really appreciated that I spoke to them in such a straightforward, down-to-earth way, which was a nice compliment indeed. And I can still hear Ray telling me, "The sooner we buy, the better." What realtor wouldn't love to have that eager young couple as clients? Am I right?

But please don't be too quick to state the obvious answer! Let's hang on just a minute and not get ahead of ourselves here, and in fact, let's come to a screeching halt. Why? Because even though that happy couple was extremely gung-ho, they really were woefully lacking in any concrete knowledge about the all-important step they were considering. Truthfully, they knew nothing! Absolutely nothing! Harsh words perhaps, but let me tell you that that scenario, along with countless other similar ones, is very common among my first-timers. Even though my clients' goal is to own a home, many have literally no clue what it is like to be a homeowner!

At least Ray and Yvonne had the common sense to admit their limitations upfront. To be frank, their lack of knowledge didn't concern me at all. Instead I was hopeful that it was an indication I wouldn't have to waste valuable time and energy tearing down a lot of preconceived notions or ideas that they had already acquired based on loosely informed or irresponsible sources.

As we began getting down to basics, we quickly established that Ray and Yvonne were almost drowning in debt. However, they didn't seem fully aware of that predicament. And why not? Well, tunnel vision seemed to be the culprit. "Our main focus during the past two years has been saving up our down payment," Ray told me. "And that's all that's really required, isn't it?"

Since they were currently living together in a rental apartment, they had assumed that having a monthly mortgage was really just the same as paying a monthly rent after you had made the down payment. Well, no, it's not. In fact, far from it! Yvonne explained, "Ray's cousin really knows real estate and he made it all sound so easy." Ouch! Oh yes, the misinformation out there is rampant and can prove to be very harmful indeed. It looked like I would have to tear down a few preconceived notions after all.

But then I figured that I could use their "bullshit baffles brains" misconceptions as my jumping-off point, so I patiently began to explain that the down payment was just one of the major hurdles for them to deal with.

I tried not to be too surprised when the next thing I found out was that Ray and Yvonne had only a vague idea of how much money they actually expected to spend on their new house. The disparity in the figures that each of them threw at me was pretty large, as were their individual living expectations. It was plain that Ray and Yvonne hadn't really discussed in depth their individual needs or desires, because just by asking a few simple questions it was quickly apparent to me that each of them had a totally different meaning for the words "Home Sweet Home."

My last big question to them was what area they preferred to live in. Once again they told me they hadn't really given it much thought. I merely said the following three words: "Location, location, location!" and then enjoyed laughing along with them as Yvonne rolled her eyes and looked slightly embarrassed. But regardless of their naïve notions regarding a house's final appearance, its location and even its purchase price, Yvonne wholeheartedly agreed with Ray when he said, "Basically we just want a nice home to live in and we want you to help us find it."

"Fine," I told them. "Let's get to work." I decided to deal with the easy part first by helping them put all their ducks in a row—that is, to identify the essentials. After all, you can't get what you want until you first know what and where that is. In fairly short order it was clear that Ray wanted to look at older houses located within a mature, established neighbourhood. But I discovered that Yvonne, who had never lived in an older house, wanted to look at houses that were as new as possible. "I really don't want a creepy old house that makes noises and stuff like that," she confessed. I had uncovered one of those "hidden objections," helping my clients solve a real estate issue they didn't even know they had. But that's all in a day's work for me.

My job entails helping the first-time homebuyer to identify their essential criteria, while at the same time reminding them to keep in mind what they can afford. I started off that pair of eager beavers by having them jointly draw up a list of "must have" primary features—with regard to location, size and price, and lots of other intangibles—for the home they'd like to live in. Must-haves don't always make a lot of sense to the objective observer, but they're always important to the people involved. For instance, a couple could insist on a large master bedroom because she had to share with her sister all her life. Or maybe they want a big tool shed because he wants to take up woodworking. Making up that must-have list wasn't such an easy task for Ray and Yvonne, since they were coming from such different points of view.

Next I had them draw up a "wish list" that contained secondary features they would like to have if possible. I pointed out that those two lists were not mutually exclusive and that once I got to the point of selecting suitable homes for them to consider, I would attempt to have some overlap, if it was financially feasible.

Lastly, I had them draw up a list of "eliminating factors" that were going to keep them from making a purchase. Usually this list of items is the easiest to come up with, because by nature people tend to have very strong and definite dislikes regarding their living space. And that rule of thumb held true for my clients too with Yvonne emphatically declaring, "For starters, there is absolutely no way I'm moving anywhere near a cemetery!" Ray quickly concurred: "Me neither. A cemetery is definitely out." Lots of buyers wouldn't feel this way about cemeteries—in fact, thousands of Canadians live with a cemetery in their neighbourhood, or a recycling depot, or hydro towers, or any number of other things that some people might not wish to have in their vicinity. But I took the feelings of my client to heart.

■ ADVICE FOR PROPERTY VIRGINS
TALKING IT OVER

If you're planning to buy a house with your husband, wife or any other partner, make sure you discuss your real housing needs and desires before getting too far into the process. What should be on the list? Location, size (how many bedrooms, bathrooms), cost (determined by what you can afford on a monthly basis) and architectural style and age of house are a good place to start.

Now then, let me think, was there anything else? Oh yeah—what about that thorny little problem with their debt situation? Exactly what were they going to do about that? Since their current financial situation was going to have a very large impact on their ability to borrow the substantial sum needed to make their dream of home ownership become a reality, their debt load had to be addressed—and the sooner, the better.

How could Ray and Yvonne believe that they had saved a respectable sum to be used as a down payment when, in fact, the opposite was true? Well, it happens all the time, actually, so some excellent advice that I freely give to anybody hoping to purchase a home is to make darn sure that all their "financials" are in order before they go shopping. This means lowering or eliminating consumer debts (such as credit cards and lines of credit that are not attached to a business), while at the same time saving a substantial sum for a down payment (with the exception of "zero-down" mortgages, you'll usually need

20% to 25% of the total sale price as your down payment). Understanding your own financial situation is so important that I don't know why it isn't taught in high school as a mandatory subject. After all, it's never too early to learn how to budget wisely. So get yourselves organized because it's time to face the facts—and the brutal truth!

I suggested that Ray and Yvonne should begin their debt management process by contacting one of the major credit bureaus to request their own credit reports. This would give them the same report that a bank or any lending institution would pull up about them if and when they were applying for a mortgage. That report is your financial reputation in a nutshell. It is a clear indicator of how you've handled your current and previous financial obligations such as credit card payments, lines of credit, loan payments, etc. Your credit report also includes your banking history, any collection agency history (if such a company was ever hired to retrieve an unpaid debt that you owed), as well as information on the public record such as bankruptcy or any lawsuits against you that were credit related. You should check it carefully for accuracy, because there can be mistakes in it, and it's imperative that mistakes be corrected.

The report you request will look very different from the one a bank will get, as it is more user-friendly and easier to understand. Read the bureau notes that explain what "hard" and "soft" inquiries are, and if you are wondering why a particular company requested a credit check, call the number beside the name and find out who they are and why they needed a report. That is how I discovered that the people who stole my ID had ordered two cell phones, and the account was more than $2,000 in arrears. It was hard work to prove that I was not involved in this transaction at all, but I finally managed it. I didn't suffer any financial loss, just a huge headache. Always follow up something that looks suspicious or makes you look bad, because the bank will use the credit report to determine what kind of risk you represent if they loan you money. Any bad debt or judgements against you, including unresolved debt that arises from identity theft, will not bode well.

It goes without saying that you don't want to have any unwanted surprises pop up just as you're hoping to seal the deal on your dream home. Unfortunately I did have to witness that embarrassment one time on a transaction, and let me tell you that it was a very devastating experience for the humiliated buyer to endure. Please do your utmost to avoid having this happen to you!

And pray really hard that you've never missed making a minimum monthly payment either—or else! Every little slip-up has been recorded. Now before I get sounding a little too preachy on this issue, it might be a good time for me to confess that unfortunately I also learned that very same lesson the hard way. Oh yes, how well I remember my naïve assumption that "nobody will ever know except me" about my convenient habit of ignoring payment deadlines or my silly errors in judgement whenever I exceeded my credit limits. Nobody ever taught me to make the minimum payment on time, regardless of how small it was, and not to wait until my paycheque came in the following day to pay off the entire amount. Seems it is a common mistake, but those reckless patterns came back to haunt me one bleak day as a slightly alarmed financial advisor confronted me with a multi-page printout that detailed each and every "little mistake" I'd ever made! As I stared at the evidence in stark black and white, I turned the colour of a beet. Luckily, I saw the forest for the trees in one hell of a hurry and immediately changed my behaviour, and I've managed to be a good girl ever since. My saving grace, with my busy schedule, was getting rid of my scepticism and accepting that pre-authorized payments on my credit cards are a really good idea!

With regard to Ray and Yvonne, they quickly made the decision to repair as much damage as possible. Probably the most important decision was to have a suspicious signifier of fraudulent activity looked into. After close inspection, the dispute was resolved and Ray and Yvonne were cleared of any possible wrongdoing. In all fairness to the couple, they had sought legal advice at the time of the dispute, years earlier, and they firmly believed that the resolution had been completed properly at that time. I'm sure you can imagine their genuine surprise when they were told the unvarnished truth! Luckily they found out about it when they did, and got off to a good start by cleaning up that mess pronto. And they didn't stop there either. The time seemed right for them to close out two rarely used credit accounts, because although neither account had a substantial balance owing, regular payments on both accounts were often missed, thus establishing a pattern of neglect. Ray and Yvonne decided to clean them both up once and for all and then cancel them entirely. All right, folks, another great decision!

Next up was the simple matter of transferring an outstanding credit card balance with its high interest rate to a low-interest loan. Then they picked up some serious steam by agreeing to focus on reducing the balance as much as possible on their current credit cards. "We've both agreed to tighten our belts," Yvonne admitted to me, "so we're going to lock up our current cards for a full ninety days!" Obviously that drastic action was going to be terribly inconvenient for them, but let's face it: it was the ultra-convenience of those same cards that had been almost lethal to them both in the first place. Well, that and perhaps their own carelessness at not maintaining those "easy" minimum monthly payments too. They were learning the hard way, but at least they were learning.

Here's another thing they were learning: borrowing money is not only a good thing, it's absolutely vital if you're going to get a mortgage. That's because the only way a lending institution will know if you're a good risk is to see the proof of it in your past dealings. In fact, if you've never had a credit card or a line of credit, you could find yourself being turned down by a bank when you need a mortgage. And let's face it: it's always fun to say a big fat "yes" to the tempting offer of a credit card, isn't it? I'm a firm believer that when the bank offers you credit, you should say "yes" and take it—but you must act fiscally responsible by managing that credit properly. That means charging responsibly, and meeting every single minimum monthly payment. That's how you establish a favourable credit history.

As you probably imagined, Ray and Yvonne's initial gung-ho desire to become instant homebuyers was dampened considerably by a large dose of reality. But having to cool their jets as they got their finances in order did not deter them from their original goal. In fact, quite the opposite was true: Ray and Yvonne had realized the need for better communication with each other and the importance of establishing a feasible plan of action. I had originally told them that I was willing to work at their pace, and due to necessity their pace had slowed down considerably. But because there was no pressure for them to jump into what could become an uncomfortable situation, I stayed in constant touch with them during their period of low activity and continued to educate them. They began by checking out the online information-sharing network of MLS. (The Multiple Listing Service is run by the Canadian Real Estate Association and the National Association of Realtors.) It shows all houses that are publicly listed and available for sale at any given time. The detailed information provided on that website is helpful because it allows buyers to easily compare similar homes within a set price range, their approximate square footage, with photos, location and sometimes even floor plans. I also recommended that Ray and Yvonne attend open houses on their own, to gain even more market knowledge. It never hurts to view a house on the market and file away some important information as a point of comparison later on. Of course, I also cautioned them that since they weren't yet in a position to buy, they should avoid falling in love with anything!

Ray and Yvonne were also receptive to my suggestion that they learn as much as possible about the dozens of convenient mortgage options they could choose from. When the timing was finally right for them, they informed me that they were in a more credit-worthy situation to get pre-approved for a loan.

◼ ADVICE FOR PROPERTY VIRGINS
MORTGAGES FOR NEWBIES

Mortgages come in all shapes and sizes, with different interest rates, amortization periods (total length of time to repay the mortgage) and terms (length of time for which the specifics of the mortgage hold true, usually one to five years). What you choose will depend on your particular financial situation and how comfortable you are with risk. See more on mortgage choices in Episode Six.

The mortgage financing pre-approval process is a very important-step that I advise all first-time homebuyers to go through because it determines their buying power. Based on the careful analysis of the financial history that you have provided, a lending institution will actually pre-approve you for a specific loan amount before you even begin looking for a home. I tell my clients that a pre-approved mortgage is so highly recommended because it indicates that your financial position has been clearly outlined to you and you know what you can truly afford. Hopefully it will keep your sense of reality in check so you do not go beyond your means when it comes time to make an offer on a home.

Why bother with pre-approval?

Getting a mortgage pre-approval is free, and there's no obligation until you make your final decision. Getting a pre-approval from a lender benefits you in many ways:

1. It determines the maximum mortgage loan for which you qualify.
2. It allows your realtor to show you a range of properties in your price range.
3. It allows your realtor to make a realistic offer on your purchase and saves time in the negotiation process.

4. It holds the interest rate for a period of 90 to 120 days, guarding you against rate fluctuations.
5. It provides peace of mind during the home-buying process, and eliminates the possibility of unpleasant surprises.

My advice is to find a mortgage broker who will look at your entire profile and then provide you with a wide variety of mortgage options from a list of different lenders. He or she should explain all those options in detail. Then you can choose which lending institution to apply to, or you can ask the mortgage broker to make a recommendation as to which is the best one for you. Once you've gone through the application process, your chosen lending institution determines the maximum amount of a loan that you are eligible for, and you'll receive a letter stating that you have been pre-approved. That letter signifies a commitment from the lender to guarantee you a loan for a specified amount of money for the purpose of a home mortgage—excluding any last-minute unforeseen financial reversals, of course.

But keep in mind that the home you ultimately choose to buy must also pass muster or "qualify" as being worthy of that pre-approved sum of money, so your mortgage lender will undoubtedly want a written appraisal from a qualified expert who will estimate the property's value. This is often arranged by the lender, but the cost (several hundred dollars) is charged back to you, the customer. The appraiser would do a comparative market analysis by comparing other recently sold properties in the surrounding neighbourhood that are of a similar age, that feature similar lot sizes and square footage, and that possess roughly the same amenities. If those comparable properties' statistics are very similar, at a similar price, that is an indication you are paying fair market value for the home. In a case like this, you likely won't have any difficulty in getting final approval.

Now I don't want to accuse all banks of being guilty, but thankfully the days of walking into any bank and accepting its first—and quite possibly only—mortgage offer are long gone. There is a lot more choice and competition in the marketplace today, and the result is a shift toward mortgage brokers: in some instances a bank employee might place only two mortgages per year whereas a reputable broker could place 20 in one month. Many personnel within a bank's employment structure are apt to be promoted in less than a year's time to another department entirely, thus making it very difficult for me to establish, and then build, a meaningful, concrete business relationship with one particular employee. In my work, I have such a strong affiliation with my preferred mortgage broker that he is willing to go that extra mile for my clients as he focuses on securing the best lending options, terms and rates available. In a real time crunch I need the ability, and want the control, to contact my broker to complete transactions in a suitable hurry—regardless of banking hours.

On a few occasions my mortgage broker has even issued a preliminary pre-approval letter that stated the buyers were pre-approved subject to receiving their officially issued letter a day or two later. And during a very hot selling period, or even on an unusually busy weekend, that helpful measure has saved some of my clients from heartbreak. I clearly remember an example nine years ago when one transaction was rescued from going south simply based on the strength of my preferred mortgage broker's trusted contacts. It truly seemed like he had managed to pull a rabbit out of the hat by convincing a particular lending company to assume a slightly riskier deal than usual. As a result that sale was completed in my clients' favour just in the nick of time. (And in case enquiring minds want to know, those first-time homebuyers have never defaulted on a payment to this day. That transaction turned out to be a "win-win" situation for all parties. Who says there are no happy endings?)

Mortgage brokers don't charge for their services, since they are paid a commission by the lender, but some people still prefer to shop around on their own. It is a very competitive field, and due to the fact that market conditions for mortgages are in constant flux, it is best to compare the rates and the terms offered by various lenders. Try not to become a rate-driven shopper because a mortgage is a complete product, and the interest rate is just one of a multitude of features that it offers.

Another advantage to the buyer from the pre-approval process is that once your realtor and all prospective sellers know that you have been pre-approved, your intent to complete a purchase appears stronger. Your offer will not have to be "conditional on financing," since you'll already have your financing in place. It gives confidence to a seller by removing the stress of worrying that an offer won't actually pan out. In a multiple offer situation, being able to remove this condition is even more important, since it may give you the competitive edge—even if your offer is lower than someone else's.

Fade out . . . fade in. After cleaning up their credit history, Ray and Yvonne's savings for their down payment had been depleted by half, so they were somewhat restricted in their price range as they went in search of a pre-approved mortgage. That was not great news for my clients, since their original spending expectations had been much higher. They were forced to alter their criteria a little bit, but they soldiered on regardless. When they had made firm decisions about the style and age of house they wanted, the number of bedrooms they needed, a few acceptable locations and the type of neighbourhood amenities they required, we all breathed a sigh of relief.

It turned out that the biggest advantage of all for this young couple was that they were willing to face the dreaded "c" word in order to become first-time homebuyers: "compromise." Both Ray and Yvonne had decided they were willing to compromise because they understood that flexibility was key. Now that brought them right up against the "s" word, which is a very close cousin to the "c" word, but even the thought of "sacrifice" didn't scare off that intensely determined couple. Ray was even willing to say goodbye to his cherished, but very expensive, motorcycle if that proved to be necessary. His bike was a classic beauty, but he bit the bullet and said, "I hate to admit it, but this baby is becoming too expensive to maintain and insure. To say nothing of the fact that it spends far too much time every year just locked away in my parents' garage for safety's sake." And Yvonne? Well, she had to sacrifice her desire for a newer built home. Instead she had accepted the inevitability that their first home wouldn't actually be their "dream home" at all, and she was determined to look on the bright side. Their first home purchase would prove to be a stepping stone. Okay, so way to go, guys! Talk about stepping up to the plate! Now I was finally ready to show them some properties.

We began by looking at two-bedroom single-family homes that were in good condition, were within their pre-approved price range and were located within the areas they had chosen. They viewed a number of listings. Although none appeared to be perfect right off the bat, that was fine since Ray and Yvonne knew from their own research that "the perfect house" is never 100% perfect. In fact "the perfect house" simply doesn't exist because there will always be something imperfect about it that the new homeowner will want to fix or change.

For instance, after one particular viewing, the reason the house with the perfectly landscaped back yard didn't appeal to either of them was simply that, although they both wanted some back-yard space, they already knew that they didn't possess one green thumb between them! The added expense of maintaining that beautiful yard wouldn't be worthwhile to them. Yvonne suggested that we "keep it simpler," and said that in fact a small patio would do fine.

The next two houses were "perfect"—they both had an attached garage, and a garage was extremely important to Ray and Yvonne because they both drove small cars and wanted the convenience, privacy and storage room that a garage would give them. But both of those houses' interiors were hideously decorated and it was nearly impossible for Yvonne to see past that.

"Keep an open mind," I encouraged her. "With just a few cans of paint, some modern light fixtures and some creative touches throughout the main rooms, your decorating alternatives will be endless. What I did with my own house, literally, was to just rip out anything that I didn't like and then changed it to suit my own taste. And since I wasn't in a huge hurry, I was able to spread out the costs over time." But I sensed that Yvonne was still unconvinced, and I was right. She told me after viewing a third badly decorated home, "I really prefer to see pretty houses if it's possible." Her remark didn't surprise me in the least, because I'll wager that nine out of 10 first-time buyers will not see the hidden potential that exists in a badly decorated house.

And so it went. A few more properties went by, followed by discussions with Ray and Yvonne about their personal likes and dislikes regarding each house that we had viewed. After one particularly long day, I suggested the possibility of viewing houses in an alternative suburban location that was farther away from their jobs and families than they had initially hoped to be. "I know that you'll be able to get more bang for your buck by moving farther away from the city's core," I offered. Timing is everything, as the saying goes, and by now they were not only willing to consider my idea, they actually agreed.

I started by showing them some potential properties on the real estate intranet (which shows all the information available for MLS properties) within that alternative area and they were excited by the possibilities. Believe me, it wasn't the first time I clicked the mouse to help locate a house. And then presto! Now it all seemed to be coming together, so we were off and running again.

First off, I showed them a really cute bungalow. "This will satisfy your lifestyle needs now, as well as for many years down the road, since I know you're not planning to move again within the next five to 10 years. Nor are you planning to have any children during that time. So although the lot is smaller than you both had initially hoped for, the house is located on a quiet street in an established neighbourhood that's considered to be a very safe area. It also has a garage and a small but suitable back yard."

Both Ray and Yvonne could see that it was a clean, well-kept home. And although it appeared small from the outside, it was surprisingly spacious on the inside. It had enough closet and storage space for their needs; however, the master bedroom and main bathroom would both need to be redecorated to suit Yvonne's taste. But she smiled and giggled when Ray said, "I'll do the painting myself, I promise." There was a cozy kitchen with appliances that would last a few more years, and the house even contained a surprise feature: a well-finished basement. And since that little gem was within their price range, and no renovations or major repairs were required, both of them were able to see the promise that it held for them if they decided to buy it.

So far, so good. The only major drawback was going to be the commute. Unfortunately, upon further reflection, both Ray and Yvonne had now decided that 90 minutes each way was a long time to spend battling rush-hour traffic every morning and every evening. And of course I could empathize with them on that score. I mean, what else could you do with those three hours each day instead? I know that almost anything else would be more productive than sitting in traffic, right? To say nothing of the extra mileage and general wear and tear on both of their vehicles.

Where did that leave us? Because of their reconsideration of the commuting issue, were we right back at square one? Hopefully not just yet, as I reminded them about those notorious cousins, "compromise and sacrifice," and that made them both laugh! "Stay focused on other relevant matters," I said encouragingly, "and spend some time in the immediate area checking out the many conveniences that the neighbourhood has to offer. For instance, the local plaza, a small community centre with a gym, and even a bowling alley are all within a short drive."

And although I knew that Ray and Yvonne were not planning to become parents any time soon, I also pointed out that there were two reputable schools within this district, which is a very strong re-sale factor.

I also asked them to take particular notice of the neighbours, since the age range of many of them was compatible with theirs. That point was obviously a big plus because Ray immediately said, "That's wicked because I'd like to fit in and feel right at home." From past experience I've learned that it's always a positive deciding factor when my clients can immediately envision a sense of community. The daily or weekly necessities, such as mail delivery and garbage pick-up, had well-established routes and schedules that had been operational for years. I even pointed out that they were only a 10-minute drive from the highway. When I left them a short while later, they promised to give that home some serious consideration. I really didn't know what conclusion they would come to. There were so many pros and cons to balance, so many options to weigh—I was glad I wasn't in their shoes!

Within 24 hours, I received a call from the happy couple. "Yvonne and I would like to take a second look at that little house we saw yesterday," said Ray. "We've been thinking about it a lot, so we'd like to go back again." No problem, I said; I would meet them there as soon as conveniently possible for the second viewing. I always encourage a second viewing before buyers make an offer on a home, and as always I encouraged Ray and Yvonne to consider that additional viewing as their very own home inspection and to not be afraid to get really specific with any questions or concerns they might have. "Collaboration is key and as your realtor I want to go out on a limb to protect you from overlooking anything," I said.

So they looked inside, then they looked outside, and then they looked inside again. Then they asked questions—lots of questions! They had been careful to compare that home's features with their lists of deciding and eliminating factors to be sure that they were satisfied.

And after they allowed for a little flexibility, Ray told me, "Although the commuting problem has the potential to be one of life's big headaches for us, we're prepared to make an offer." What great news! I looked over at Yvonne who smiled broadly and nodded her head in agreement.

But wait just a minute, because we're not out of the woods yet. I had informed Ray and Yvonne that the house had already been sitting on the market for more than 30 days without any offers, while other comparable properties usually sold in much less time within that area, so they could feel hopeful that we could get the seller to stop fixating on the price he wanted and to instead start thinking about the price he would accept. Even though Ray and Yvonne's first offer was a reasonably good one, it was a lower price than what the seller was asking for and the seller wasn't happy. It took some skillful negotiating, followed by some tense moments, a lot of hand-holding and more than a few cups of coffee, but eventually after the fourth round of information was passed between that seller and my clients, a firm deal was accepted, at what in my opinion was fair market value. Hallelujah!

I am frequently asked if I get a "rush" from my job. When this question comes up, I always think of the metamorphosis that Ray and Yvonne went through during their home-buying journey. They are a perfect example of the satisfaction I get when I'm able to take a very naïve couple of first-timers and lead them by the hand, and witness their growth, throughout that convoluted process. The 11 months that I spent working alongside that couple was both a challenge and a pleasure for me. When viewing potential properties with them, I initially had to point out the visually appealing elements that they should say "no" to, and convince them to concentrate on the more functional aspects of a property and why they should say "yes" to those features instead. But toward the end of their home-buying process, both Ray and Yvonne were on occasion able to beat me to the punch on those same matters. What a great chuckle we all had at my expense! But they knew I was being sincere when I told them, "I am so relieved that you're finally getting it."

In the end I helped that cheerful, newly enlightened couple make what I considered to be the best choice for themselves. And I know that they would agree, because when I made a surprise visit to them on their moving day, taking along some homemade pizzas (hey, I'm Italian, so I never need an excuse to cook, or to eat either), let me tell you that their unbelievably proud and smiling faces said it all.

Ah yes, the comfort and joy—and the pride too—that come with owning your very first home!

New Kids on the MLS Block

In which Mike and Angela learn the ropes of working with a realtor, and in which Sandra has no time for sitting on the bench

"Sandra! Sandra! What's taking so long?" My father bellowed so loudly that the whole house seemed to shake.

"All right, I'm coming, Dad. Just give me a minute."

"Hurry up, Sandra. You know we don't have all day."

I cursed silently before calling out, "I'll be right down."

But less than 10 seconds later he bellowed again, "Sandra! We have to get going." His sharp tone indicated that he really meant business, so I dashed out of the bathroom and started rushing toward the stairs while still buttoning up my blouse with one hand and desperately trying to straighten my unruly hair with the other. The last thing I needed right at that moment was to be suffering from another bad hair day! But I certainly knew better than to mention that minor irritation to my agitated father because it would just go right over his head anyway.

As I started down the stairs I could see him rapidly pacing back and forth in the front hall, determined to wear a hole in the rug. When

I was still two steps from the bottom I announced "Okay I'm here" as I leapt off the staircase and landed right beside him.

"Finally! Always late, ever since you were little."

I just nodded silently in reply.

"Have you got the camera?" he asked.

"Yes, Dad, of course I've got the camera." I sighed deeply.

"Okay then, let's go."

My very nervous and excited father, while reaching to open the front door, looked sheepishly at me and asked, "What? Who says a father can't be proud of his own daughter?"

I just nodded silently once more, as he blushed a deep shade of tomato red.

"Okay then, let's go! Before it's too late to get a good picture, because you know what I always say."

"Yes, Dad, I know what you always say." Then, playing the moment for all it was worth, I responded with my best impersonation of his own low gruff voice: "You better hurry up, Sandra, because the sun won't wait for you."

"Well, you got the words right," he said as he desperately tried to keep a straight face, "but who was that talking? Jimmy Durante?"

And we both burst into loud laughter because, as much as he hated to admit it, my dead-on impression of him always tickled his funny bone!

As I began to follow my happy father out the front door, he abruptly stopped and playfully asked again, "Sandra, have you got the camera?" I just nodded while gently pushing him toward the car.

As we pulled out of the driveway, he continued to mutter to himself about the sun going down, while I continued to curse the darn humidity and the disaster it was making of my hair! For me that was the real tragedy because, just for the record, there was little chance of the day's sun disappearing anytime soon—according to my watch it was only a few minutes past noon!

Why was my dad so excited? Well, earlier that same day he had spotted my very first "bench." That's right, you've all seen them before, those benches that can be found at bus stops and in other public areas displaying a realtor's picture along with the appropriate contact information and number for that realtor. Those benches are used as a popular form of advertisement, and even though I had already been a realtor for two years by that point, and had been reasonably successful from the get-go, I decided that it wouldn't hurt to have a bench to assist me in getting my face and name out there even more.

So just as a FOR SALE sign provides a visible neighbourhood presence for a realtor and that realtor's company, a bench ad keeps the realtor's name and image in front of the public during a slower period of activity. Once a potential homebuyer has seen your name or image an average of only three times, they start to recognize you. If their perception is that you're successful enough to have been around a long time, what can they lose by calling your number?

When I told my parents of my promotional plan, my dad practically started counting down the days until my bench appeared. And then on that fateful day when he finally spotted it, he became as excited as a little kid let loose in a candy store. He just couldn't wait to brag to his gang of poker buddies in Florida about his successful daughter. Thus the necessity for that fateful day's rushing around—he wanted pictures as proof to accompany his many letters. (Just between you and me, the cold, hard fact that I was paying dearly for that bench was lost on my dad entirely!)

When we turned that final street corner, there it was: my bench. The ad was simple and direct and it looked good, so I must admit that I was very pleased with it. I was truly thankful that it didn't look gauche, because I've learned that the more professional you are about your advertising, the more trusting your buyer will be. That buyer will automatically benefit from the realtor's image, as well as the credibility of the realtor's company and its marketing expertise.

And when it came to location, I seemed to have hit the jackpot since my bench was in a great spot. It was prominently positioned at an intersection that had a busy strip mall and was smack dab in the middle of an area with a constant flow of traffic. And there were no other competing benches within the vicinity, so how could I possibly ask for more?

In no time flat my dad started burning through six rolls of film as he directed me to sit on the bench, stand beside the bench, lean over the bench, look at the bench, touch the bench—holy mackerel, it seemed to me that there wasn't anything legally permissible that I didn't do to that bench! Who knew my dad was such a director? I was actually relieved when he finally admitted, "I'm out of film."

Then on the much less stressful drive back home—because Dad had finally stopped rushing around like a maniac—I was able to take a closer look at my nervous father, and when I did, I smiled with grati- tude. His worrisome attitude was kind of cute and it went without saying that his strong belief in me as a realtor was second to none, so I was happy for him that he derived such simple pleasure from that bench. If he wanted to trumpet my small success to his cronies, and blow his own horn at the same time, then so be it. I just hoped those folks in Florida would be too busy reading his letters to notice my hair in those photos, because that day's frizzed-out "do" was definitely a "don't." Yikes!

MEET MIKE AND ANGELA

Well, that sign worked! Timing is everything, and while sitting at a red light one afternoon, Mike had noticed my bench and immediately asked his girlfriend, Angela, to jot down my name and number. As a result of that red light, a few days later I met the two of them at an open house I was showing. Mike's firm handshake and direct gaze told me that he was going to be all business. After talking briefly we agreed to meet again in my office the next day.

When we met, I sensed that I would need to gain Mike's confidence by impressing him with some solid facts. I was right: Mike was definitely an information seeker, or "statistic watcher," as I like to refer to those types. I took the time to review my résumé in depth with him and Angela. I let them know about the average ratio of homes that I listed and then sold, and that my number of exclusively represented buyers who ended up making a property purchase was very high. I also provided them with unsolicited references, and I let them look over a variety of sample documents that they would be presented with at the appropriate time (and ultimately end up signing) if they were to purchase a property from me. I made a mental note that Mike was extremely appreciative of that "upfront glance."

I told them both some of my own real estate experiences and I happily offered some personal information on myself, such as the area where I lived and why I had chosen that particular location. It was at that point that Angela politely interrupted me by asking, "So then you must know my cousin Mario?"

I laughed and said "Angela, I'm Italian and you're Italian so we both know plenty of cousin Marios. You're going to have to tell me which cousin Mario you're referring to."

She laughed loudly, and then she and I played a quick game of what I call "Italian geography" so that we could figure out who our mutual "cousins" might be. Because not only is every Italian person totally convinced that he or she is closely related to every other Italian person, it's also all about what village your family comes from back home!

Even though Mike was amused by our antics, within a few minutes I managed to steer the conversation back to the original real estate matter at hand with a fairly accurate impersonation of Tony Soprano: "Buy land, A.J., because God isn't making any more of it." I am happy to say that both Angela and Mike caught my reference and fully appreciated it. (And I have to admit that I wasn't half bad. I mean, I could impersonate my own father no problem, as well as various relatives and neighbours, but until that very moment it had never occurred to me to attempt the big guy, Tony Soprano himself.) Shortly thereafter it was time for Mike and Angela to leave. They assured me they would look over the material I had supplied them and they would be in touch before the week was out. I let them know that I looked forward to receiving their follow-up call.

(Oh, and just for the record, I also do a mean Adrianna!)

Now, in any given situation, it's possible that one partner within a couple could prove to be difficult. It's all relative, given people's individual personalities and how I perceive them—and vice versa. There could be complications that I'm not immediately aware of. For instance, I once encountered a man who proved to be very contentious because he plainly didn't want to deal with a female realtor, likely due to attitudes he'd inherited from his cultural background. But since his wife's family was supplying the down payment that was driving the sale, and I was their choice of realtor, they insisted that he deal with me. Needless to say, he was not a happy camper throughout most of our interactions but that didn't faze me in the least. Because once I understood his hidden objection, I knew it was up to me to work with that resistance and to form an alliance with him—and his wife.

And since every situation is different, I am prepared to deal with every type of customer possible with respect and integrity. Over my years of experience, I've met a wide range of sellers and buyers; some were extremely superstitious, some had champagne tastes but only a beer budget, some couples played a game of good cop-bad cop with me. The husband of one couple wanted to buy within the neighbourhood that he and his wife had grown up in because that location was a comfort zone for him, but his distressed wife couldn't wait to get as far away from that same neighbourhood as possible! Some first-time homebuyers have a general fear of committing to the purchase of such a big-ticket item and that often paralyzes decision making. Others, due to the politics of their relationship, have a fear of commitment to each other and that situation can be downright impossible to manage! Unfortunately I have witnessed a few "happy" relationships end rather abruptly within the emotionally charged atmosphere that surrounds a first-time property purchase.

But whatever the various circumstances might be, the important objective for me is to not patronize a buyer in any way. I rely heavily on my natural instincts and my warped sense of humour (maybe you've noticed it?) to guide me while I make an honest attempt at understanding and accepting people for themselves. Like every realtor should do, I try to remain fair, assertive, friendly, trustworthy, dedicated and communicative.

THE ROLE OF THE REALTOR

I enthusiastically greeted Mike and Angela when they returned to my office for a second round of fact-finding and "getting to know you." I gratefully thanked Angela for bringing me her favourite pesto sauce recipe, and when I promised to reciprocate by giving her a delicious family recipe for *ail e olio* with hot peppers, which my parents used to eat at 5 a.m. on a Sunday morning after staying up all night playing cards with their friends, her eyes lit up!

Mike wasted no time as he politely but firmly laid it on the line. "We really want to buy a house, but we've held off on signing any agency agreements thus far because we haven't been satisfied with any of the agents we've met with. So we're both hoping that you can change that for us." As I nodded, Mike continued without hesitation, "I hope you don't mind that we want to ask you some more questions."

"Mind?" I replied. "Not at all. I love answering a potential homebuyer's questions because it helps me to gain your trust, so fire away." And boy did he ever!

"Okay, could you let us know how you go about conducting business? And how that would differ from another realtor?"

"I'd be happy to. But to begin with, realtors are people and since no two people are exactly alike some points of comparison will be difficult to make. So let me start by telling you both that I see myself as the ultimate behind-the-scenes player whose goal is to work comfortably with my clients in an atmosphere of mutual respect, and to help them fulfill their expectations of home ownership while helping them to avoid the pitfalls. I listen closely to their desires and their objections, and then do my utmost to empathize with those points because I like to work with everybody. And, to the best of my ability, I must figure out each buyer's unique personality, so that I can focus on and bond with that personality. I like to present a relaxed but authoritative role model that my clients can relate to and trust because, let's face it, trust is the key element in all business relationships. After all, what good is a team leader who hasn't gained the loyalty of the team members? And thanks to my years of full-time, hands-on experience, I'm also very patient and resourceful." I paused, then laughed as I said, "So how am I doing so far?"

Both Mike and Angela joined me with their own chuckles and grins, as I continued.

"I will gladly work at my client's pace and I will be sure to keep them focused when their mind wanders from fatigue or anxiety, both of which are almost inevitable once the going gets tough and the pressures from decision making threaten to overwhelm them."

"What about negotiating an offer on our behalf?" Mike asked.

"Real estate is essentially a game with clearly defined opponents. Make no mistake about it, the gloves can come off during a heated negotiation. But I firmly believe that a dedicated realtor who comes to the negotiating table properly prepared with statistics, crucial knowledge and unbiased information will be able to serve her clients efficiently and well."

"Where do you find that information?"

"From a variety of professional sources. In order for me to be an effective negotiator, I have to be extraordinary at networking, as well as at marketing. I need to find out as much as I can about any other pending purchase offers so that, working together with my clients, we can strategize to beat out any possible buying competition, at the most affordable price. I also have to be able to identify how the opposition— the seller's realtor—operates. And I must be fearless when it comes to pulling off an in-your-face confrontation with that opponent if it's necessary. As a real estate veteran, I'm able to avoid intimidation and manipulation from a seller's realtor by relying on that pre-planned strategy and my own skillful persuasiveness to see me through."

"But what happens if they don't back down?" Angela asked tentatively.

"Well, I just don't give up until I've worn them down and they see it my way," I shot back.

When Angela had finished laughing, she said, "Hang on. Before you go any further, you keep saying 'realtor.' Is that the same as 'agent'? Because, to be honest, I've heard both of those terms so often, I just assumed they were the same thing. But do you mind clarifying that for me just so I'm sure?"

"Certainly," I said. "An agent is quite simply any person who is legally licensed to sell real estate, whereas the term 'realtor' is a trade-marked name that comes with a few restrictions attached, since only agents and brokers who are members of the Canadian Real Estate Association can use that term. Extensive training and continuing education are required to achieve that professional title. CREA's primary mission is to represent its membership at the federal level of government and to act as a watchdog on national legislation that pertains to the real estate industry. It's the Real Estate Business Brokers Act that governs all realtors. Realtors within the province of Ontario must also follow a very strict code of ethics that is administered by the Real

Estate Council of Ontario, and there are similar codes and councils in other provinces. I am happy to say that throughout my career I have never had any grievances brought against me at any time. Finally, realtors must adhere to regulated standards of business practice that are designed to protect the buyer's best interests."

"You also said broker, so ...?"

"A broker is any experienced agent who has worked in the field for a minimum of two years and who has also passed a more extensive qualifying exam. Every real estate office must have a broker of record."

THE MLS SYSTEM

"Let's back up a minute," Mike suggested. "I'd like to know how some friends of mine were able to find a house quite easily on the Internet, but Angie and I haven't been able to do that even though we've been looking for months."

"I'd be glad to clear up the Internet confusion for you because there is a mistaken perception in the minds of many homebuyers, especially first-timers, that the information they are able to access on real estate consumer websites, like the MLS system for example, is the exact same information that a real estate professional is privy to. Wrong, wrong, wrong! I refer to those who think they know it all as mere 'surfer boys' because in reality those edited listings found online only represent the tip of the iceberg. And because those public listings are sometimes three to 10 days behind the listings that a realtor has access to view, a specialized property might sell within a week's time, therefore never even getting posted onto the public MLS system!

"The development of the MLS concept has significantly advanced the professionalism and efficiency of real estate sales since a realtor has exclusive access to much more additional information than what the public sees on those same listings—critical and confidential information such as a property's listing date, its expiry date, security issues, previous selling prices, required deposits, if there have been any recent repairs or upgrades, how soon the seller wants or needs to move, how long that seller has lived there, as well as other personal data regarding that property's seller. And it's that vital insider information that can play a significant role in determining how I can provide an accurate property evaluation for you—supported by an effective negotiating strategy—prior to submitting your purchase offer."

"Is there anything else?" Mike asked.

"Absolutely. It is also important for potential homebuyers to know that an experienced realtor would have invaluable insights regarding a particular property's eliminating factors as well. And let me assure you that negative property information—such as limited parking options, being far from public transportation or too close to a hydro station, that the home itself has reached its full potential or is maxed out (which means that a new owner can't build up another level or expand it in any other way), constrictive municipal bylaws, a nearby vacant lot that could be adversely built on, or even if a particular property backs onto a local restaurant's adjacent property which could result in unpleasant odours or even rats—will most definitely not appear on a public Internet listing for obvious reasons.

"As well, current information concerning the local market could be supplied by a realtor's own office, while zoning and development updates may come via civic authorities. Either way, these aren't posted on the public website and realtors have the experience and expertise to interpret that information correctly to use it for the homebuyer's advantage. Thus, a competent realtor will outline the advantages and the disadvantages of each area, each type of home and each feature that's available to you so that you don't have to drive all over hell's half-acre, wasting your own valuable time, and still not accomplishing much! With so many pieces of information to pull together, a realtor needs to use time wisely and productively, so be respectful of your realtor's time. A 'looky-loo,' or tire-kicking session, can become a real pain in the neck in a real hurry! Keep in mind that every property is unique, therefore sourcing out hidden details on each one for the potential homebuyer's benefit is where the professional realtor's expertise comes in."

"So our friend basically had beginner's luck with the MLS then?" Angela asked.

"Perhaps."

And so it was on that note that we said another goodbye to each other. Mike had requested some time to digest that day's information. And since I sensed a subtle turnaround in his original reticence, I was happy to let him have the time he needed—and I was darn sure that that couple and I weren't done yet. Why? Well, thus far I was able to provide answers to the questions that Mike knew to ask. But what about the questions that he didn't know to ask? I was definitely hoping for the opportunity to provide him with those answers, too.

QUALIFYING THE BUYER

Sure enough, we were all seated together again in less than a week's time and it seemed that I had barely sat down before Mike's next question was headed my way!

"If we decided to have you represent us, and we are leaning toward that happening, could you tell me how that goes down?"

"Absolutely. I begin by 'qualifying' the buyer so that I can focus their search criteria, help them align their goals, priorities and buying capacity, and get their home-buying process rolling smoothly. To qualify a buyer means that I have to ask three essential questions—the same questions that I ask every potential client—which are these: are you currently working with another realtor? If so, that becomes an ethical issue for me because I don't want a client to run to a competitor with the exclusive knowledge that they glean from me—or vice versa. Second, I ask: are you pre-approved for a mortgage? Often the answer is no, so I then explain how pre-approval works and suggest ways that they can improve on their borrower profile and maximize what they can afford. Third, I ask: when do you want to move? This is important since both time and timing are always important factors in real estate transactions.

"I also do my utmost to educate my clients. I watch, listen and ask probing questions regarding a potential buyer's current, as well as future, property needs. I listen very closely to what my clients are saying and without being a nosey-parker I probe for their motivation. Sometimes they have already made a decision regarding an important point, but they aren't aware of it. So I merely express it for them by repeating back what I hear from them. As well, I listen to what they're objecting to. Then I crack those objections to get to the yolk, which is where their real objection is hidden. And then once that is pinpointed I can sell to that, or come in through the back door and surprise them.

"For instance, when it comes to location, I look into what changes have occurred recently in the buyer's chosen area and why some people might be moving out of that area. That way I could possibly spot a potential problem that a homebuyer wasn't even aware of. And in that way I've already fixed a problem for them—before they even knew they had it!"

Mike and Angela exchanged approving glances with me on that point while I took a deep breath. Then I continued, "Or I'll hear through the grapevine about an overly anxious seller who must sell a property quickly to satisfy their own needs, such as a last-minute job opportunity or financial hardship that's motivating them to make a fast, clean transaction that will be low on offers, conditions and possibly price. And with Christmas fast approaching, let me tell you that, contrary to popular belief, it's actually an advantageous time of year to go house hunting within certain price points, because traditionally fewer other buyers are out looking at that time of year. Therefore the chances of getting caught in a bidding war are minimal."

"I'm liking what I hear, so don't stop there," Mike joked.

"Throughout the entire process I feed off the buyer's energy, while keeping them comfortable. Perhaps some essential criteria has to be changed and priorities need to be re-established. No problem: together we can discuss possibilities and I can hopefully suggest a suitable compromise because getting creative does solve problems. I might need to remind the buyer to keep an open mind, but at the same time to also keep their dreams anchored in reality! For instance, I remember having to convince one homebuyer to sell her furniture because it was so oversized that she couldn't find a house that it would fit into comfortably. So I gently reminded her, on numerous occasions, to stop putting the cart before the horse and that she should buy furniture to fit a house instead of the other way around!"

"That won't be happening to us because we're minimalists," Angela said with a laugh.

"What type of contract will we sign?" Mike asked.

"I will only accept clients via a Buyer Representation Agreement, which is a legally binding contract. That agreement does not obligate you to buy, but you must obligate to the contract. This means that you will work exclusively with the agent, thus enabling the agent to get paid by the seller. By working with only one agent, the process and its results are greatly improved. I'll keep your personal and financial information confidential and I'll negotiate the best deal regarding price and conditions on your behalf and with your explicit approval. I can become a shield between you and all other parties as a way to protect your best interests. There is a written expiry clause in every client's purchase offer because that document is by nature very time sensitive. At a predetermined deadline, all details of that particular offer will automatically become null and void, which means that you are never tied into something that doesn't work for you. And remember that hiring a realtor is a great value for every homebuyer, because the seller pays the realtor's fee!"

WHAT TO EXPECT FROM YOUR REALTOR

I finished my conversation with Mike and Angela by explaining that a realtor under contract owes "fiduciary obligations" to his or her clients—and so much more. Here's the short list of what that means. A realtor will

- present all properties that match the buyer's criteria
- provide fact sheets on those properties when appropriate
- refer the buyer to other professionals (such as home inspectors and lawyers) as needed
- prepare comparative market analysis reports and analysis
- provide pertinent data regarding municipal zoning laws
- remain non-emotional and objective, enthusiastic and energetic, patient and diplomatic
- anticipate problems, then take charge and follow through
- avoid any situations that would involve a conflict of interest
- refrain from discrimination
- pay strict attention to disclosure laws
- give the buyer the facts and analysis of the facts using her knowledge and expertise
- disclose market conditions that govern the purchasing process
- coach the buyer during multiple offers and offer negotiations
- reply to all correspondence
- coordinate the closing details

Fade out ... fade in. Mike and Angela eventually purchased a very attractive, well-kept bungalow located in a residential neighbourhood that they really liked from the moment I showed it to them. The home was located in an area that featured a greenbelt, which added a slight touch of sophistication to the surroundings and would also be an asset to them when it came to re-sale, since walkways, bike paths and dog runs surrounded by beautiful, mature trees never go out of style. But don't think their purchase was a slam-dunk by any means! The seller, both frustrated and desperate, must have been relieved when the final sign-back—number 11—took place. Eleven? That's higher than usual because although the average number of sign-backs ranges from three to seven, in this instance both sides drew a hard bargain against each other, with Mike being his extra-cautious self the whole way. And there was nothing wrong with that.

The decision-making process is different for every buyer—at one end they can be fairly quick and easy, while at the other end they are very emotional, fearful and agonizing. There's also the simple "process of elimination" type in the middle, like Mike. He was a keen researcher who was very methodical and who really liked evaluating data. No problem: patience is a virtue!

The three questions that I am most asked by first-time home-buyers are should I buy now? Can I buy it? And how do I make that purchase? Well, because the hard answers to those seemingly easy questions are entirely personal and remain dependent upon each homebuyer's individual set of unique circumstances, it's impossible for me to state a generic or "pat" answer to them. So instead, when I'm asked those questions, I suggest that I'd be happy to sit down with the homebuyer to exchange some stories and advice and then we can take it from there. The lesson is *find a realtor that you trust, then listen to what they have to say.*

Oh, and just in case you needed confirmation, I now have proof that it really is a small world after all! When I answered my phone many months later, I instantly recognized Angela's voice. But I must admit that I was in the dark as to why she was calling me "cousin." She explained that via a very circuitous route—her Aunt Bonita, who was in town visiting from the old country, had received a letter from a relative who had a brother who lived in Florida, and the brother's letter contained a picture of a real estate agent, whose father lived in Toronto—and, well, you get the picture! Yes sir, the photo that Angela's aunt referred to was a certain picture of yours truly and by the sounds of things it had racked up more frequent flyer points than a carrier pigeon!

After listening to that strange coincidence of connections, I nearly fell out of my chair laughing when Angela asked, "By the way, my aunt wants to know what was with your hair in that picture, anyway?"

"Oh, Angela, you'll never believe it, even if I tried to explain," I said, through tears of laughter.

"It was your father, right?"

"Yes, sort of. I mean my dad and the weather, but what made you ask that?"

"Well, according to my Aunt Bonita ..."

Angela and I ended up staying on the phone for a full hour as she repeated some of the funniest stories that her aunt had heard secondhand regarding my dad when he was a small and evidently very precocious child. And that tenuous connection was all it took for Angela to declare us to be "cousins"!

After we hung up, I quickly called my dad and tried to playfully rub his nose in some of that long-ago dirt. But he wouldn't bite—until I got home that night for dinner. And then he came clean as the stories poured out of him, stories that were so hysterically funny that as I heard each of them, I thought I was going to bust for sure. My dad? Who knew?

One week later there I was, back on my bench, with my dad once again snapping away, getting more pictures. But at least that time I was surrounded by new family, new friends—and a new hairstyle!

Avoiding the Pitfalls

*In which Sandra navigates the dangerous waters of divorce,
and in which Niall and Bob take the home-buying plunge
after a home inspection steers them away from disaster*

I was having a really tough time trying to sleep the night before my "big day." My anxiety level was so high I'm sure it could have set a new record on the Richter scale! After all, it wasn't every night that I had to face the fact that I'd be walking into a lawyer's office early the next morning to get a divorce. Strangely enough, the only previous instance when I could remember having experienced such a sleepless night was due to a high level of anticipation, rather than anxiety, and that was the night before my other "big day"—my wedding. Talk about irony! I wanted to laugh, but I couldn't. The stress, the pain and the shame I was feeling were indescribable.

Oh sure, I knew better than to indulge in a pity party for one by simply reminding myself that countless other women had endured the same traumatic experience. But even so, I have to confess that my personal sense of failure at that precise moment was overwhelming, because when I was younger I was certain that I was destined to achieve some spectacular feat and appear on *Oprah* as a result! I'm not kidding, what better recognition could there possibly be than an internationally watched, on-air hug from the strong, smart and secure Ms. Winfrey? Besides, admit it, doesn't everyone want to be on *Oprah*?

Okay, all kidding aside, even though the specifics of my spectacular achievement had been a little hazy in my young mind, I had still managed to convince my younger self that at the very least I was going to grow up and be able to solve everybody's problems. So where had I gone wrong? Because there I was instead, all alone and facing the realization that I couldn't even solve my own marriage fiasco.

In an attempt to banish those confusing, negative thoughts, I reached over to the night table for a really trashy novel to read. In no time at all I was knee deep in Monique's sordid problems with Lance— and believe me when I tell you that her problems made my current situation pale by comparison. I mean, that poor misguided gal was really in a pickle!

A few hours later I marched into that lawyer's intimidating office with my dignity securely wrapped around me like an imaginary mink stole. I had resolved to remain as calm as possible and let the law take its course. Then, come what may, I would deal with the fallout as an independent, newly single woman. So I kept my head held high and silently congratulated myself on the wise decision to wear a skirt that reached mid-calf, because even when I was seated, that discreet skirt length hid my badly shaking knees! At one point during the proceedings, I glanced over at my soon to be ex-husband with a slight mixture of frustration and sadness, even as I acknowledged to myself that "it takes two to tangle."

In a far shorter time than I had thought it would take, the decisions were made, the details were finalized, the nightmare had ended, and I left that impersonal office in the same composed-looking manner in which I had arrived. Luckily, my fabulous, imaginary mink stole had not slipped an inch! I stoically walked straight to my car and locked myself in, very cautiously drove around the city block, pulled over to a quiet, relatively private area, then I totally lost it and just started bawling like a baby! Mink, shmink—where was my dignity now? After some time passed, the hysterics stopped and I slowly gained control of my fragile emotions. I popped a CD into the player and cranked it up full blast! Oh yeah, now I was cookin'! I started to belt out the lyrics to every Prince song at the top of my lungs to help me clear my head and to pump up my energy as I drove across town to get to work.

What? Why are you surprised? I was divorced—I wasn't dead!

HOW IDEAS GET STARTED

When I eventually arrived at the small coffee shop that I owned, my mood was pleasant and I instinctively jumped into the fray of the afternoon lunch rush and began serving the customers their lattes, cappuccinos, decafs, herbal teas, sandwiches, salads and desserts. The time flew by and before I knew it, it was almost time to call it a day.

And that's when it happened: a semi-regular customer came into my shop and started bragging about the two real estate deals that he had just closed, back to back. What a relief it was to hear some good news.

"Congratulations, Steve, this one's on me," I said. Then he smiled and thanked me as I placed a hot coffee and fresh slice of cake in front of him.

About a week later, I gave Steve a call and asked if I could pick his brain about a business problem I was facing. It was actually something I'd known about for some time, but due to the upheaval in my personal life I had left it simmering on the back burner. Steve agreed, so when we met I asked him for some general facts and statistics regarding the current real estate market within my shop's immediate area. Then I asked him for some specific pointers in dealing with my own predicament, because right at that moment I was extremely undecided as to what I was going to do: my landlord had recently sold the building that my coffee shop was located in, and I'd been given an unofficial heads-up that, sooner rather than later, I would have to relocate.

Quite logically and sensibly, Steve started discussing the options that were available to me, and outlined a few possibilities for me to consider. What a relief it was to know there was a light at the end of the tunnel. But then Steve paused for a moment, cleared his throat, scrunched up his face, and as I braced myself for some bad news, he blurted out, "You know, Sandra, you could just give up your shop entirely and go into selling real estate yourself."

Can you imagine my shock at that comment? I honestly think my eyebrows hit the ceiling—and temporarily stayed there—because I had never, ever considered that option before. Why would I now?

"Where in the world did that come from? Me? Sell real estate?" I laughed out loud at his preposterous suggestion. "Steve, if you couldn't already tell by now, I know practically nothing about the real estate market. And what I keep hearing about it from others seems to be the high risks that are involved, the demanding clients you have to deal with and all about every realtor's long, exhausting hours. No thanks, I sure don't need that stress. Why would I want to be on call every day and night just to please someone else?"

"Well, it's really not so different from the schedule and the stress you already have with this business," he replied.

Touché! I had to hand it to him, he'd scored a valid point there! Don't get me wrong, I loved being my own boss, but the intense responsibilities and general worries were beginning to take their toll. I was on my feet all day, I had to finalize every decision, sign every cheque, cover shifts for sick employees, haggle with the bank, and most importantly I had to try every trick in the book, as well as invent a few new ones, just to stay one step ahead of the national coffee franchises that were springing up on every other corner and threatening my business. But I shook my head "no" and laughed once more.

Steve persisted, "Sandra, do you know how many cappuccinos you have to sell just to match the commission you'd earn on only one property sale?" He smiled wickedly at me as I shrugged and continued sipping my drink. Then he casually scribbled a number down on a napkin and slid it over to me. I tried not to register too much surprise as I glanced at it indifferently. His sly wink indicated that he was being serious, as well as totally shameless!

When I thought about that conversation again a few days later, I had to admit that although Steve's idea did sound tempting financially, I couldn't seriously consider it. The timing was totally off due to the collapse of my marriage and the many changes that I now had to deal with. And since I knew that the words "recently divorced" were going to take some time getting used to, I was smart enough to realize that my plate was full. Besides, I saw my small coffee shop as an extension of myself and my lifestyle because it was an immediate connection to my community. So when the time came and I would have to move it to another location, so be it. But to give it up entirely? No way!

Another three years zipped by before I finally did "close up shop" and stopped pouring coffee for others. Unfortunately, the area that I had re-located to hadn't been as successful as I had hoped for, and to be honest the growing competition was simply crushing me. So although it had been fun while it lasted, I read the writing on the wall, and admitted to myself that the time had finally come to call it a day. Coincidentally, at just about that same time, my friend Debbie had proven to be very successful in an entirely different phase of her own career. She encouraged me to take a similar plunge at trying something new. I listened closely because I figured if Debbie could hike herself up another rung of the ladder of success with her skinny chicken legs, then it was definitely time for me to take steps in that same direction!

Now I don't care how corny this little confession will sound, but I literally had a tear in my eye and a lump in my throat on the day that I closed my shop's front door for the last time. I walked away slowly, resisting the urge to look back, knowing that I'd permanently divested myself of that phase of my life. I was investing in a new future with a new motto: "Work smart, not hard"!

MEET NIALL AND BOB

Naturally I recognized the address I was headed to on that particular day for my afternoon appointment. Even so, as I stepped into my client's office I couldn't help but reflect on the strange coincidence that his office had formerly been my modest coffee shop. What a curveball! I looked around at the many changes and smiled to myself. Then, after a moment's reflection, I reminded myself that I wasn't there for a stroll down memory lane. No, instead I was there to pick up first-time homebuyers Niall and his partner, Bob, so I could accompany them on their second viewing of the old Victorian-style home they were hoping to purchase.

Once we arrived at our destination, I'm happy to report that everything went smoothly. The floor plan of that four-level house suited their needs perfectly, it had the required number of bedrooms and bathrooms, a separate dining room, a beautiful winding staircase and a loft upstairs that could be easily converted into a personal, compact-sized gym as they planned. And since the house had been renovated within the past five years, and had been extremely well maintained since, the hardwood floors throughout were also in great condition, and the kitchen's major appliances and its other upgraded materials still looked like new. There was a fenced back yard that was a definite necessity for their two Dalmatians named Sonny and Cher, whom the men didn't want to keep confined indoors. There was a large deck off the third floor that was fairly private and suitable for entertaining. And talk about the perfect location! The funky downtown neighbourhood was within a comfortable walking distance to the local upscale shopping district, as well as to a very beautiful public park where they could exercise their pets. Last, but not least, it was also conveniently close to public transportation that would be handy for Niall, so what more could they possibly ask for?

As I was compiling the data for their offer, Niall voiced a legitimate concern. "Sandra, we think it's necessary to have an extremely thorough home inspection by a competent and experienced inspector. My sister neglected to have that type of procedure done when she purchased her first home a year ago. And unfortunately as a result she's now heavily involved in some very serious, expensive and nasty litigation. Needless to say, both Bob and I are willing to do whatever it takes so that we don't end up in that same kind of mess." My ears were on full alert, because it's always important for me to "hear" my client's objections, whether real or imagined, and Niall's feeling on that particular point was clearly understandable!

So I started by telling them both some good news. "A home inspection actually costs very little and it's an essential policy of mine to request that my clients have one completed before they purchase a property. The purpose of a home inspection is to make each new homeowner aware of any significant defects in the house that may put them at personal or financial risk in the near future. And in your specific case an added advantage will obviously be for your own security and peace of mind, so it makes perfect sense for you guys to pay a little now in order to save a lot later on." They were happy to hear my enthusiastic support for their concern.

"But I do occasionally have homebuyers balk at the idea of a home inspection," I said. "The usual excuses are that it's just one more expense they didn't need right then, or that they really didn't think it was necessary, so they weren't going to bother with one. When that happens, I make certain those buyers sign a Statement of Risk Acknowledgement that releases me, and the real estate company I work for, from all potential consequences, responsibility or obligations for any costs or damages that might result from their homebuyer's decision not to have proceeded with the recommended inspection."

I went one step further to mention some other cases I'd encountered in which the sellers had decided to have an inspection completed prior to listing their property for sale. That way, they could deal with any major problems before they were noticed by potential buyers (and other home inspectors working on the buyers' behalf), problems that might have soured a transaction altogether.

I also pointed out to Niall and Bob that it's fairly standard procedure for a homebuyer's mortgage broker, or their lending company itself, to require that a "subject to inspection clause" be included in the buyer's offer to purchase. That clause can act as their own safety mechanism against a seller's misrepresentation. Then, contingent upon the final information reported and its acceptance by your lender before your mortgage is finally granted, that condition may release the buyer from any obligation to purchase the property if the inspector finds major faults in the building. Although it doesn't happen too often, I do remember when one of my clients had their sale revoked by their lender! The legitimate reason for that drastic step was that the seller had improperly installed UFFI (urea formaldehyde foam insulation), a potentially toxic insulation substance that was discovered during the lending company's mandatory appraisal inspection.

I also informed Niall and Bob about another item that should be a standard part of every real estate transaction. "I'll include a condition in your offer that will stipulate that you receive a copy of a disclosure statement from the seller regarding the property. This provides the homebuyer with documented proof, and not just a verbal assurance, of the property's condition."

"That's great, thank you," Bob said, with obvious relief.

I explained further. "Within that disclosure statement, the seller must include relevant information stating all land and building defects, because a seller who fails to reveal a property's defects could be held liable for that omission. The disclosure statement should also indicate any potential or recurrent problems with the home that may require future repair work as well. By disclosing upfront everything that is wrong with the property, there is no attempt at deception. That puts the ball in your court as to how you'll choose to handle any problems you find out about."

Since both men nodded their approval, I continued, "If you choose to accept those problems as yours, there can be no reason for complaints or possible lawsuits later on. *Capisce?*"

"Yes, we *capisce*," laughed Bob.

BUYER BEWARE: THE PITFALLS OF DISCLOSURE STATEMENTS AND HOME INSPECTIONS

Can all disclosure statements, or Seller Property Information Sheets (as they're called in some provinces), be guaranteed for accuracy? Well, unfortunately, that's like expecting every seller to be 100% truthful and 100% knowledgeable about their own property, including latent deficiencies. Obviously honesty is the best policy, but some sellers may attempt to cloud the facts a little— in their own favour, naturally. The possibility that a disclosure statement might be inaccurate is the number one reason to insist on a thorough home inspection to begin with. I prefer to assume that the sellers are acting in good faith, but it's best to take precautions anyway. So when you receive your copy of the disclosure statement, be sure that you read it closely and in its entirety prior to the home inspection. And be sure that you hire a highly recommended, dedicated inspector because, unfortunately, home inspection in Canada is an unregulated and ungoverned industry, with no standards or criteria controlling its members except those imposed by the various inspectors' "associations." Because there is no formal licensing of home inspectors, it is incumbent upon that industry to police itself and weed out any "pretenders" with limited qualifications who have imprudently decided to call themselves home inspectors.

Even so, as in every industry, a few bad apples still manage to slip by. Which reminds me of the time I met an "actor" at a social function. He was quite attractive and very personable, but because he didn't look immediately familiar, I politely asked him, "What have you been in that I might have seen?" I found out that he had no formal, accredited training or even a current performing résumé, so how he thought he was qualified to call himself an actor was certainly beyond me!

Be sure to protect yourself from running into a similar situation when you hire a home inspector, because you'll want to invest your complete trust in a knowledgeable individual. There is obviously much more at stake than a brief embarrassing moment!

I made some suggestions to Niall and Bob. "I have put together a list of inspectors whom I am happy to refer to you. I suggest that you contact those potential inspectors one on one, and ask enough questions to satisfy your peace of mind. Find an individual who inspires confidence, clarify what his liability insurance covers, ascertain his degree of skill and competence, and request references. Then, when you have a top choice, be certain to check out a few of those references. Do not leave anything to chance because although home inspectors are liable for their errors, omissions and outright mistakes, every inspector's final report will undoubtedly contain sufficient disclaimers ..."

"Do you mean loopholes?" interrupted Niall.

"I hesitate to use the term 'loopholes' because that implies fraudulent practice. But the inspectors' contracts do protect themselves from assuming liability if a problem is overlooked. It is entirely up to both of you as the potential homebuyers to perform your own due diligence regarding this very important hiring matter."

"Any suggestions?" Bob asked, as he looked a little uncertainly over at Niall.

"Sure. For starters, I can recommend a well-respected industry organization with rigorous standards of practice that you can check with. It's called the Canadian Association of Home and Property Inspectors and it sets minimum standards of professional conduct, educates its membership and imposes mandatory liability insurance requirements. But remember that it's not necessary for a home inspector to be affiliated with that particular organization, or any similar one, so take all necessary precautions before hiring your final candidate."

"Anything else?" Bob implored.

"Well, a little piece of personal advice. If it's at all possible to hire an inspector who's a Virgo, then please do! Because although on a daily basis those analytical, perfectionist nitpickers are critical enough to drive anybody crazy, those characteristics are the exact same qualities needed for a successful home inspecting gig!"

"And who do we know that's a Virgo?" Bob jokingly asked.

"Your uptight mother," Niall snapped.

"Yes, but she thinks her criticism is constructive and that her complaining is an admirable trait because she's ..."

"Just trying to be helpful, dear," Niall interjected in an overly sweet tone.

"You've got that right, and we both know she'll never change," laughed Bob.

GETTING THE MOST FROM A HOME INSPECTION

I strongly suggest that you accompany your inspector—whether he's a Virgo or not—during the entire inspection procedure if possible. That way you can see exactly what he sees and be able to gauge his reactions accordingly. Be sure to stay out of his way so you don't impede his progress, but don't hesitate to ask questions whenever you feel it's necessary. Oh, and that disclosure statement you have on file from the seller? Be sure to take it along and ask your inspector to pay particularly close attention to anything that might look problematic within any listed areas.

The inspector will visually inspect the home's basic components: foundation and/or crawl spaces, chimney, roof, garage, driveway, eavestroughs, soffits and fascia, basement, drainage, staircases, floors, walls, ceilings, fireplace, doors, windows, attic and garage. He'll assess the quality of any renovations. He will also observe the operation of the house's various systems and their components too:

plumbing, electrical, furnace, water heater, air conditioning, insulation, ventilation, ductwork, appliances, light fixtures, and make all of the necessary notations. As well, he may check for any signs of rodent infestation or insect infestation. A thorough home inspection will take approximately three hours to complete since it actually covers more than a thousand checkpoints around the property! So don't be alarmed when your inspector insists on crawling around in the attic, or climbing up to the roof despite nasty weather conditions. He is just "doing his job."

Upon completion of the inspection, the buyer will receive a detailed, written report of the home's present condition. That comprehensive itemized report should be a professional, unbiased and unemotional assessment. And because the potential buyers are just days away from making an extremely large financial investment, they should take the time to scrutinize that report with a fine-tooth comb, asking for any puzzling issues to be fully explained, before they give their final approval and acceptance of its findings. The report could include information regarding any substandard elements, the estimated life expectancy of expensive items to replace like the roof or the driveway, some preventive maintenance ideas and their costs, as well as estimates for how long it might be for major repairs to be needed (such as a new roof) and ballpark figures for how much repairs and improvements might cost.

Unfortunately, when Niall and Bob's home inspection ended, the report noted that an infestation of termites was suspected. Termites? Yuck! Don't even get me started on how much I detest creepy, crawly bugs—and termites sound particularly disgusting.

■ ADVICE FOR PROPERTY VIRGINS
True Tales About Termites

Termites are tiny wood-boring insects that are extremely destructive to homes and other buildings. They have been around since the beginning of time because they are adaptable to ever-changing environments.

The most common type found, subterranean termites, is extremely tough to control. They're of increasing concern to homebuyers in North America because they can cause serious structural damage.

Termites live in the soil, but feed off the cellulose in wood, breaking it down and returning it to the soil. Be forewarned that any untreated wood that comes into direct contact with the soil surrounding a home provides a perfect entry point for those destructive, menacing insects. And because they basically never stop working and eating for even a minute out of the day, their ability to tunnel their way through a home's wooden structure and leave it destroyed is truly frightening. An average termite colony is over one million strong, and thanks to the fact that they remain unseen and cause their destruction under the surface, they can be very difficult to detect. If they are found in a home's support beams, thereby jeopardizing the integrity of those beams, they can put the entire home at risk!

Even though circumstantial evidence raised concerns for Niall and Bob's home inspector, he would not commit 100% to a full declaration of a termite infestation without further investigation, which he recommended should take place. As he candidly admitted, "After thirty years on the job, my eyes are well trained, but it's impossible to see if there's any serious damage beneath the surface, because even I don't have x-ray vision!"

Now, as can be expected, my clients weren't about to take that potentially explosive "possibility of termites" situation sitting down, and I didn't blame them. Nor were the sellers, who seemed quite devastated—and quite genuinely shocked—by the inspector's findings. Like most sellers who find themselves in this situation, these particular sellers insisted that they had not been aware of the situation, and had not deliberately neglected to divulge such vital information in their disclosure statement. And let's be honest: how many people do regular checks of their basements for signs of termite damage? It's easy to see how this could be overlooked, even by the most honest sellers.

The seller's vehement claim to be innocent of any such subterfuge sounded genuine and the seller's realtor insisted that the possibility of termites was not deliberately concealed information, "because that's not something my clients should have been reasonably expected to know."

Even so, Niall and Bob could have walked away right then and there, refusing any further consideration to conclude their purchase. Before that happened, I said, "It can't hurt to follow up on the home inspector's recommendation for further investigation just to see where such an investigation might lead. And since the sellers realize that the final sale of their property is hanging in the balance by a very slim thread, I'm confident that they'll agree with my suggestion."

Well, not only did the sellers quickly agree, but in a show of good faith they also agreed to pay for the cost of having a professional pest control inspector conduct an in-depth investigation. It was quickly scheduled for the next afternoon.

A professional termite inspector will poke holes into a home's wooden structure with a sharp tool, searching for samples of evidence that a termite colony exists. However, since some evidence may not be easily accessible within a cramped crawl space or attic, it is very important to ask specific questions of the current owners. Had there ever been a previous infestation? If so, how extensive was the damage on that occasion? What method of treatment was used at that time? Does the neighbourhood have a history of, or a bad reputation for, similar infestations? These questions must be answered before accepting an inspector's "all clear" because the cost to treat an extensive infestation can be unbelievably high. I remember the time a realtor acquaintance of mine told me that she'd once had clients who had to shell out more than $20,000 to fix their new property's termite problem within the first six months of purchasing. In that instance, the buyers had gotten caught up in a frenzied bidding war and had—against the advice of their realtor—waived their right to a home inspection in their purchase offer. It's tempting to remove all conditions when you're bidding against others, but the information you get from an inspection is just too valuable to forego—if you hear about a really serious problem, you may decide to lower your offer, or walk away from the house altogether. Unfortunately for those buyers, they were forced to pay through the nose for their error.

Fade out ... fade in. Let's return to Niall and Bob's dilemma. When the pest control inspector's report indicated that an infestation definitely did exist on the property, the sellers again maintained that they had never experienced a prior problem, and they hadn't been aware of the current one. Fine. In that case, there were some necessary questions to ask: would the sellers be willing to fix the problem themselves? If so, how soon could that take place? Or would they substantially lower their asking price for the property instead?

After careful consideration, the sellers agreed to pay for the treatment of their home to have the termite infestation eliminated, as well as to have the existing damage repaired. That decision was acceptable to my clients as long as a condition of the home passing one more, final inspection was also honoured, thus making the property's final sale contingent upon finding no further evidence of the infestation. If it didn't pass that final inspection, my clients would walk away once and for all. And that arrangement was agreed to by the seller.

When I reminded Niall how much he had insisted on a thorough home inspection, he laughed. I don't think even he expected that his tenacity on that point was going to result in a total of three inspections!

And so, all-out war was declared on the termites! A chemical barrier had to be established between the ground and the seller's home, and the treatment procedure required specialized chemicals that are not available to the general public. Those unique chemicals must be administered under very strictly controlled conditions by professionally trained experts, because the treatment method to eliminate termites is much more specialized than the procedures required to eliminate other insects. Just so you are aware, while the procedure is effective against the elimination of the termites, it will not damage the indoor air quality of the home's environment itself, nor does it cause any damage to the interior's paint, furniture, possessions, etc.

Success! Or as Borat would say, "Good times!" Niall and Bob were soon enough the proud new owners of a unique old Victorian home in a beautiful, mature neighbourhood. Since a homeowner cannot get termite insurance, they had armed themselves with enough practical knowledge regarding the necessary safety tips to protect their property from any recurrent infestations. They would avoid all direct wood-to-ground contact, trim or remove all trees, shrubs and vines from actually touching their house, schedule a termite inspection on a yearly basis, remove all excessive moisture from around the home's foundation, purchase a warranty with sufficient liability protection from a reputable pest control company, and learn about the necessity, along with the methods required, to specially treat any new wood that is going to be used for future exterior renovations. I had to applaud them both, because in no time at all they had practically made themselves experts on the subject!

MORE HOUSING HAZARDS TO KEEP ON YOUR RADAR

Now then, let's leave the world of creepy, crawly bugs behind to take a minute to discuss the still-controversial situation that surrounds the home insulation substance known as UFFI (urea formaldehyde foam insulation). Although the substance was permanently banned in Canada in 1980, it could still be hidden within the walls of homes that are for sale in today's marketplace, and therefore it remains a potential problem for first-time homebuyers to be aware of. Prior to being banned, UFFI had been government-approved so it was popularly used in the 1970s as an effective method for insulating homes built during that time. As well, UFFI was sometimes injected into older, pre-1970s homes as a method for re-insulating them. If UFFI was properly installed, the homes that contain it should be free of contamination. And since they pose no threat, those homes can be insured by the Canada Mortgage and Housing Corporation.

But if UFFI was improperly installed (which is what happened in my previously mentioned client's unfortunate case), a potential lender could decline financing. More than that, improper installation can cause very serious illness to the home's inhabitants due to a hazardous level of formaldehyde within their living environment. If the insulation's ingredients were not mixed properly, that damaged insulation released unsafe quantities of formaldehyde gas into the home's atmosphere, causing a potentially dangerous situation. It is the level of toxicity that can prove to be injurious, and not the formaldehyde gas itself, because believe it or not every home does have formaldehyde gas inside. Formaldehyde is found in many other products, such as aerosol sprays, dry-cleaning chemicals, natural gas furnaces, cigarette and cigar smoke, and lots of other things. Because our environment is not entirely free of it, the concern and controversy revolve around the "acceptable" degree.

That concern and controversy are more than a nuisance for those homeowners with a home that has (or once had) UFFI, because its reputation is usually far worse than its effects. Even improperly installed UFFI ceases to have much of an impact on the air if it's left undisturbed (as is the case in most houses). Air quality tests are done every day on UFFI homes, and often those tests prove that the air quality in those homes is no worse than in other homes.

Nonetheless, during a professional home inspection, the inspector will routinely remove electrical faceplates from the interior walls to look for evidence of UFFI. He will also closely examine the exterior walls for telltale drill holes where UFFI would have been injected into the wall cavities of the home. Safety tests are also administered inside the home to establish the exposure limits and level of formaldehyde gas within the interior to determine that its level doesn't exceed an acceptable standard.

As a concerned realtor, I do my utmost to protect my clients from that potentially hazardous substance by determining whether or not the home they are interested in purchasing is currently—or had ever been—insulated with UFFI because, besides the obvious safety threat, those types of homes also have a stigma about them as being "unsafe." That unsafe reputation has an extremely negative impact on a property's re-sale value. If there is any question of UFFI in a house you're considering, I would highly recommend that a clause be written into your offer for your own protection, although it may already be a standard clause in the Agreement of Purchase and Sale where you live. The sellers must govern themselves accordingly and be truthful in their disclosure statement that the home is not now, nor ever has been, insulated with UFFI. If evidence of UFFI is found during the home inspection, the offer to purchase could be automatically withdrawn.

Termites, UFFI, what's next? Athough the threat of lead-based paints or asbestos being found in homes has lessened over time, a buyer must still be vigilant in performing their due diligence regarding those toxic substances as well. In very old homes, for instance, lead-based paints can still be present under layers of newer paint, so beware. Any lead-based paints are a dangerous contaminant, and therefore an extreme health hazard. A new homeowner, unaware that lead-based paint has been applied on walls that he wishes to knock down to carry out some renovations, will be exposed to that old toxic paint during the process.

A similar situation could also occur during the removal of asbestos. Minute mineral fibres of that cancer-causing material could remain in the air for weeks. In some older homes asbestos could be found in the following areas: concrete roofing shingles, asphalt floor tiles, insulation on oil and coal furnaces or on boilers and hot water pipes.

Fireplace flues could also be lined with asbestos. But if the asbestos fibres remain "lockedin"—that is to say, the shingles are not crumbling, the tiles are not chipped, the lining is not cracked—then the substance itself actually poses very little danger to those inhabiting the property. So it would be highly advisable to just leave well enough alone. Perhaps imagining a very large DO NOT DISTURB sign posted near those specific areas will do the trick!

As you can see, for a first-time homebuyer there's always something to watch out for in the world of real estate so that you don't get blindsided by an unseen threat. And I think the same goes for life in general, don't you? The good news is that there are ways to protect yourself, the most important one being this: *hire a reliable home inspector, and specialized inspectors when necessary, and follow up on any information that sounds risky or expensive.* Your investment could rely on it.

By the way, in case any inquiring minds want to know—and I'm sure there are a few who do—I actually rebounded fairly quickly from my unhappy divorce experience. No, I wasn't exactly out dancing in the street within a week of those legal papers being finalized, but I wasn't numbed into senseless inactivity either. I was comforted by knowing that I had done my best to make my marriage work, and that I'd only given up once it became obvious that my emotional and physical health were at stake. Thanks to the love and support of my close-knit family, along with some very concerned friends, I just didn't allow myself to become despondent. Instead I did my level best to stay focused, to remain positive and to concentrate on moving forward. And if I let some of the little things slide, big deal. I noticed that the world didn't stop spinning. So I figured that maybe I was meant to go through a little hell first, before discovering that whenever I did cut myself some slack it felt great. So I kept doing it! No more making mountains out of molehills for me.

I also made sure that I went to practically every comedic film I could find, because I've always believed that laughter truly is the best medicine. It's the kind of medicine that I can never get enough of, because there's just nothing like enjoying the cathartic release of a really loud snorting laugh at some imaginary character's onscreen foibles!

I also remember enjoying a girls' night out with some of my closest friends, women who were either struggling in their relationships or were also, like me, "divorcées." Don't you just hate that word? But I guess it's a sign of the times that there are so many of us who now fall into that category. We all had a ton of fun just getting silly and letting off a whole bunch of steam. It felt great to laugh a lot, to cry a little and to tell the cute waiter, "Okay, I'll have one more. But it's the last one. And I really mean it this time!" As we sat there sharing our war stories, I found out that my own experience wasn't really all that horrible in comparison to some of theirs. It had been very unpleasant, don't get me wrong, but it hadn't been debilitating. And even though it was true that I had learned a few of life's lessons the hard way, I could honestly say that I was thankful to have gained those new insights.

Before I could dredge up too many unhappy memories, one of my girlfriends piped up with her story of having seen a television interview with the voluptuous blond bombshell Zsa Zsa Gabor as she spoke about her multiple marriages—and subsequent divorces. When the interviewer suggested that perhaps the glamorous Zsa Zsa's infamous party-girl lifestyle didn't lend itself to a simple life of housekeeping, the not-so-dumb blonde's eyes flashed wickedly as she wittily responded, "Dahling, I am an excellent housekeeper really. Because you see, dahling, I never keep the husband, but I always keep the house!" And so it went. What a night—we had a blast. But, unfortunately, what a morning after too!

Shortly after my marriage ended, I had indulged in a little "shoe therapy" that perked me up, and soon after that I also splurged on a vacation to Mexico. But on both occasions I was proudly spending my own funds, and not my ex-husband's. And since there were no children or long-term financial issues between us, I found those circumstances made it easier to pick up the pieces and move on. As you know, I also channeled a great deal of energy into my very demanding small coffee-shop enterprise.

I also even managed to find a little bit of spare time to expand my interests into a few recreational areas as well. I've always thanked my lucky stars that I was born with a thirst for knowledge. As well as having an inquisitive business mind, I have an insatiable curiosity for personal pursuits too. Although it's quite possible that curiosity has actually killed a cat at some point, so far it hasn't done me any harm!

And so, as I casually sat outside the other day enjoying my sun-drenched patio while mulling over the somewhat meagre, but personally significant achievements of mine that I could hopefully discuss with my best friend Oprah, I heard the phone ring in the other room. Before dashing to get it, I silently prayed that it would be her show's booking agents calling to inquire about my availability. Naturally I would act humbly surprised while I resolutely assured them that I was indeed willing and able to appear. But it was just a wrong number.

Hey, not a problem. Patience is a virtue, and when it comes to *Oprah*, I'm ready for my close-up!

4

Taking It All On

In which Sandra snaps out of daydreaming mode to help Mustafa, a first-time homebuyer with big dreams for home ownership, renovations and becoming a landlord—all at once

If only life were perfect! What a wonderful world it would be if that were even remotely possible, don't you agree? Contemplate the amazing possibility of living a stress-free existence, all the minor daily hassles that currently irritate each of us eliminated. And just think of all the free time we'd have on our hands if we were suddenly blessed with absolutely no cares or worries. Last but not least, for a really perfect life, there would no longer be any life-threatening diseases or dangerous environmental issues that currently plague us as they spiral out of control and threaten our very existence. Well, for the gift of an entirely perfect life, I know I'd be willing to sign on the dotted line.

Is daydreaming one of your favourite pastimes? It is for me. I did it a lot as a small child when I was bored stiff at school. Go on, admit it—you probably did too! The possibility of fun and games in the playground filled with those big rain puddles that sat silently tempting us just outside the classroom window sure looked a lot more interesting than those math problems up on the blackboard, didn't they? And which one of us can honestly say we weren't watching the clock with eager anticipation when we knew the recess bell was just about to ring? Especially when we all knew that simple sound signalled our chance at a temporary freedom, endless pranks and oodles of excitement.

Even though I no longer have a daily recess to look forward to, I still allow myself the pleasure of daydreaming. And when I can find the time to indulge that whim, I love to take full advantage of it by just sitting still and allowing my mind to temporarily shut off from the steady drone of facts, figures and worrying obligations that are crowding it. I chill out by thinking about a perfect world instead!

I was enjoying such a deeply blissful state of mind late one afternoon when my phone rang sharply, snapping me back to reality. When I answered it I was greeted by an eager voice asking if I was available for a meeting. As always, my response was a firm "You bet I am."

MEET MUSTAFA

The next morning I met with a first-time homebuyer named Mustafa, who told me that his objective was to purchase a property that he could renovate fairly cheaply, because his plan upon completing the renovations was to rent out half of the home in order to help pay the mortgage. The rent would provide him with an added source of income to help him pay off the mortgage.

"No problem," I answered with a smile, since I'd previously dealt with my share of buyers who wanted to purchase a "fixer-upper." I had even joked to one of those clients—and now to Mustafa—"A diamond in the rough is probably the only kind of diamond that Elizabeth Taylor doesn't collect!"

But wait just a second. Had I heard correctly? Did Mustafa also say that he was going to rent out half the home? Yes, in fact, he had, which was all well and good in theory. But when I heard his clarification, I asked, "Do you realize the enormous undertaking that you're facing by becoming a first-time homebuyer as well as a landlord?" He responded by shrugging and giggling nervously before saying, "I know it will be a lot of work."

Now that was an understatement if ever I heard one! "So, let me get this straight: first-timer *and* fixer-upper *and* landlord—all in one fell swoop? Mustafa, is your middle name 'ambitious'?"

As his giggles grew louder, I deadpanned in my best Cuban-accented Ricky Ricardo impersonation, "Lucy, you got some 'splainin' to do!" Mustafa's nervous giggles turned into a loud guffaw!

Once he had managed to catch his breath and settle down, Mustafa began, "A few years after my parents emigrated to Canada, they were able to purchase a second home to be rented out as an income-generating property. Since both of my parents are accomplished medical professionals with very good earning power, and I was an only child, they felt that their surplus income would be wisely invested in a rental property venture. And it appears that their decision was a wise one, because within a little less than twenty years that property of theirs is now totally mortgage free."

"That's wonderful," I said.

He continued, "And fortunately for my parents' sake, their various tenants throughout that entire time were all law-abiding, respectful families who were reasonably easy to deal with, so my parents were never confronted with any of those aggravating, typical landlord-versus-tenant type of headaches. You know, like having somebody skip out on paying their rent or causing a lot of property damage, whatever."

"Fortunate is right!" I concurred.

"So, as you can see, my parents have set an excellent example for me to emulate regarding a successful property purchase and its management."

"They sure have," I agreed.

"And now, after some careful consideration and research, plus the fact that I've always been an overachiever"—more giggling—"I think

I'm finally ready to play copycat and take a giant step forward. So that's why I'm here."

"Who doesn't love a daredevil?" I said.

"Or a daydreamer?"

Okay, that did it for me right there. Little did Mustafa realize how much he and I had in common regarding that word! So I wished him a great deal of success with his venture, and then got right down to brass tacks to help him put his plans into motion. Just a few days later, and armed with my short list of appropriately selected properties in hand, we set off to "see the wizard"!

GOLD MINE OR MONEY PIT?

Before Mustafa and I arrive to view our first property I'd like to clear up a few misconceptions regarding fixer-uppers in general.

Although it's true that a fixer-upper property should be on the market at a substantially lower price because it needs work, potential homebuyers must also keep in mind that a fixer-upper is only truly cheaper if its defects are fixable at an affordable price. Otherwise, a property that was supposedly a bargain could turn out to be a money pit instead! The best way I can suggest to avoid that hellish money drain from happening is for homebuyers to deal with realities and not fantasies, which means keeping their eyes wide open to fully understand the severity of each fixer-upper's specific problems. Although some homebuyers might possess an enviable entrepreneurial spirit, they often lack the precise knowledge required to correctly estimate the renovation time and the financial outlay that will be required to make a wise fixer-upper purchase. You should also remember that essential financial factors such as the property's closing costs and its monthly carrying costs will tie up a big chunk of your investment capital. Any mistakes in under-estimation can end up biting those homebuyers in the bum by severely impacting, if not outright destroying, their profit potential in the future re-sale price. That equals a lost opportunity.

Other obvious questions will undoubtedly crop up, questions such as was it really worth the extra time, the extra money, the extra effort and the extra inconvenience? If the answers to those questions are "no," maybe an already decent-looking and appropriately priced property should have been purchased right from the word "go" instead, because it would have saved the unsuspecting buyers from financial hardship and mental meltdown. And in some cases, even from a close friend or family member smugly braying, "I told you so!"

WHAT WILL THE BANK SAY?

There are financing issues to consider, too. Where will you get the money for the mortgage and the renos on top of that? You'll find that the words "expensive" and "extensive" are not always welcomed with open arms by lenders. Keep in mind that your lender will qualify a mortgage limit based on the *current condition* of the property you want to buy, not on the property after its repairs, simply because any number of adverse circumstances could crop up to keep those repairs from ever getting done. Some lending institutions may balk at lending the necessary funds to make that investment purchase at all—until the renovations and repairs are complete, even though the renovations and repairs obviously can't be completed until the property has been purchased. Some banks will allow you to borrow more for renovations (on top of your mortgage), but don't count on it. Unless it's clearly spelled out, you should expect that none of your pre-approved mortgage amount can be set aside for, or get applied to, those pending renovations or repairs. To finance a fixer-upper, a few additional appointments with a few additional lenders might be in the cards before the right lender is found.

■ ADVICE FOR PROPERTY VIRGINS
Reno Financing with CMHC

If you don't have enough money for a 20% down payment on your house purchase, your lender will require that you seek "mortgage loan insurance" through the Canada Mortgage and Housing Corporation (CMHC). This program costs you a bit extra, but it might make it possible for you to get the financing you need.

You may also qualify for a program at CMHC called "purchase plus improvements." It allows you to add the cost of renovations into the purchase price of the home—and use the higher post-renovation value as the value by which to calculate the mortgage amount.

This program is limited to renovations that are no more than 10% of the purchase price or current value. There are hoops to jump through with a program like this, but it's well worth looking into.

As well, for any homebuyers also wishing to become landlords, the eventual income from a rental unit cannot be used to qualify them for a higher pre-approved mortgage amount. The maximum amount granted will be for the actual purchase price of the property only, and you'll still need to show an adequate down payment and adequate employment income. Any attempt to increase the mortgage limit by using the projected rental income would unfairly enhance the homebuyer's current financial circumstances, and obviously the lender would be careful not to allow that to happen. It is only after rents have been collected that they can accurately be called income. Taking in rent will increase the homeowner's future financial status only—not their current status.

FIRST TIME'S THE CHARM?

Now that doesn't mean that a first-time homebuyer can't make a lucky strike on a fixer-upper. It just means that nothing is ever as easy as it first seems. In fact, it's very gullible of a potential homebuyer to assume that finding an inexpensive fixer-upper, buying it, repairing it and turning around and re-selling for a tidy profit is a piece of *gateau*. Contrary to a commonly held belief, not every fixer-upper can be re-sold for a mighty profit within a very short period of time. In my experience, the buyers who think that way are usually the ones who have never done it before. Be careful not to over-romanticize your expectations.

Instead, be extra cautious when purchasing a neglected property at a comfortable price. You want its price to remain comfortable even after factoring in the cost of the necessary renovations and their inevitable delays.

■ ADVICE FOR PROPERTY VIRGINS
THE POWER OF TWO

All potential fixer-upper homebuyers might want to acquaint themselves with the number two. Why? Because it may cost them two times the amount of capital they had originally budgeted for, two times the patience to deal with the unexpected stress—and those repairs will inevitably take two times as long to complete as they had originally expected! Keeping that thought in mind, the necessity for very careful planning and management is obviously of the utmost importance. Thanks to a more accurate plan of attack from the beginning, when all is said and done, those properly informed homebuyers will hopefully come out as contented winners instead of ticked-off losers. It's no fun for anyone when a homebuyer's precious dream turns into their worst nightmare instead.

TEARING DOWN MISCONCEPTIONS

A close cousin to the fixer-upper is the "tear-down." That usually refers to a small or very decrepit house that's in bulldozer condition but sitting on an attractive piece of property. A homebuyer might be tempted to purchase the house with the specific intention of tearing it down and replacing it with a brand-new, larger house that fits comfortably on its larger lot. Many homes exhibit excellent potential to become tear-downs for a savvy homebuyer—however, beware the best-laid plans of mice and men! Often those speculative plans can become sabotaged by unseen traps, so remember to follow the facts and not the scent. Especially not the scent of easy money!

The scent of easy money is exactly what lured a greedy builder to a street where I lived. He tore down an original bungalow and replaced it with a "McMansion" because he believed that if he built it, they would come. Unfortunately for him, that new XXL-sized house was constructed to be impressively large and impressively showy. It was built right out to its legal limits, thus making it seem like a giant polar bear squatting on a toadstool. Needless to say, it stuck out like a sore thumb on our street filled with bungalows. The developer had "over-improved" for the area.

But was that McMansion just an early indicator of progress, you ask? A sign of what might happen to that neighbourhood in the future, perhaps? Or was it merely an example of an overzealous builder with more money than taste? Well, in that particular instance, it appeared to be the latter because the home sat empty for seven months with no offers at all. Which actually wasn't too surprising, considering that surrounding homes were selling for less than half of that property's over-inflated asking price. Its interior had been decorated in a very pretentious manner with an obvious lack of balance between beauty and functionality. It was trying too hard, "showing off," which proved to be another turnoff for potential buyers. When a home lacks character or charm, it's about as appealing as a piece of dry toast! Mmm ... no thanks.

So what happened? Did it ever sell? Yes, it did, but for far, far less than what the ambitious builder had originally intended. He reluctantly lowered his asking price by a substantial amount and even humbly admitted to his realtor that his plan had obviously been ahead of the market. He was right on that point, at least. Most homebuyers won't want to spend their hard-earned million dollars on a property located within a half-million-dollar area when they could make a much wiser purchase simply by going directly to a more upscale location instead.

Fade out … fade in. When Mustafa and I arrived at our first designated property, he took one look at what greeted him and his enthusiasm went right out the window. Now, to be fair, that house and its surrounding property did not show well. There was zero curb appeal—both the house and yard needed a heaping helping of TLC! Even though the property met the essential criteria that Mustafa had outlined, it was obvious by his shocked reaction that he wasn't expecting the dose of reality that greeted him. But hey, welcome to the world of fixer-uppers where it might be necessary to put aside an initial negative reaction to the home's physical appearance, since that can always be changed anyway.

Another reason for the lower asking price on that particular property was its location within what was considered to be an up-and-coming neighbourhood—which means the neighbourhood was on the cusp of being turned around and revitalized, but not quite there yet. Adventurous homebuyers can seize upon an opportunity within such an area—or get left out in the cold. Because once that up-and-coming area has actually "arrived," you'll find that its property values have increased dramatically as well. A reality check might be in order to remind yourself that up-and-coming is not spelled "picture perfect"!

Mustafa, after viewing the home's interior, which was not as badly neglected as its exterior, said, "I don't think I'm going to bite." We were out of there and moving on to the next possibility.

Although the next property we viewed had been listed "as is," and was also quite needy, Mustafa's initial level of acceptance of it was much greater. That agreeable opinion on his part was due mainly to the property's location since the neighbourhood was a more desirable one with many well-maintained homes. To be honest, that neighbourhood would have been out of Mustafa's reach under regular circumstances since even its entry-level price point was dangerously close to the top of his pre-approved mortgage amount. But by saving money on that "slightly spoiled tomato" I'd found lurking within an otherwise unspoiled batch, he might be able to take a step up to that entry level.

That one, however, wasn't meant to be either, due to Mustafa's rejection of its floor plan. Unfortunately, the location of its main staircase conflicted greatly with the mental image he had in mind for the placement and design of his rental unit. And since the cost for the additional construction work involved in repositioning the staircase was not in his current budget, we moved on again.

Approximately a week later, we viewed a much older house that really exhibited some raw potential. Its curb appeal wasn't award worthy, but it was certainly acceptable. And since it was already early fall, I suggested that the yard work enhancements weren't an immediate priority; he could conveniently put them off until the spring instead. When it comes to fixer-uppers, it's usually necessary to pick your battles and to complete the work according to priority. And since landscaping improvements only tend to increase a property's yield by roughly 30%, whereas a new bathroom and a new kitchen usually present a payback of anywhere from 75% to 200%, or more, Mustafa smiled and agreed.

We entered the house with high expectations, and once inside I could see that this home's interior was meeting with Mustafa's satisfaction. I watched closely as he took his time to look intently at the bones of the building's structure to help him determine its suitability for his remodelling plans.

"Once the renovations have been completed as I imagine them," Mustafa said, "I can totally visualize a very comfortable finished home that will give both my tenant and myself plenty of room, and plenty of privacy too."

"That sounds ideal."

"But I'd like to have my cousin take a thorough look at this place before I finalize my decision."

"Is he a licensed building contractor?" I asked.

"Um, not really."

"Is he a professional home inspector?"

"Not exactly, he's more like my secret weapon," Mustafa said with a giggle.

"Well, it's always nice to have a secret weapon," I told him, "but it's far more advantageous to hire an experienced home inspector who really knows his stuff because you wouldn't want to encounter any expensive hidden problems later on. And I could certainly offer you some recommendations for a few who are worth their weight in gold."

"Sure, thanks," he replied unconvincingly. "But do you mind if I call my cousin anyway?"

"Not at all, be my guest," I responded. I am always more than happy to supply my clients with pertinent facts, as well as professional observations gleaned from my years of experience when they pertain to a given situation. It's not my position as a realtor, however, to impose my personal opinion onto my clients since the final decision on all matters remains their responsibility.

In the early evening, Mustafa and his cousin met me at the property. After a very fast look around, the cousin stated that he had no major objections. "You know, buddy, this place is a real find," he declared. Then he turned to me. "In fact, if he doesn't end up buying it, would you give me a call?"

"Hey, don't go getting any ideas," Mustafa said teasingly. "She's my realtor and don't you forget it."

"Thanks for the compliments, guys," I said, playing along, "but flattery will get you nowhere. Mustafa, you and I have some serious work ahead of us if we're going to get started on that offer."

"Yes, boss!" he giggled nervously. He thanked his cousin and we left.

In the time it took for us to drive back to my office, Mustafa told me that he was reconsidering the need for a professional, unbiased home inspector after all. Hmm, so much for his secret weapon! He didn't explain why and I didn't ask, but I can't tell you the immense relief that I felt for his sake. So I smiled sincerely and said, "I think you'll be very happy if you do decide to get another opinion."

"I think so too, but I'm not going to tell my cousin yet," he giggled.

Now don't get me wrong: Mustafa's cousin seemed like a terrific guy, but just between you, me and the lamppost, his idea of a complete home inspection consisted of only checking out the obvious and that really frosted my flakes! After all, installing a kitchen cabinet would seem like no big deal on the surface; however, a huge problem could be looming underneath when it's discovered that the plumbing is in the wrong place. Yikes! And because I've seen a few unfortunate and costly errors like that occur, I'm leery when a client prefers to substitute their friend's or family member's untrained eyes for those of a qualified expert's.

My objective when preparing Mustafa's offer to purchase was not only for him to acquire the property at a reasonable price, but also for him to be able to complete the renovations and repairs in a realistic and timely fashion. Mustafa's dream of generating a second income wouldn't be a full-fledged reality until a tenant was installed who was paying a monthly rent—in his legally retrofitted, fire-code-approved duplex. He was far too smart to ignore the high risk of accepting a tenant under lesser circumstances. And in a perfect world, I was even hoping that Mustafa would also have a small reserve of capital set aside to help cover the costs of any unforeseen emergencies.

Since re-sale homes, unlike newly built homes, do not come with a warranty, all building material specifications, installation procedures, and construction techniques would have to conform to the latest municipal building codes regarding health and safety issues such as ventilation, fire safety, etc. Meeting all those specific conditions would take time, money—and building permits.

"Oh, and about that contractor," Mustafa began, but then just left that thought dangling in the air for a moment while I inhaled sharply. "Well, I've already decided that I'm definitely going to hire a professionally licensed contractor, so don't worry," he informed me.

"An extremely wise move on your part," I responded, as I exhaled slowly.

"And I guess that means I'll have to compromise a little by doing the painting myself," he said, with his trademark giggle.

"So who doesn't love compromise?" I joked.

WORDS TO THE WISE ABOUT FIXER-UPPERS

Any number of major problems could crop up to drain you financially when you're doing the fix-ups on a fixer-upper. Here are some of the major categories of repair to watch out for.

Structural

Major structural elements include the roof, foundation and the framing members (wooden joists, beams and wall studs that make up the structure). Problems can arise in the attic or basement because of dampness, inadequate ventilation, improper levels of insulation and improperly installed vapour barriers. Excess moisture can lead to mould and mildew formation, and ultimately the deterioration of the wooden framing members that support the house. These are almost invisible, but often very costly, problems to repair.

If you're feeling drafts of cold or hot air (depending on the weather at the time you're looking at a house), there could be problems with air leakage. An inspection for structural problems will help to pinpoint how that air is getting in, so that the proper method of sealing the leaks can be determined. An inspector or contractor should look especially closely at the attic and basement. Even though a poorly insulated attic is usually relatively easy to repair with insulation, weather stripping and caulking, health and safety standards have to be adhered to because insulation materials must be handled with care.

How often have you heard somebody say, "We don't like to entertain in the basement because it's always so cold down there"? Significant heat loss is obviously the reason! Basements, like attics, can be insulated and sealed to make them more comfortable, but it's much easier to do so before a renovation is complete than after. Any finished basement should be inspected carefully for the quality of its construction, insulation, and how well it's been waterproofed prior to finishing—but be aware that these can be difficult to determine once drywall and flooring are in place. If you detect any signs of moisture—if the air smells musty, or you can see mildew or efflorescence (mineral deposits) on walls or floors—you know there could be much bigger problems with moisture lurking under the surface. These, too, can be costly to repair.

Mechanical

Major mechanical systems include the electrical, plumbing or heating (often referred to as HVAC or heating, ventilation and air conditioning). If you buy a fixer-upper that's in need of a mechanical retrofit, which would involve the installation of an entirely new system or the modification of an existing system, you're looking at a big-ticket item.

While you're replacing or upgrading major mechanical systems, it's wise to include as many energy-efficient measures as possible. Over time, those measures—whether they involve major outlays for mechanicals, or low-cost strategies such as caulking or weather stripping—will ultimately save you a bundle on heating and cooling costs. When an old furnace or boiler needs to be totally trashed, for instance, replace it with a new, high-efficiency model that will reduce heating bills and make the home's indoor environment more comfortable. Keep in mind that all retrofit repairs must comply with current municipal building codes and bylaws, which can add to the cost.

But let's look at worst-case scenarios—scenarios that are, unfortunately, relatively common. I've heard of contractors or electricians uncovering an old breaker panel in the wall—with brand new drywall installed over it. For one thing, it's illegal to close in a circuit panel of any kind. For another, it likely indicates that the current seller (or a previous owner) is trying to cover up an outmoded electrical system known as knob and tube wiring. Knob and tube wiring acquired its name from the insulators (or "knobs," shaped like caps on tubes of toothpaste) that were used to keep the wires isolated from other objects, and the ceramic liners (or "tubes") that were needed to pass those wires through wooden joists in the building. Knob and tube wiring represents the first generation of electrical wiring; what was sufficient then is no longer suitable for today's lifestyles, which demand much more electrical energy. Because knob and tube wiring is generally insufficient for the levels of power now used on a daily basis, the risk of fire has become a primary concern.

Knob and tube circuits also functioned without a ground wire, which explains why they are so susceptible to blown fuses. Sometimes, in an attempt to avoid those constantly blown fuses, homeowners would subject the wiring to damage from higher current levels by "over-fusing" the circuits with in-line splices. Hello? What were they thinking?

Modern electrical wiring standards include a safety ground conductor, as well as a junction box for containing the electrical connections. A modern system will have an efficient electrical panel with room for additional breakers to help avoid the power outages that happened in the past with knob and tube wiring. (Oh, and aluminum branch circuit wiring is stigmatized because it's also considered to be a fire hazard, so ask your inspector to watch out for that as well.) Today's thermoplastic wiring systems are contained within one plastic sheath that is more water resistant and better protected than earlier systems. The amount of exposure for knob and tube wiring left it vulnerable to rodents or pets.

(Hold on, did someone mention pets? Well, when I'm not carefully watching my own cute, little bunny, that pampered fluff-ball loves nothing better than to chew on wires from lamps, telephones, CD players, and every available appliance. Due to her sharp teeth and non-stop nibbling, I'm constantly putting all electrical cords out of her reach. She has chewed my carpet, and my new couches but I never stay angry with her because I'm a pet lover and my little bunny is by far the cutest pet imaginable. I even celebrated her birthday recently with a very noisy party—and a carrot cake, naturally!)

Okay, where were we? Oh yes—problems with knob and tube wiring. Here's another biggie. An acquaintance of mine who has owned the same home for 30 years was recently told by her insurance broker that she would have to replace the knob and tube wiring in her house by a specified deadline or she would have her policy cancelled. She called me to ask if she had any recourse. Unfortunately, this is what I had to tell her: "It's nearly impossible to get an insurance policy nowadays if knob and tube wiring is present. Although a diligent researcher might luck out and find an insurance company still willing, based on the proper documentation, to insure such a residence, most companies will definitely refuse to do so!" However, because of the inherent safety issue, knob and tube is more than just an inconvenience for homeowners, and so I suggested that she contact the appropriate government representatives by calling the Electrical Safety Authority. They will conduct a free, thorough inspection of a home's electrical system. If those experts could pass her system in its current condition, then her insurance company could not deny her a policy.

As a general rule, knob and tube should be replaced completely. And it won't be cheap. Expect to spend thousands of dollars, with the price going up with the size and style of the house, and the number of electrical fixtures. The amount of finished space will also affect the price, since electricians have to work harder and longer to fish wires through finished walls. An unfinished basement is, therefore, something of an advantage if rewiring is needed.

What about the condition of that fixer-upper's plumbing, which is another major mechanical system? Before you assume that it's all fine just because the taps turn on, find out how old the system is and what it's made of. Galvanized pipes can usually be found in homes that are more than 50 years old, and although galvanized plumbing was initially used to reduce or even eliminate rusting, unfortunately those pipes didn't live up to their promise. In fact, they are susceptible to corrosion from the inside out, with the rust accumulating over long periods of time. When you turn on an infrequently used water faucet and a disgusting brown liquid pours out, you've probably got galvanized pipes—not to mention a potential health hazard.

Rusting can also cause a reduction in water pressure because the pipes' interior passageway has grown smaller, a lot like a clogged artery. The worst-case scenario would be a blockage that causes those pipes to burst. And due to that potential danger, many homebuyers are now being refused insurance on properties that contain galvanized plumbing. Ideally, copper pipes should be used for all plumbing systems instead. An even newer (and some say better) option is flexible tube plumbing—but you're not likely to find any of that in a fixer-upper!

Copper pipes or not, the water intake pipe should be inspected for size. Why? Because a pipe that's only half an inch in diameter will not supply a two-storey house with the water pressure needed to function properly—and I'm pretty sure I'm not the only person who hates trying to shower and shampoo while standing under a tiny trickle of water! Like so many other repairs around the house, replacing the water intake pipe can be a complicated and expensive undertaking.

■ ADVICE FOR PROPERTY VIRGINS
GETTING REAL ABOUT RENO COSTS

I hate to curb your enthusiasm for fixer-uppers, but you should know that the most expensive fix-it items to crop up may not even be obvious to you at first. Don't fixate on ugly wallpaper or pink bathroom fixtures. In the grand scheme of renovations, those don't add up to much because they're just cosmetic. Remember that if it looks bad on the surface, what's under the surface is probably far worse. And structural and mechanical systems will cost much more to repair or replace than you might think.

The numbers might still work in your favour—but get estimates from reliable contractors and other specialists, and do your number-crunching using realistic figures.

SO YOU WANT TO BE A LANDLORD?

Having a separate apartment in a house is a time-honoured way to help pay off a mortgage. But as easy as it sounds, and as often as you've heard of it being done, you need to know a thing or two before you start putting up walls and tucking that extra bathroom under the stairs. Being a landlord is a serious responsibility.

A rental unit or "second suite" is a self-contained, private apartment that is located within a house. Many such units are basement apartments, but in larger, older homes it may in fact be the entire first floor or second floor of the house. An attic apartment is also possible. As a landlord, you must be aware of the rules, rules and more rules that you will have to confront. Every municipality will have its own local zoning bylaws, fire codes, and building and housing safety standards that you are required by law to meet. Those laws and standards can vary from city to city, but the following guidelines will hold true almost everywhere in Canada:

- A second suite must have its own separate entrance, separate kitchen and separate bathroom.
- There may be minimum size requirements for each of those rooms.
- There will be a minimum height requirement for an attic or basement suite.
- There must be the proper fire separations between the second suite and the rest of the house.
- There must be a second entrance or exit that can function as an escape route in an emergency.
- Adequate and functioning smoke alarms and carbon monoxide detectors must be installed.
- There may be parking restrictions or requirements (such as one legal parking space for each unit in the house).

Once the legality of that second suite has been established, an inspection followed by a letter of compliance will need to be issued by the local fire department, confirming that the unit has indeed met with the municipality's fire code. You'll need that very important "all clear" or you might face serious ramifications when trying to collect on an insurance claim.

THE DREADED "R" WORD: RESPONSIBILITY

Needless to say, there is a great deal of responsibility involved in being a landlord—and very hefty penalties for non-compliance with zoning bylaws and health and safety standards. Get properly prepared if your goal is to become a landlord. Let me be the first person to tell you—from my personal experience—that it is definitely not a responsibility to be taken lightly.

As I've already begun to explain, it's essential that you research the legal obligations of being a landlord so that you have a clear understanding of your rights, as well as your obligations. The relationship that you establish and maintain with your tenant will be governed by the Tenant Protection Act (which varies from province to province). A tenancy agreement is also subject to the governing laws found within the national Human Rights Code. Now, obviously, mutual respect and acceptance of a stranger's possibly annoying differences is a good starting point between the parties involved, but that's simply not enough. So, are you catching my drift here? *Do not enter into that landlord battlefield without the proper armour to protect you.* No way, no how.

Fortunately, in some cities there are non-profit legal clinics available to provide information, advice and referrals to landlords to inform them of their rights and responsibilities. You might want to seek them out because it is incumbent upon you to do your own due diligence—and then to do it again—with regard to that extremely important undertaking. Good luck!

Fade out … fade in. So whatever became of Mustafa? Well, I'm happy to say that he did purchase that fixer-upper he liked so much. With the financial help of his devoted parents, he was even able to hire an extremely capable building contractor to carry out the necessary renovations and repairs. Although the contractor's bid was high, Mustafa and his parents knew that the essential work had to be done properly—or why even bother doing it? Because, after all is said and done, who wants to end up having to repair the repairs?

Luckily, the chosen expert was fully licensed, as were all of his employees, which is not always the case. That factor is just another example of the many small details for first-time fixer-upper homebuyers to keep in mind if they want to avoid possible lawsuits. Because, most assuredly, a total stranger will sue you in a heartbeat if injury or accident happens while they are working on your job site. So reduce your risk of liability and check out every contractor's licensing and insurance before you sign a contract with him. Unfortunately, "Tinker Bell" will not suddenly appear and sprinkle some fairy dust all over that new property to magically transform it into a castle—that is just not going to happen in this lifetime!

That's not what happened for Mustafa, either, but his situation did turn out well. So well, in fact, that it would be easy to envy him just a little. When he called me recently to let me know that he had found a suitable tenant and that he really enjoyed being a landlord, he also invited me to his "official housewarming to check out the renovations party" that he had planned for the following week. I immediately accepted.

What a pleasant surprise greeted me on that big night, because the place looked wonderful. What a difference! I was so happy for Mustafa and all that he had accomplished. Clearly it must have been a long haul for him, with a lot of planning and hard work required, but there was every indication that it had all been worth it.

"Sandra, you made it," Mustafa yelled from across the crowded room.

"You bet I did," I yelled back.

Moments later I was introduced to his wonderful parents, who expressed their pride in him for all his hard work and tenacity. In no time flat it seemed that I was surrounded by his many other equally proud relatives and friends. Whoa boy! I sensed this was going to be one very boisterous celebration. And it was.

Before leaving, I asked Mustafa, "So, even in your wildest dreams, did you ever think it would turn out so perfectly?"

Ever the optimist, he immediately replied, "Absolutely!" And then he giggled!

The Condo of
Their Dreams

*In which Claudia and Grant experience love at first sight, and
in which Sandra does not regret raising her career sights above
her mom's expectations*

In my family, I am the youngest of three girls. Although I was an hon-
our roll student in high school, I was never encouraged to plan too far
ahead when it came to significant decisions regarding my future.

"Sandra, this report card is wonderful. But do you need these high
marks to be a secretary?"

"Secretary? Mom, what are you talking about? I don't want to be
a secretary."

"Why not? It's the best job out there. All you do is pick a big company that'll give you a nice weekly paycheque, show up for work on
time and then after a year or two ..."

"After a year or two what?"

"You marry the boss and settle down."

"And then what? Live happily ever after? Oh my God!"

The roll of my eyes accompanied by my loud sigh of aggravation
could not have been more dramatic. Unfortunately my histrionics were

in vain because my mom actually believed that her advice was helpful—she had no idea how short-sighted her outlook truly was. And Lord knows I'd heard her advice often enough to realize she was being completely serious, because it was the same ridiculous advice she had relayed to my two older sisters on countless previous occasions as well.

I also remember watching David Letterman's short-lived morning show on TV when I had a spare during my school schedule. Try as I might to explain to my mom that I really did have a spare, she just wasn't buying it. She was convinced that I was skipping school and therefore doomed to fail. So do you see what I mean about not being encouraged to plan for my own future? Why should I bother with such a mundane task when my mom was convinced that the man I would marry would also do all my future planning for me instead. But who was kidding whom? Me, marry the boss? Yeah, fat chance of that!

Luckily my enjoyment and appreciation of my very first part-time retail job had made it possible for me to contemplate other options. Because I learned that I liked working as well as being creative, and especially liked interacting with the public, I figured that maybe one day soon I would even be the boss. Hey, why not? I definitely knew that I needed steady challenges, and I also knew that in order to find them, it was up to me to think outside the box. You know, "the box"—the one that stifles innovative thinkers, the one that demands you play it safe, the one with the constricting view that obliterates all others. Yeah, that box. Well, fortunately for me I decided that was not the box I intended to live in. No way, José, not in this lifetime.

Fade out … fade in. Well, surprise, surprise, because now the shoe was definitely on the other foot. Probably due to the empty nest syndrome, my mom seemed to have undergone a significant change in her outlook. My mom had become unbearably bored. She was bored with running the household, she was bored with travelling to Florida just to visit with old people (especially since she wanted to hang out with Ricky Martin instead!), she was bored with the general sameness to her slow-moving days, and she was especially bored playing cards with her sneaky relatives.

So what did my mom do? Without any warning—or even prior experience, for that matter—she invested some of her savings into a decrepit flower shop and went to work! It's interesting to see how the passing of a few years can put an entirely fresh perspective on things, isn't it? But wait, because it gets even better: not only did my mom get out of the house and go to work, but she loved her very first job so much that, within two years, she bought out the original owner of the business and became the boss! Needless to say, my sisters and I teased her mercilessly.

My mother's flower shop hummed with constant activity. There was a steady stream of customers and deliverymen coming in and going out, all day long. And it seemed that the phone never stopped ringing from the minute she opened up each morning until the time she pulled the heavy door shut again each night. When my own schedule permitted, or at extremely busy times of the year, I liked to pitch in and help out my mom as much as possible.

There were always special occasions for customers to celebrate: birthdays, bar mitzvahs, weddings, retirements, anniversaries, holidays. And there were also those unhappy occasions that required condolences, such as illness or death. At almost any time of the year, bouquets of freshly cut and artfully arranged flowers, or easily maintained potted plants, are in demand.

But when it came to Valentine's Day ... Yikes, don't even go there! I had literally never seen so many long-stemmed roses in my life. To say nothing of the chaos! Or my mom's taut nerves! The labour-intensive days leading up to that special holiday required additional staff just to record all the orders and to re-stock the inventory shelves. Hectic days were followed by late, stressful nights when my mom and I spent additional time carefully coordinating the inevitable "D-day." Yep, when it came to that all-important "delivery day" schedule, we were forced to strategize as though caught in the middle of my mom's very own war zone to meet the special demands and last-minute changes, and to accommodate the personal requests regarding each order's vases, baskets, ribbons and personalized messages. The pressure on my mom to make everything perfect on behalf of her valued customers was very intense. Thanks to our plan of attack, and a little luck thrown in for good measure, the day would go off without a hitch and we would somehow survive for another year.

Even luckier still, a few days later my sisters and I would spend some time relaxing at a nearby spa where we indulgently treated ourselves to the "Principessa for a Day" special. I honestly don't think those estheticians had seen three more exhausted people in such desperate need before.

When I closed down my small coffee shop and began working on a "strictly temporary" basis with my mom, I found some extra time to myself and decided to put those hours to good use by finally enrolling in those real estate courses that I'd been considering. Bingo! I immediately loved them. I sensed that I was making a significant change for my future as I eagerly soaked up the pertinent information. My mind was a sponge! No matter how much I learned, though, I wanted to know more, and faster.

But then the inevitable happened.

"Close the fridge door," my mom snapped. "That must be the tenth time I've had to tell you today."

"Sorry, Mom," I called out, and then quickly did as she'd asked while thinking that I wouldn't put it past her to have actually kept count!

"Are those prom corsages nearly ready?" she asked tersely.

"I'm just finishing up the last one now," I answered. But I'm not even sure that she heard me. Whoa, talk about being in a bad mood.

You see, my mom had foolishly allowed herself to hope that I'd work in her shop forever. Although I had outlined my "strictly temporary" plan to her in the beginning, and she had willingly accepted those terms, it was evident that since I had earned my real estate licence and had accepted a job with a reputable brokerage firm, the storm clouds were brewing.

For the past two weeks, my mother's daily mantra had become "I don't know how I'm going to get along without you." Oh, and naturally a few tears were thrown in for good measure. Aren't Catholic mothers wonderful? Yep, all the signs indicated that I might as well pack my bags because clearly my mom was preparing to take me on a guilt trip!

Fortunately I didn't have time for it. Just two weeks later Claudia and Grant were sitting in front of me at my new office, telling me how much they wanted to purchase a condominium. Did I mention that, thanks to the start of my new real estate career, I loved my life?

MEET CLAUDIA AND GRANT

"We're on a very tight budget, so we know what we can afford and what we can't. And since our research indicated that buying a condominium is generally less expensive than purchasing a single-family home, that became the deciding factor for us," said Claudia.

"And the pool and the gym," laughed Grant.

"Oh yes, the allure of the amenities," I teased.

"That's right," Grant continued, "because staying in good shape is a top priority for me. I take my daily workouts pretty seriously, so having immediate access to those two features is a really big turn-on. Especially since at this time there's no way we could afford to purchase a property that included a pool, or had enough room for a home gym."

"And just between us, I really hate doing housework!" Claudia said.

"Don't we all?" I immediately responded.

"I mean, the apartment we're in now is fine as far as that goes, but the thought of having to keep a smelly, dirty basement clean just makes me nauseous!"

As our lengthy conversation continued, we covered the details of Claudia and Grant's "essential criteria"—their must-haves, their wish list, and their eliminating factors. And based on the information they shared with me, their preference for a condo did sound like the perfect choice for them. These days, condominiums are "hotter than a pistol" due to their affordability, their availability and their many conveniences, all of which appeal to many first-time buyers, buyers like Claudia and Grant. In fact, the rate of first-time buyers who will purchase a condo is projected to double within the next few years! Contributing factors for that trend are the ever-increasing number of young single buyers, as well as young couples who are willing to raise their families within the condominium complex environment. Since many condo buildings provide excellent security features, are located close to workplaces and schools, and are convenient to public transportation, condo living apparently won't be dominated by retired folks for much longer.

An evolving real estate market is changing some of those traditionally held attitudes for first-time homebuyers like Claudia and Grant, whose dream home may no longer include a house in the suburbs with a fenced-in back yard and a double garage. And there seems to be no end in sight for the condo's popularity to wane, either: a quick glance out almost any window from almost any office building in any major urban centre will almost certainly reveal that construction is under way on another shiny new condo building. The only drawback to this kind of activity is that the condo re-sale marketplace is a competitive one, and the percentage of your return on re-sale may not be as high as for a single-family home. A word to the wise, therefore: purchase an average to smaller unit rather than the largest one, which is more likely to appeal to other buyers and will give you a better return on your investment when it comes time to sell.

Some very good news for selective first-time buyers is that the days of the boring cookie-cutter condo unit seem to have gone the way of the dinosaur. Many developers are keeping a hop, skip and a jump ahead of the condo craze by providing discerning buyers with features, upgrades and amenities that have been purposely streamlined to appeal to the unique lifestyles of a diverse, expanding and individualized populace. And I am not simply referring to the ultra-luxury condo complexes where money is not an issue, because it is now quite common for many starter units to feature a variety of affordable upgrades for buyers to choose from. First-timers can customize their living spaces, too, without breaking the bank.

And yet, despite those savvy builders who are going the extra mile by putting together the most desirable package of attractive features, flexible financing and competitive prices to entice buyers, I still remind all first-time condo buyers that the old rules regarding their "dream home" (or "dream condo") still come into play. No living space is ever 100% perfect, so compromise remains a reality for them to confront when making their final decisions. It may not be possible to get the square footage you want, *and* the amenities you'd like, *and* the best view on the highest floor.

■ ADVICE FOR PROPERTY VIRGINS
FROM THE BANK'S POINT OF VIEW

You'll find that financing requirements will be affected when you come to buy a condo. For example, your lender will include half the condo fee (which covers maintenance and repairs to the building and common elements, but more on that later!) in your debt calculation when you apply for a mortgage. There's nothing quite comparable when you're purchasing a single-family property. That condo fee will be added to the monthly expenses that you'll have to carry—a figure that always includes mortgage payments and interest, municipal taxes, and utilities—and that higher figure will have an impact on the total amount the lender will approve for your mortgage. However, that initial drawback can also be a blessing in disguise for the condo buyer, because by knowing the fixed monthly maintenance cost in advance, you can budget accordingly.

For Claudia and Grant, I had in mind a particularly popular lake-front condominium complex whose units I had recently shown to other first-time buyers. It had been expertly constructed by a reputable developer, and many of those units had already sold to other young professional couples. I instinctively felt that Claudia and Grant would feel right at home there. I selected four different units for them to view, units with very different floor plans but all of them reflective of the couple's essential criteria.

"What a great building!" Claudia whispered as we drove up to the front door.

"Wait until you see the inside," I replied.

"This place looks too good to be true," Grant said after we'd crossed the foyer and entered the elevator. "Are you sure it's within our price range?"

"Yes, the asking price for each of the units I'm going to show you falls within your pre-approval amount."

Grant smiled and looked over at Claudia, who smiled back at him and whispered, "So far, this place definitely feels right for our lifestyle."

Chance, fate, serendipity—whatever! The condominium complex was just what Claudia and Grant had been looking for, and they didn't waste any time in making decisions. By early evening I was busily negotiating on their behalf for ownership of the unit they had chosen. That was only possible, though, because by the time they saw that building we had already gone over a great deal of specific information regarding the purchase of a condominium and how to take full advantage of the lifestyle opportunities that it offers. Let me touch on some of those important aspects now.

CONDOS, FROM THE GROUND UP

The first thing to know about condos is that you will never actually buy the structure that you live in. Instead, you are simply purchasing the interior space occupied by a particular unit—you don't actually own the walls. Now if you decide to decorate those walls with some wonderful paintings, then clearly those paintings belong to you, but not the walls themselves. And you don't own the roof or the floors either. Huh?

Well, the difference comes in the legal structure of a condo versus a single-family home. A condominium is a corporation of shared ownership, and that legal structure can be applied to just about any type of property: a high-rise building, a four-unit house, a resort property, and even vacant land.

The type most people are familiar with is a structure that contains many units—from about six units right up to units that number in the hundreds. When you purchase a condominium unit, you "share" with others in the ownership of the building's actual structure and the land on which the condo complex is situated. In effect, you are buying a piece of the pie rather than the whole pie. As one of many owners, you are responsible for paying a monthly fee to the building's condominium corporation to oversee the operation, maintenance and repair of the building's assets and those areas that are considered "common elements." Common elements could include the parking facility, sidewalks and surrounding grounds, hallways, amenities such as the pool and gym, elevators, the plumbing and electrical systems, etc.

By law, every condo corporation is guided by a board of directors consisting of unit owners who have been elected to those board positions. My advice to all first-time condo buyers? Get involved as soon as possible by seeking out a position on your building's board so that you can take an active, participatory role in those decision-making processes that will affect your lifestyle. Speak up and help to guide those important policies, rather than just following along blindly and muttering under your breath every time you are told, "No, you can't do that."

The complex's condo corporation will hire a property management company to act under its guidance to ensure that those policies or its "covenants, conditions and restrictions" are properly enforced. In other words, you have to follow the rules or you'll be sent to the principal's office! Well, not quite, but make no mistake about it: there will be plenty of rules and restrictions. As I tell my first-timers, those rules are generally a good thing.

On the other hand, if you're thinking about owning more than one pet or consistently hosting late-night parties or subletting your unit or even considering hanging a Christmas wreath or other religious item on your front door—double-check the fine print first!

Speaking of fine print, you'll want to examine closely a number of documents before purchasing a condominium. One very important document is the "status certificate," which lays out exactly which expenses are the responsibility of the condo corporation, which are the responsibility of each individual owner, and which are to be shared by all owners collectively through their monthly maintenance fees. It will also confirm whether the unit's previous owners have fulfilled all their obligations to the condo corporation. As the new buyer, you must be sure that important piece of paperwork is up to date at the time of your purchase or you could get stuck with some of the previous owner's debts!

And don't stop there, either. The new buyer must meticulously review all of the other relevant condo corporation's documents as well: the financial status of the condo corporation, the seller's disclosure statement, the corporation's articles of incorporation, the declaration of its covenants, conditions and restrictions, annual reports, the minutes from previous board meetings, applicable municipal bylaws, etc. Only by doing this can you be aware of your personal rights and obligations, as well as the obligations of the condo corporation, so that you are not left in the dark regarding any important matters. To avoid any confusion by a first-timer attempting to deal with all that "legalese," I not only suggest that they review the documents with their lawyer but I also make it a condition of my client's Offer to Purchase that their lawyer must have the chance to review that complicated documentation with them.

When the appropriate time arrives, the new buyer must be certain to hire a professionally qualified home inspector who specializes in condominium inspections. Always hire someone who is very knowledgeable about and experienced with the common problems found in condominiums. Their assessment of the common areas (such as roof, plumbing system, hallways, stairways, elevators, heating and air conditioning systems, surrounding land, pool and other amenities) is extremely important, since you, as a buyer, will be one of the individual owners within that complex to own a proportionate share of those areas. A new buyer doesn't want to get stuck finding out after they have just moved in that any of those common areas is in need of an immediate repair!

Inspectors will also check exposed areas like balconies, decks, patios, outside windows, doors, etc., to assess any damage that may have been caused by inclement weather. As in other building structures, evidence of wood rot, peeling paint, cracked sealants and so on must be noted—and dealt with. Who will pay for what? That's a very good question, and the answer depends on where a specific problem is located. Location will indicate who is liable for the repair cost. All those answers can be found in the very thorough documents that were provided to you as the prospective buyer. You remember those, don't you? That's right, those extremely important papers that you had your lawyer review in detail.

PROS OR CONS? IT ALL DEPENDS ON YOUR POINT OF VIEW

On the one hand...

You're probably already aware of some of the drawbacks to condo living: there tends to be less privacy than in a single-family home; you'll have very little control over the already established maintenance fees; there is likely to be limited parking for yourself or your guests. And, as already mentioned, there are the rules, rules, rules!

On the plus side, you won't be responsible for any snow shovelling or lawn mowing, cleaning out the eavestroughs, or climbing a ladder to make the windows shine. It's possible that dry cleaning services, a convenience store and DVD rentals will be available on the premises. There may be a social convener to arrange group excursions, and there's a high probability of indoor gym or swimming facilities. There's also the elegance factor of a 24-hour doorman to announce your guests!

More on maintenance fees

A common myth regarding condominiums is that their maintenance fees rise steadily and sharply. Most of the time, that's far from being the case. In a smaller low-rise building with a limited number of units, each owner would be responsible for paying a larger slice of the maintenance pie. However, in a very large complex with a couple of hundred units, obviously the opposite would be true. It's up to the buyer—with help from their realtor—to investigate precisely what the condo fees will encompass, how often they are increased, and the reasons for those increases. Keep in mind that the basic monthly amount will be calculated according to the square footage of the individual unit.

If you're shopping for a condo and looking at maintenance fees, make sure you're comparing apples to apples. You may notice that fees will vary greatly from one complex to the next. The difference often comes in the amenities included in those fees. For instance, one complex's fees may include two parking spots and the unit's utilities, while another complex offers a storage locker and a 24-hour concierge, and yet another complex's fees only make provision for one parking spot and a pool. Since options will differ from one condo building to another, so will the fees to maintain those options. You have to be ready to comparison shop if you're going to ultimately make the best selection to fit your needs and lifestyle. After all, why pay for the maintenance of a pool if you don't even swim?

And don't be like me when I'm shopping for a business suit or some other item of clothing. After a hectic afternoon of shopping, I've forgotten which suit was in which store and at which price, and out of pure frustration I end up buying the suit that's closest at hand, regardless of price. Keep track of the different fees as you shop for a condo, but especially make note of what those fees represent—because it's a lot more expensive to end up with the wrong condo than to end up with the wrong business suit!

With regard to utilities, many owners question if they are paying more than their share. First of all, keep in mind that the overall charge for heating, for example, shouldn't be extremely high: your condo will be naturally insulated by virtue of the fact that you have neighbours on three or four sides, and that your front door opens out into a warm hallway, rather than to the cold outdoors. The only exception may be a corner unit that has more windows.

Even so, there is a trend nowadays for some condo developments to have separate heat pumps for individual units. Therefore, the unit owner pays only for what they use. In the case of a "snowbird," that means they'd pay next to nothing during the cold winter months because their unit's furnace would be off while away for an extended period of time sunning themselves on a tropical beach. Obviously, that same unit's hydro bill would be substantially lower too during that period since lights and appliances would not be in use either.

Those oh-so-special assessments

By law, a condo corporation must maintain a reserve capital fund for the purposes of paying for the repairs or replacement of the complex's common elements and other assets. Such an expense is one that wasn't budgeted for in the regular maintenance fees and that cannot be fully covered by the balance currently in the condo corporation's reserve fund. The cost for such major improvements—which might include roof replacement, a new garage, a new elevator system, exterior window replacement, outdoor sidewalk reconstruction or an unusually high deductible from an insurance claim—will be evenly divided among the individual unit owners to cover the shortfall for that assessed amount.

I always caution all potential buyers to inquire about the possibility of any pending "special assessments" because they do not come cheap! If a special assessment is imminent as you are about to purchase, your realtor may be able to negotiate that the current owner must be responsible for paying for it—especially since that special assessment was levied while they were still the legal owner. Or perhaps your realtor may negotiate to have the condo unit's price reduced to reflect the cost that is about to become your responsibility.

A buyer must be certain to make the proper inquiries so that they aren't in for a rude awakening, because after the sale has been finalized, the owner has to pay for any special assessments levied.

But can you play football in it?

Condos often get a bad rap for being too small or too cramped. Once again, that's not always the case. Besides, when was the last time you played a game of touch football inside a three-bedroom bungalow? Try to remember that more house does not equal more happiness. Instead, look for ways to maximize the space of the condo to meet your urgentneeds and let organization become your best ally. Downsize your accumulation of possessions if necessary, and purchase furniture that is appropriately scaled to fit with a condo's size and lifestyle. Make the condo as functional as possible. Perhaps a futon within a designated home office would be the appropriate answer to being able to accommodate the occasional out-of-town guest. Many complexes provide storage lockers, which can be used to store bikes, hockey equipment, holiday ornaments and other items that aren't used on a regular basis.

Tenants: new friends or nuisances?

Some condo owners want to purchase their unit for investment purposes. They'll buy the unit and then rent it out as an income-generating property. This use may not be permitted by the condo corporation, however. Whether it is or isn't, the first-time buyer should be aware that a complex with too many tenants could spell big trouble because those "non-owners" usually lack "pride of ownership," and in its place is often a more casual or uncaring attitude instead. Tenancy tends to put a really heavy strain on the building overall and on its amenities in particular, and in some cases, it is also more difficult for rules to be enforced against tenants when the condo's actual owner is not physically on the premises to carry them out. A number of lending institutions will refuse to even sanction a condo mortgage if the tenant ratio within a complex is higher than 25%. Due diligence is required by a potential buyer to ascertain the tenancy situation.

Another word of caution about tenants. Be especially aware of a condo building's tenant ratio if that building is located near a major college or university since the majority of tenants will invariably be students. Whoa—down, boy! Don't start growling at me for slamming students! Because I'm not; I'm merely stating a possibility that could prove to be bothersome to some owners—though other owners might enjoy having the garden, gym and rooftop patio scattered with an increased number of dating possibilities! Either way, knowing who your neighbours are, or are likely to be, is a very important factor for complete enjoyment of any community.

MORE FINE PRINT: INSURANCE!

Protect your investment by getting the proper insurance contents and liability from a reputable company that provides prompt and efficient service and expert advice. Far too many first-time buyers think their monthly condo fees will cover them from loss or damage when that is not the case: in fact, your condo fee will only include fire and extended coverage insurance for the building and its common areas—not your individual unit and its contents.

Do not neglect the important step of getting contents and personal liability insurance, because your possessions (computers, furniture, clothing, electronics, etc.) are more valuable than you think, once you start adding them all up. Work with your insurance agent to make sure that all your valuables are insured. All items should be properly identified and evaluated in order for that vital information to become part of your insurance policy. And if you buy any funky, expensive artwork, make sure you keep those receipts to verify its worth. Someone less knowledgeable might only see a painting with two big blue stripes on it—and challenge you accordingly! Make sure your liability covers negligence because accidental damage may happen.

A low-cost condominium homeowner's insurance package will also cover you for improvements that you make to upgrade your suite. Therefore, when you decide that ceramic countertops should become granite instead, that won't be a problem.

THE PERILS OF PURCHASING A "VIRTUAL" CONDO

When you purchase a condo from plans, the process can be very different from buying a unit that already exists. The buyer must sign an agreement of purchase, which is a legally binding contract, with the developer. The advantage of buying from plans is that the buyer will have a wider selection of floor plans, unit locations and finishing options to choose from. The disadvantage is that the condominium developer will likely insert a clause that says the move-in date can be pushed back if the buyer's unit hasn't been completed by the occupancy date. That, unfortunately, happens with great frequency! In fact, the entire building must be hazard-free and up to the required municipal safety codes—with elevators functioning properly, sprinkler systems functioning, etc.—before the building can be declared fit for occupancy.

One simple clause can give the developer the option to delay a buyer's occupancy date, which may cause the buyer untold grief if they have already sold their previous dwelling to coincide with their planned move-in date. It's not the sort of clause that developers will deviate from, since it protects them from being exposed to the cost of penalties for delays. If a delay happens, notification must be sent in writing to the buyer or to their real estate lawyer, but even so, a letter doesn't help put a roof over their head, does it? What happens then?

Well, to begin with, the inconvenienced buyer will clearly have to find a temporary living space, as well as possible storage space for their furniture and other belongings. And after that it's anybody's guess as to what other hassles could crop up for each individual: longer commute times, school reassignment headaches, additional financial expenditures, etc. So a word to the wise is to always have an affordable and convenient backup plan in case of being faced with that type of emergency.

Your realtor, if he or she is experienced in new condo sales, can offer valuable advice regarding whether or not an anticipated move-in date seems realistic, so don't hesitate to ask this important question.

Fade out … fade in. Condos, townhouses, lofts, co-ops—what's the difference? Claudia and Grant did inquire about lofts at one point, so I'll let you know what I told them.

"A traditional loft features an open floor plan and high ceilings, along with exposed pipes and support beams, larger windows and possibly concrete floors. There are usually wide central hallways inside the building, and very few internal walls inside each unit. A loft tends to be the ultimate open-concept environment, so keep in mind that sound travels and a floating staircase isn't safe for children. Many lofts have been converted from old warehouse buildings, former office buildings, old apartment buildings or no longer used factories.

"Keep in mind that not every loft means that its airy, open space has been wisely used. Unfortunately, some lofts resemble nothing more than a tacky mosh pit! An eccentric artist friend of mine lives in a loft conversion that features a lot of unusual brickwork and glass ornamentation. During daylight hours, with the sun shining in, you have never seen anything so beautiful in your life! However, when night time rolls around … Well, his bedroom is located directly above the kitchen, and it is only accessible by a ladder rather than a staircase. That's a very bold bohemian touch for the right homeowner like my friend, but what happens when it comes time for him to sell? I can guarantee you that any potential homebuyers who suffer from bad knee joints or vertigo will not be in a rush to make an offer!

"Because many older loft buildings tend to be located in dicey sections of the city that are rundown or slightly out of the way, the square-footage costs of a loft may be less than if the same unit was located on a major downtown street instead. But don't start counting your savings just yet, because within those questionable areas there tends to be a higher incidence of criminal activity and that could put the kibosh on a future sale. On the other hand, there may always be some adventurous first-timers who will prefer the trade-off of a bohemian lifestyle to a property in Pleasantville."

Claudia and Grant's purchase process didn't present them with any major hiccups. But before they could blow out the candles on a celebratory cake, there were some concerns and compromises that had to be addressed.

First of all, upon reading through the minutes from the previous year's board meetings, Claudia and Grant discovered that the delinquency rate was quite high when it came to some of the present owners not coughing up their maintenance fees when they were due. As well, there were repeated complaints about a particular security issue, and a continued fire hazard from some negligent owners who refused to stop operating barbecues on their balconies. Although it appeared that perhaps the financial stability of the condo corporation might be at stake, the concern turned out to be a case of a property management company that just wasn't on the ball. And in newer buildings where the board of directors might be a little green still, poor choices do get made. Claudia and Grant investigated the problem and were reassured that the property management company was in the process of being replaced.

Second, Claudia and Grant had to compromise on the view. A high-rise condo—especially a penthouse suite with panoramic views, a large balcony and western exposure that provides afternoon sun and sunsets—can be a little piece of heaven. But be aware that heaven comes at a price: condo units increase in price by several thousand dollars per floor within a high-rise complex. Developers tend to reserve the largest suites with the best views and most convenient parking spaces for those upper floors. So Claudia and Grant bit the bullet and agreed to purchase a unit located on the seventh floor instead of the fifteenth. To them, the view wasn't radically different anyway.

■ ADVICE FOR PROPERTY VIRGINS
Hey, Where Did My View Go?

Only pay for "protected" views!

Before purchasing a condo in the sky, verify that your unit's breathtakingly gorgeous view is lawfully protected. Are municipal zoning laws, building regulations or environmental restrictions on the books to prevent someone else from destroying your fabulous view? Don't pay a premium for that view only to lose it a few years later—along with some of your investment. Never assume that your view will last forever. Check into the area's future plans, and get written assurances from the developer.

SOME FINAL WORDS TO THE WISE

Every real estate purchase is an individual one. But if there were some rules about condo buying that might apply to everyone, I'd highlight these:

- Always look at the bones of the structure: how old is the complex, how many units are there, and how well does the particular unit for sale suit your needs? Does the unit offer individuality and character as well as utility?
- Look carefully at the complex's turnover rate and its tenancy ratio.
- This point will apply most to buyers in high-density cities, where parking is at a premium, but when it comes to the optional parking spot that goes along with your unit—buy it! If you don't, you may be kicking yourself later because prices for parking spots in many condominium complexes have skyrocketed. However, if buying a parking spot isn't an option, you might want to look into whether the building's developer is getting the income from its rental fees, because, in my opinion, it's best to avoid a situation where the important amenities aren't owned by the condo corporation. Each condo corporation should have ultimate decision-making power over all of its amenities.
- Another big trend is for environmentally friendly concerns to play a bigger role in the construction of new condominium

complexes. I can assure you that statistics indicate this "going green" trend is here to stay. Many first-timers are asking more and more questions regarding environmentally friendly building practices. So find out before you buy: What are the energy efficiency measures in place? What environmentally conscious construction techniques are builders using? What are the innovative green initiatives incorporated into my specific unit? Condo owners want to create their own environmentally aware living space—and I'm all for it.

⁑⃗

I have enjoyed my career as a realtor so much that I've never for a minute questioned my decision to enter the wonderful, wacky world of real estate. And what a cast of characters I've met during these past 10 years! Fortunately, my real estate highs have outweighed my real estate lows, to the extent that I honestly couldn't even imagine where I would be now if I'd followed my mom's advice. Marry the boss? *Not!*

What I studied at university has been more valuable to my career than I could have imagined. I earned an honours Bachelor's Degree in sociology, with a specialization in crime and deviance, and a minor in languages. Granted, I haven't exactly been out solving any crimes during my career, but I've noticed that I am able to draw upon some of what I learned and apply it to particular situations that help me discover and understand a buyer's motivations or their fears. It helps to be aware that any number of various sociological and psychological aspects can prove to be the driving force behind a final decision.

Claudia and Grant are part of a growing number of buyers who are looking to condos as a practical and luxurious option to single-family dwellings. Every demographic is represented in the condo rush as condos offer a more affordable choice in prime locations, a maintenance-free lifestyle, and the ability to lock the door behind you and travel the world. Claudia and Grant love their condo complex so much that they often don't even leave the grounds on weekends, preferring to use all the amenities, including the party room and rooftop barbecue lounge. The resort-like feel helps them relieve the stress of urban life, and makes them feel like queen and king of the castle.

Mustangs and Mortgages

In which Sandra's Aunt Cecilia displays her backbone on the dealership steps, and in which Lauren finds a safe haven in the sky

Life was never dull when my Aunt Cecilia was around. The room would light up from the moment she entered it, and the atmosphere would crackle. Her charismatic personality was magnetic and her loud laugh seemed to be contagious … at least to me … but apparently not to my father! Even though there was no love lost between my father and my aunt, I recall him laughing affectionately as he said, "That sister-in-law of mine's a real character, that's for sure. She could sell ice to the Eskimos and charm the birds out of the trees at the same time! But I'm also warning you: be careful not to cross her … or else."

My two sisters and I especially loved our Aunt Cecilia's weekly visits because we knew she would always have some family gossip, silly jokes or funny stories to tell us. One evening, she had barely arrived and removed her coat before she had launched into a comical aria about the previous weekend's chain of events. In no time flat, the three of us were squealing with laughter.

When she forcefully stubbed out her cigarette while proclaiming, "What a complete bunch of idiots!"—well, that did it! I laughed so hard I had to bolt from the front porch into the house, silently praying I'd make it to the bathroom in time before I peed myself.

Then I shouted, "Aunt Cece, wait for me! Don't tell any more until I get back."

Now, truth be told, our grandmother had already told my sisters and me about the story of Aunt Cecilia's day at the car store," as she called it. But hearing that earlier version as it made the rounds of our relatives (in record time) wasn't anything like hearing the juicy details directly from my aunt's mouth. With eyes like cold marble, she grandly divulged those details to her three wide-eyed little nieces with enough dramatic flair to make Meryl Streep green with envy!

After I was back out on the porch, my aunt lit a fresh cigarette and continued with her tale. "I mean, I bought that damn car from them less than a month ago. And I paid for it in cash. Every penny! So to have that silly jerk pretend not to remember who I was made me so mad I wanted to kick him in the behind!"

"But I hope you didn't," my sister gasped.

"Of course I didn't; you know I'm a perfect lady."

My sisters and I were totally convulsed over that "perfect lady" comment, since my beloved Auntie Cece wasn't exactly known for her impeccably dainty manners. No, there would be no mistaking my aunt for a convent-raised nun anytime soon! I don't want to give the wrong impression, because she was never openly rude or hostile to anyone, but she was "quick on the drawl" and was known to "shoot from the lip." Her well-aimed sarcasm would unfailingly score a bull's eye!

"No, instead of kicking that fool in the backside, I very patiently proceeded to tell him that my car's radio didn't work. I also told him that I'd already called up his company's repair shop on three separate occasions to report that to them, but that I'd received nothing more than a polite brush-off each time. I told him that I had no idea why someone in repairs wasn't calling me back to make an appointment to just fix the problem. Especially since the radio's parts were all under warranty and I was able to drop my car off at their shop whenever it was convenient for them. I told him I didn't like getting the runaround and that I was so unhappy with the lack of customer service, that out of sheer frustration I'd decided to come by the showroom in person to ask him for some advice on how to handle the situation."

There was a deep inhale, followed by a pregnant pause, followed by a slow exhale of smoke before she continued. "But he just looked at me like I was off my rocker and tried to dismiss my legitimate complaint by declaring, 'Maybe you don't know as much about radios as you think you do. Are you sure you're turning the right knobs?' The right knobs—yeah, right, who did he think he was kidding?"

My aunt paused again to pull on her cigarette before she continued. "To add insult to injury, he kept insisting that because the car was new, it had to be my problem and not the car's problem."

There was a slight pause for dramatic effect as she narrowed her eyes before quietly saying, "And then he said it."

"Said what?" asked my sister, right on cue.

"That condescending know-it-all actually said—and I quote—'After all, women know nothing about cars.' Needless to say, I couldn't believe my own ears. I just could not believe that lousy SOB had the nerve to make such an insulting remark. Can you?"

My sisters and I sadly shook our heads in unison, looking like matching bobble-head dolls, I'm sure.

"I felt my pulse racing and my heart thumping in my chest. And I was convinced that, at any second, steam was about to pour out of my ears while I stood there struggling to control the urge to knock that good-for-nothing creep flat on his behind."

"Didn't you say anything?" I asked.

"Not at first!" my aunt roared. "I was so completely dumbfounded that I was speechless. Me … speechless! Can you can believe that one?"

My sisters and I squirmed and giggled as we anticipated the story's big finale. Our beloved Auntie Cece didn't disappoint us. She sprang out of her chair, took another huge drag on her cigarette, paced back and forth for a moment, and then stopped abruptly to take a turn at looking each one of us square in the eye before continuing her feisty tirade.

"But after I recovered from my initial shock, I said plenty. I let him have it from both barrels. I told him that I wasn't going to move my car until it was fixed. But he still played dumb. So I thought to myself, 'Enough already with the lame excuses.' Even though he claimed they weren't capable of fixing my radio, I knew that I was very capable of fixing them. So as I resisted the very tempting urge to knock that fool right into next week, I stated that I would be reporting this incident directly to the manufacturer. Then I turned and left as quickly as I could. But apparently I wasn't quick enough because I heard him snickering behind my back just as the office door was closing. And that was the last straw. That smug low-class snicker made up my mind for me as I stormed furiously across that lot. Forget the manufacturer—now I was ready to call his bluff! So I started up the car and then I drove that beautiful new, fully paid for, Mustang convertible of mine right up those cement steps of that stupid dealership until it ground to a halt. And then I leaned on the horn for a full minute before I flung open the door, got out and marched back into that damn showroom. I must've looked like a thundercloud, but I didn't give a damn because you should have seen the looks on their faces! *They were priceless.*"

The three of us laughed like crazy as our aunt took a final pull on her cigarette butt before letting it drop and grinding it out with her high heel. Then she threw her head back and joined us with her own loud laughter. Many minutes passed before we had all calmed down again. But just as my aunt was about to pick up her conversation from where she left off, my mother called from inside the house. "Girls, time to wash your hands, dinner's ready. Cecilia, could you please bring them in with you?"

My aunt shouted back, "Sure thing, hon," as she winked broadly and motioned for us to follow her into the house. Then, before leading the way, she patted her stiffly sprayed upswept hairdo, smoothed her skirt and squared her shoulders. My Auntie Cece was so beautiful and elegant, and yet so courageous and strong, that I wasn't quite sure if I was following Dusty Springfield onto a stage, or following General Patton onto a battlefield!

By the way, did they fix the radio? You bet they did … right on the spot.

A ROLE MODEL WITH MOXIE

It should come as no surprise that my funny, loveable, tough-as-nails aunt was a favourite role model of mine when I was growing up—much to the chagrin of my parents. Whenever I lost my temper I'd let loose with a few choice swear words that I'd learned courtesy of Aunt Cecilia! Oops … nobody's perfect.

Besides influencing me to be a bit of a diva, my mentoring aunt also nurtured my budding independent streak by encouraging me to accept a dare, to treat everyone as an equal and to voice my opinions in a clear and direct tone of voice. Her willingness to confront adverse situations head-on, with her fearless "take no prisoners" attitude, certainly rubbed off on me.

My aunt was an intelligent, liberated and proud woman who was probably born a generation too soon. Because although she was a trailblazer at her workplace—she was an administrative executive with a leading airline company—when it came to her creative ideas and economic skills and marketing expertise, she remained a victim of her era's male-dominated big business practices. She earned a good salary, but received very little company recognition for her enviable achievements. That highly sought-after promotion up the corporate ladder never materialized because there was always a male counterpart lurking in the wings, ready to usurp her position.

Although my aunt's dream for corporate recognition remained stifled for the most part, she knew how to live large in other areas of her life. And one of those areas where she chose to expand her awareness was, surprisingly, within the precarious world of stock trading. Very diligently, on her own time, she learned as much as she possibly could about risk versus opportunity. And then, against the loud complaints of her immediate family, she announced that she was ready to take the plunge and make her first pork-belly purchase. She was determined to put her money to work for her instead of listening to her father's counsel about hiding her savings under a mattress!

Well, talk about preparation and determination paying off. In no time at all my aunt was successfully trading up a storm—and that storm was paying dividends. The naysayers of the extended family were eventually proven wrong, because she hung in there with her stock trading endeavours for many years and consistently earned a profit.

It was her one-two punch of hard work and financial acumen that enabled Aunt Cecilia to purchase her fabulous new Mustang *in cash*. If she hadn't had the cash, the law of the time would have required a man's signature on the paperwork needed to secure a bank loan. And as you've probably already guessed, my strong-willed aunt was having none of that, thank you very much. She was proud of her money-earning achievements and she knew that her cash was the same colour and value as any man's.

My aunt loved to travel to the many foreign job postings that her company offered. She would work for a few months and then enjoy a brief vacation before returning home. So I wasn't too surprised the day she announced that she was off to the pineapple capital of the world: Hawaii. When she returned home, she declared that it had been her favourite exotic location yet. She couldn't stop talking about what a great time she'd had splurging on enjoying herself in every conceivable, self-indulgent way. I just loved hearing her fascinating stories as she showed me countless photographs of the island's beautiful, untouched beaches and its strange, lush vegetation, while the ocean surrounding that magnificent jewel of an island looked so pristinely clear and blue that my eyes hurt just staring at the pictures of it.

Approximately two months later, my aunt dropped a bomb when she informed her family: "When the time comes, I'm going to retire to Hawaii." Her parents did not like that idea at all so they tried talking her out of such a silly notion. But to no avail because once my aunt's mind was made up … that was it.

More forceful than her parents' disapproval, though, was the law of the day. At that time, the real estate market was closed to single women—even a woman wanting to make an all-cash sale. That's right—she was refused because property could only be sold to a man or to a couple. It was that same hurdle all over again: first the car and then the property. The mere thought of having to play by that ridiculously sexist law angered my aunt a great deal. She couldn't knuckle under and accept it either, since she had already kicked one boyfriend to the curb, and she hadn't exactly been out shopping for his replacement!

But retirement dreams die hard. Aunt Cecilia asked her father to co-sign the necessary papers so that her beachfront property sale could be completed. He refused to do so. His reasons were many, but the biggest stumbling block was ultimately just good old-fashioned fear. Because he was basically a very simple, uneducated man, the intricacies of my aunt's international real estate transaction were just too involved for him to grasp. He was convinced that either the realtor, the real estate lawyer, the bank—or possibly all three of them in cahoots—were out to separate Cecilia from her nest egg. And there was no way to convince him otherwise. There was to be no retirement for my aunt on her beloved island of Hawaii. For so many reasons, that was a shame—not least because the steady appreciation of that prime piece of property through the years would have made my aunt an exceedingly wealthy woman!

I'll always remember the sacrifice that my aunt made when she accepted her father's adamant refusal to help her buy that longed-for Hawaiian "dream property." Even though she initially fought him tooth and nail, when she realized that the battle was creating a rift within the extended family, as each relative weighed in with their opinion and chose a side, she simply stopped the battle. Although her heart was truly broken, my aunt understood that her father's deep fear was actually motivated by his love and concern for what he truly thought was best for her. And so to keep peace in the family above all else, like a dutiful daughter she took it on the chin and accepted his decision with grace. And then she never, ever spoke about that incident again. Ever!

Is that class or what?

MEET LAUREN

When I first met Lauren, her mannerisms and slightly over-the-top laughter reminded me right away of my Aunt Cecilia. I found out soon enough that her business smarts were very similar too, although in Lauren's case she did indeed have the prestigious title and the corner office from her company that she merited. Hurray for changing times!

"How can I help you?" I asked Lauren when we first met.

"I'm looking for something located downtown that's fun, but it has to be affordable too," she said. "You see, thanks to my recent split-up, the shackles have come off and I'm not putting them on again for the sake of an expensive house. I want to live in a house—not be married to it!"

"Not a problem, you won't have to be," I replied.

Lauren was in her late twenties, recently divorced, childless and looking to become a first-time homebuyer. (My aunt, on the other hand, had not married until her mid-thirties, had one child and then divorced. She temporarily moved back home to live with her parents. What can I tell you? Moving back home is the Italian way.)

Because Lauren's newfound freedom was so important to her, she stressed vehemently that she wanted a property that would still allow her the financial leeway to pursue an eventful single lifestyle to its utmost. She wanted a safe location, she didn't want to sacrifice her level of comfort, and she also insisted on a property that was easy to maintain.

"I don't want to be bogged down by time-consuming chores, either. I'll certainly load up and empty the dishwasher, but if I have to worry about mowing or watering the lawn, or raking and disposing of the leaves, or shovelling the sidewalk or driveway, I'll pull my hair out!"

"Your hair is safe with me," I joked.

"I really want the option of just grabbing a few things and taking off for the weekend whenever the mood hits me," Lauren told me.

"Then let's get going on making that option a reality," I said with a smile.

There were other essential criteria for me to consider before I began compiling a list of appropriate properties to discuss with Lauren. But if you're already catching my drift and thinking what I'm thinking ... then give me a C, give me an O, give me an N, give me a D, give me another O ... and what have you got ... CONDO! Say it again ... CONDO! One more time ... CONDO!

Yep, we're on the same wavelength.

For some first-time homebuyers—just like Claudia and Grant in the previous episode, and now Lauren—condominiums provide an entry-level, low-maintenance, affordable option of home ownership. They also offer a fairly carefree lifestyle and a built-in sense of safety, which covered the essential criteria Lauren had indicated were important to her. Her home would be more than just a living space; it would also be an investment that would benefit her on re-sale, due to the large and growing pool of potential buyers—trends are showing that baby boomers' kids will most likely purchase a condo because that's what they'll be able to afford. I was glad to see that, aside from the

empowering psychological and emotional benefits that she was looking forward to, Lauren already knew it was a wise financial decision
not to over-buy her first time out on her own.

SINGLE BUYERS RULE!

I'm sure I don't need to tell you that the real estate landscape has dramatically shifted since the days when my aunt tried to buy her own
home. In my Aunt Cecilia's time, due to rampant sex discrimination,
societal prejudices or even personally held negative opinions by some
banks and real estate companies, almost any single woman would
have been laughed right out of a mortgage broker's office. Without a
husband, there would be no house for her—and obviously no need for
a mortgage. It was the same near impossibility for a single woman to
get a credit card in her own name. And when a married woman was out
in the workforce, her income was routinely discounted on a loan application since most banks of that era assumed that she would inevitably
give up her job at some point to stay home and have children. Was that
a narrow-minded outlook or what?

In our present-day society, women are capable of accomplishing
things that their mothers would have had to fight tooth and nail for
… and did. In recent years women have also begun to account for
a greater number of college graduates than men. As a result, many
women are now financially independent earlier in life, with the same
resources that men have: money, social status and power. This represents a social and economic shift.

Since many women no longer require a spouse's additional income
to maintain their chosen lifestyle—what I call the "no longer dependent on a man" type of equality—more women than ever are looking
beyond an asset-based mating decision. They may choose to remain
single until later in life instead. Those women whose earning power is
considerably higher than it was in previous decades now wield consid-

erable clout of their own. They have discretionary purchasing power, can become wise investors and solidify their financial independence, and control their own cash flow.

Those same single, confident, knowledgeable women are becoming real estate savvy too—from an earlier stage in life. They're no longer sitting around waiting for a husband's financial terms or his list of essential criteria to be dictated to them regarding a property purchase. Single women are taking the lead for themselves and building up valuable equity while realizing the benefits of home ownership. And it's not a small minority who are doing this: the numbers of single women homebuyers is an impressively large demographic within the marketplace. In fact, single women are outnumbering single men nearly two to one when it comes to making property purchases today, whereas that ratio was equal years ago. If that isn't proof we're no longer living with Stone Age stereotypes of hunters and gatherers, you could sure fool me!

The forecast is for that gap to widen in the coming years as well, as single women first-timers like Lauren continue to out-buy their single men counterparts whose sales purchases are projected to remain the same. Those single bad boys are golfing, vacationing and partying more—which isn't a bad thing since now is the time to enjoy life. It seems they prefer their freedom and the convenience of renting over making the commitment to finally settle down with property owner-ship. But I like to say "everything in moderation," because those men could have it all if they were to plan properly.

CONDO SAFETY FACTORS

The first condominium complex that Lauren and I visited was an older, well-established one. The unit we viewed was large and airy. Lauren liked its layout and appreciated that the seller had kept it in immaculate condition. Her interest was piqued by the high-quality upgraded materials—flooring, cabinetry and countertops—that the seller had recently installed in the kitchen. However, she was greatly dismayed by the incessant barking of a neighbour's dog that could be heard very loudly and clearly the entire time we were viewing that particular suite. Was that dog an indication of trouble ahead? I couldn't definitely say, so I offered to put on my Nancy Drew hat and do a little investigating.

While reading through the minutes from the previous two years' board meetings, as well as its financial records, I quickly noticed a number of disturbing factors, and barking pets would be the least of Lauren's worries if she chose to move into that complex. Apparently a very costly refurbishment to the sewage system was planned for the complex within the coming few months, and since older condo complexes generally tend to require more maintenance due to their aging facilities, the owners were also facing imminent upgrades to the parking area and garbage removal system. Why go on?

When I suspect that a seller is exhibiting a general lack of integrity by attempting to hide a property's flaws, or by making serious omissions on the disclosure statements that are required by law, that becomes a moral issue for me. So when I indicated to Lauren that she would be facing construction hassles along with the possibility of a steep increase in her monthly maintenance fee right after moving in, her response was "Cheque, please!" We were out of there.

The next condo for Lauren to view was located within a beautiful condominium complex that was designed around a central courtyard and situated within a private, gated community, which provided its owners with a strong sense of security. That complex also featured a lot more streetlights on its roads and pathways than are usually found on similar city streets, so that feature also appealed to her. And since she instantly fell in love with the unit, I thought she was ready to start packing!

But instead, after a night's rest, and a second viewing, and her admission that it was "almost perfect," Lauren finally decided that the complex's location wasn't centrally located enough with respect to her other needs. We bid that beautiful complex farewell and moved on. Quite a few more times, actually.

But before I get to Lauren's eventual first-time purchase, let me take a moment to discuss the issue of safety in a little more detail since a single woman homebuyer's concern for her own safety is obviously of paramount importance to her. Safety tends to be of greater concern to women than to men.

As a realtor, I therefore have to be keenly aware of a specific area's reputation for safety—or lack thereof. Now it's a no-brainer for most homebuyers to decide, on their own, to steer clear of those sketchy areas that are known outright for being unsafe. But it's almost always up to me to steer potential homebuyers away from any questionably safe areas should they show a naïve interest in them.

But before trashing one "unsafe" location and declaring an alternative area as being "safe," we should first qualify the word *safe*. Although one part of a city may have a relatively low rate of repeated break-ins, it could still suffer from other illicit criminal activity such as prostitution. Conversely, an extremely upscale area with its gorgeous ravine properties and expensive foreign cars in the driveway won't have those same hookers out front plying their trade, but the incidence of multiple break-ins could be higher than the city average. Thieves are after money and expensive possessions, so they'll obviously target those affluent areas. (Many times a home is broken into simply because a thief is looking for a set of car keys! Wherever you live, be sure to limit access via a garage door that leads directly into the house.) Areas that are known specifically for their night-time drug-peddling activities could suffer from a poor daytime reputation because of that same un-savoury "druggie" element lurking around. Lastly, a quick read of the daily headlines reminds us that violent crimes can be random, which indicates that crime doesn't play any favourites with regard to where it occurs. So what's a gal to do?

After I supply the potential homebuyer with as much concrete information as I have on hand with regard to a specific area's safety record, I always suggest that they do their own homework in greater depth. A fact-finding trip to a specific area's public library, or to its local police station to have the crime statistics properly analyzed, could be very revealing and helpful to that homebuyer before she makes an offer to purchase.

Once that offer has been submitted, the purchaser's home inspector will check for basic safety features such as proper locks on all windows, as well as on balcony or patio doors, dead bolts on main doors, and smoke detectors and carbon monoxide detectors on every floor of the building. Sliding glass doors, especially, need adequate locks—the standard latch mechanism isn't good enough. As an added precaution it never hurts to insert a blocking device into the track of these doors to offer further resistance to any intruders. For that purpose I personally use the handle of my old hockey stick and it fits perfectly. I used that stick for road hockey when I was a child, and then again for floor hockey when I was playing in a recreational women's league.

■ ADVICE FOR PROPERTY VIRGINS
SECURITY MATTERS

For a single woman's peace of mind, I strongly advocate a properly installed and maintained high-tech alarm system as a means of additional security: it's fairly affordable, a good investment and its warning signage may act as a deterrent, which provides a level of comfort for the inhabitant. But keep in mind that security officers do not necessarily carry weapons and will call the police if a violent crime is in progress. Send for the police instead and hope that the police force's response time is speedy.

Fade out … fade in. Let's not keep Lauren waiting any longer. The comfortable two-bedroom condo unit that she finally decided to purchase was located in a fairly new, pet-free, high-rise complex that boasted a dynamic urban location—which was good news for her social life. It would be easy to maintain thanks to the condominium corporation's qualified service staff and it had features especially designed to appeal to single women such as larger wardrobe closets and smaller appliances that were more energy efficient. And that particular condominium complex also had many additional security features and precautions: restricted access within many parts of the building's interior; round-the-clock surveillance cameras on each floor; an extremely well-lit underground parking lot with limited accessibility; a panic button that connected her unit to the 24-hour concierge in the lobby; closed-circuit TV monitors in each elevator; and even night-time security guards who patrolled the grounds.

Lauren had done her due diligence with regard to the complex's history and she was very satisfied with what she found. It was evident that she felt a sense of pride and accomplishment from achieving that first property purchase all by herself. Many women, like Lauren, are "nesters," and she had just found hers.

It's very important for every first-timer like Lauren to have their mortgage structured with the best possible terms most suitable to their unique financial circumstances right from the start. And since the differences between the many types of mortgages available are plentiful, be certain to discuss the pros and cons of those available options with your own reliable licensed mortgage broker to avoid any confusion. You definitely want to get correct answers and expert advice from an individual who can help you make an informed decision.

WHAT'S IN A MORTGAGE?

If you're a first-time homebuyer, you're probably aware of a little thing called interest rates. The interest rate on your mortgage will have a huge impact on how much you pay for your house over time. You're probably also aware that interest rates don't remain stable (is that an understatement or what?). The good news is that for some years now, interest rates have been at historic lows, making it easier for first-time buyers to get the mortgages they need, even in high-cost housing markets.

Let me backtrack just a little, and excuse me if I'm telling you things you already know, but I'm going to give you some really simple facts about mortgages. When you buy a house, the full sale price must be paid to the party who sold it to you. Since most people don't have hundreds of thousands of dollars just kicking around in their bank accounts, they have to get a mortgage from a bank or another lending institution to make that big whopping payment at the outset. A mortgage is any loan that uses real estate as security. "Security" means that if someone can't make the mortgage payments on their house, the bank can take possession of that house, sell it, and get its money back.

I'm going to simplify things again here by saying that your mortgage payments every month are made up of two basic amounts: principal and interest. (Sometimes taxes and insurance are included too, but let's not get too complicated.) The principal is the basic amount that you owe on the house—that is, the price you bought it for, minus your down payment. The interest is the amount that the bank charges you for the use of its money. You could think of it as a rental fee: you don't have all the money up-front, but they do, so they charge you a fee (which is expressed as a percentage of the total amount owing) until you can pay the whole amount back. The length of time it takes to pay back the mortgage is called the amortization period, and it can range anywhere from five to 40 years. Until recently, the most common amortization period in Canada has been 25 years. Now within that amortization period, a mortgage will also have what are known as "terms." These are shorter periods of time—usually five years—during which you and the bank will negotiate the exact conditions of your agreement: the interest rate, how often you make your mortgage payments, and so on. At the end of each term, you can usually renegotiate the conditions of the mortgage for the next term. The biggest thing to affect the terms of your mortgage is the interest rate.

And, since interest rates fluctuate, and interest rates affect how much you pay to your lender ... well, that's why there are a lot of ways in which lenders and borrowers try to protect their own interests. Here are some of the mortgage options that are available to homebuyers.

A **fixed-rate mortgage** indicates that the monthly interest rate the homeowner will pay is fixed at the outset of the mortgage term, and will remain there until the term comes to an end. In other words, your mortgage payments will be exactly the same amount throughout that time, which some people really like because it's predictable and easier to set a budget. Even if the prime lending rate (what everyone simply calls "interest rates") goes up, the homeowner is protected from additional cost. Sounds peachy keen, right? But what if those rates drop? In that case, the unfortunate homeowner cannot benefit because their fixed rate wouldn't be able to follow that positive market trend.

An **adjustable-rate mortgage** (sometimes called a **variable-rate mortgage**) would fluctuate with changing interest rates in the larger economy. Those adjustments to a mortgage usually take place on either an annual or semi-annual basis. There are also certain limitations put into place regarding how much the mortgage amount can rise over the life of the mortgage (its amortization period). That important stipulation alleviates a common misconception among first-timers that they'll spend sleepless nights worrying that their interest rate will shoot sky-high without any warning, thus forcing them out of their own house—and into the poorhouse.

An **open mortgage** offers the option of pre-payment. That is a privilege wherein the homeowner has the right to make additional payments on the outstanding principal over and above the monthly payments. So if you win a lottery or receive a sizeable inheritance, you can pay off your mortgage without a penalty. Aren't you lucky? But be forewarned: you'll almost certainly be charged a higher rate of interest from the outset to have that option built in.

A **closed mortgage** is the reverse situation. The homeowner cannot repay the principal amount earlier than the end of the mortgage's lifespan. So if you win a lottery or receive a sizeable inheritance and are tempted to pay off your closed mortgage, be forewarned that you will get hit with a stiff financial penalty!

A **portable** or **transferable mortgage** indicates that you can carry your present mortgage terms with you if you sell your house and buy another one. You avoid having to pay any early discharge penalty fees when you are ready to purchase your next home. However, you'll most likely need to keep exactly the same terms or your interest rate may change. If, for instance, you buy a larger and more expensive house, and you need a larger mortgage to go with it, your transferable rate will probably have to be blended with the current interest rate at the time you buy. And the bank will still want proof that the new property you're buying is worth the money they're lending you, so expect to pay an appraisal fee.

An **assumable mortgage** is fairly self-explanatory in that the new homebuyer merely assumes the current seller's mortgage conditions. However, this mortgage type doesn't seem to be as common these days as it once was.

Sometimes a seller who has a lot of equity in his or her house (if it's fully paid off, for instance) will be willing to offer a private mortgage to you, the buyer. This is called a **seller take-back** or **vendor take-back mortgage**. Because it's private money, the interest rate will likely be higher than if you were to go through conventional bank financing. The advantage is that a private lender may not require as much documentation of income as a bank would. Again, this is a fairly uncommon practice these days.

There are some nontraditional mortgage choices also available today, especially as banks and other lenders acknowledge the needs of the new demographic of single homebuyers and try to accommodate them (within reason). Some first-time homebuyers can qualify for **low cash-down mortgages**, if they have an exceptionally good credit history and proof of excellent cash flow.

As well, some financial lenders are helping low-income applicants qualify for loans, which is particularly beneficial to single mothers. About 25% of that demographic spends more than half their yearly income on housing, compared to single fathers who only spend 10%. With more financing options available, single parents without a large nest egg may take their first step onto the home ownership ladder a lot sooner than was previously possible.

▉ ADVICE FOR PROPERTY VIRGINS
THE GOVERNMENT IS HELPING TOO!

The government of Canada allows first-time homebuyers to withdraw up to $20,000 in an interest-free, tax-free loan from their Registered Retirement Savings Plans. To qualify, there are a few stipulations: the funds must have been in that RRSP for a minimum of 90 days prior to their withdrawal, and to avoid a tax penalty the full amount must be repaid within the next consecutive 15-year period, according to a set schedule of yearly minimum payments.

Another possibility for first-timers in Ontario is the land transfer tax refund. With this refund program, the homebuyer could qualify for a maximum refund of up to $2,000.

For the record, our savvy first-timer Lauren chose an adjustable-rate mortgage in order to capitalize on the low interest rate that it offered at the outset, while also hoping the rate wouldn't increase. Since current indicators along with the upcoming forecast are both in her favour, well, good choice, Lauren!

Yes indeed—hurray for changing times. And hurray for my Auntie Cece too! I realized from a fairly young age that she was a tremendously brave lady who was made of much stronger fabric than most. In my teens, I read a line in a book about the extremely beautiful and courageous actress Lauren Bacall in which someone complimented her by saying, "She wears her balls for earrings!" I was immediately reminded of my own strong-willed aunt. She was never encouraged by her family to develop into the ambitious over-achiever that she became—it was her relentlessly independent drive that motivated her to stretch and reach beyond her immediate circumstances. My aunt has lived her life with great self-respect and pride, courage and freedom, supreme self-confidence and dignity—and a volatile temper!

Yep, my beloved Auntie Cece did it all. She paid her own way, she bought her own jewellery and she lived with no regrets. Thanks to my vivid memories of her outrageously funny behaviour, her incredibly generous spirit, her intimately shared secrets, her astute business advice, her unconditional love—and even her potty mouth!—she remains an inspiration to me to this day.

7

Big, Bad Realtor

In which Sandra takes the once-bitten, twice-shy Jill and Henry beyond their suspicions and fears about realtors—and walks them right through the front door of their new townhouse

I'm fairly certain that everyone finds a good reason to say "never again" at least once or twice in a lifetime. And then maybe even to repeat that phrase once or twice more—and naturally to *really* mean it each and every time. Well, since I'm only human, I've also faced those types of circumstances on many different occasions. For instance, each time I devour an additional helping of delicious risotto I promise myself that it will definitely be the last. But somehow that promise manages to get broken on a fairly regular basis because, well, let's just say that when it comes to risotto, I could practically live on it!

Along with some spicy salami, hot crusty bread and vine-ripened tomatoes with buffalo mozzarella, of course. And let's not forget the freshly grated Parmigiano-Reggiano, which, by the way, is the only grated cheese to use because there'll be no Grana Padano for me!

Oh and while we're talking about guilty pleasures, what about the fabulous "Sunday Sauce" that is typical to my ancestors' central Italian region of Abruzzi? It is so unbelievably good that I swear it's as therapeutic for your soul as chicken soup. I love it! Although it's actually prepared like almost any other sauce, the secret ingredients are its special herbs and spices. While the sauce simmers away, whole chunks of meat—pork or sausage or meatballs or ribs—are thrown in. Then, after some more stove time, that mouth-watering delicacy finally gets served over rigatoni, penne, linguine or spaghetti noodles and ... *tanto gusto*! When it comes to such delicious foods, how in the world could I say "never again" and expect to make it stick?

On the other hand, there have also been those rewarding instances when I was able to stand tall as a result of my determination to mean what I said. One such memorable instance when I did utter those infamous words—without looking back—was when I kicked Prince Charming to the curb. And that happened shortly after I had just dumped the biggest loser of all time! Whoever said that dating was easy?

Now I'll get back to the prince in a minute, but first let me give you a little background on "the biggest loser." What was I thinking when I started dating that guy anyway? You honestly can have no idea how incredibly naïve I was concerning him. To say nothing of how blind I must have been too, because everybody else around me—my trusted family, my best friends, my loyal co-workers—had already warned me that the smooth-talking macho man was going to be trouble. But warning signs? What warning signs? He didn't look like trouble to me.

Rather than listen to all that well-intentioned advice, I tempted fate. Within a few months fate had grown tired of watching me make a fool of myself and had graciously intervened. I was able to get out of that sour relationship before any real harm was done—sort of.

So there I was, right back where I'd started, trying to appear lively, intelligent and carefree while enjoying the wonderful world of dating. And that's where Prince Charming comes in.

Now when that too-good-to-be-true guy first arrived on my doorstep, I'll admit that I was sceptical about his motives. But I was determined not to be hard-hearted since having a chip on your shoulder is never an attractive look, and besides with my luck the chip probably wouldn't match my shoes and purse! And because I also believe that I shouldn't judge a book by its cover, I figured there would be no harm in at least taking a look at the first few pages, so to speak. But I didn't dive headlong into the story with the prince, and thankfully my cautious approach paid off. By our fourth date, his actions and words had started reminding me uncomfortably of the big-time loser, and my antennae were up. So that's what they meant by warning signs! At that point I silently reminded myself of my "never again" promise when it came to smooth-talking guys and decided to cut the evening short. And I do mean short because I practically told Mr. Charming that my number had just been changed to 1-800-GET-LOST!

There I was *again*. Still alone, and zero for two. But I never doubted for an instant that I'd made the correct decision about dumping those two guys. And even though nobody ever said that being single was the new black, I never allowed myself to get bitter. Nope, no sour grapes for me, because by nature I am an eternal optimist. Besides, the only time I like to hear the word "bitter" is when it's immediately followed by the word "chocolate."

But try explaining that never-say-die outlook to a nervous couple like Jill and Henry. They epitomized the old cliché of "once bitten, twice shy," having had a horrendous experience with a realtor whom they felt was far too pushy for his own good, far too greedy for his own gain and far too insensitive to their specific needs—and that's putting it mildly. So when I stumbled upon that information while casually chatting with them at a party, and innocently mentioned that I was a realtor, well, I could almost see them checking out the top of my head for a set of horns. If looks could kill, I think I'd be writing this book from beyond the grave.

Although I was initially taken aback by their scornful reaction, I wasn't personally offended in the least. I mean, how many people do you know who refer to lawyers as sharks? Apparently a great many other people want to lump realtors in with those dangerous bottom-feeders too. No, not the lawyers—I'm referring to the sharks! So when I meet a "realtor hater," I generally don't take the bait because I've learned from past experiences that nothing positive can be accomplished that way. Instead, I choose to conserve my energy, wrap up the conversation as quickly as possible, then smile politely and extricate myself from the situation.

However, even after taking those usual steps, I still found myself being sought out by Jill and Henry later in the evening. What to do then? Since you already know that I'm not the type to duck and take cover when a challenge presents itself, you won't be surprised to learn that I became determined to change that couple's mindset, if possible, by leaving them with a different and more positive image of a realtor. After all, we're not all ogres! After allowing them both equal air time to vent their spleens about their unhappy past experience, I subtly went to work. And before you could belt out the chorus to "R-E-S-P-E-C-T," Jill and Henry had graciously accepted my business card and promised to stay in touch should they ever find themselves needing the services of a realtor.

MEET HENRY AND JILL

When my phone rang five weeks later, I told Henry, "Of course I remember you and I'm very happy to hear from you, so just let me know how I can help you out."

"Well"—he hesitated slightly—"we thought we'd like to speak with you about buying a place to live."

"I'm all ears. When would you like to do that?"

"Do you have any time later this week?"

"I sure do."

And so, a few days later, first-time homebuyers Jill and Henry—who had recently become engaged to be married—joined me to begin the process of finding them a suitable property that would satisfy their lifestyle needs. After discussing the pros and cons of the many alternatives I presented them with, they decided to purchase a townhouse. Although their jointly made decision was based on a few different factors, a genuine sense of urban community living was the most significant factor for both of them.

Henry was a suit who worked regular business hours in a busy accounting firm, but away from the office he was an extremely relaxed, sociable guy with a dry wit who enjoyed kibitzing and hanging out.

"I don't want to waste my time doing chores around the house all weekend long because I am just not that lawn-mowing, snow-shovelling kind of guy at all," he adamantly stated.

"So a home in suburbia sounds like a no-go," I chuckled, as Henry nodded vigorously.

Jill, who was a personal fitness expert with irregular hours that were always being shifted around to accommodate her clients, found herself running in and out all day long. She also wanted to avoid the suburbs because a lengthy commute two or three times a day was not her idea of fun. And considering the outrageous gas prices these days, along with those two horrid driving seasons (winter and construction), can you blame her?

So, contrary to many other first-time homebuyers who are able to acquire a more affordable property only by ending up miles from the downtown core, Jill and Henry were going to substitute the cost of commuting for a higher property cost instead.

Although some of their friends had chosen to live in a typically urban, high-rise condominium complex, Jill and Henry had ruled out that option for themselves. The apartment building they were currently residing in had undergone a constant changeover of tenants during their five years living there, with the majority of those newer tenants being much younger and successively noisier. Due to that aggravating circumstance, Jill and Henry really wanted to avoid anyone living directly above or directly below them. In fact, their growing disdain for apartment living was the catalyst for them to re-evaluate their current circumstances and become homeowners instead. They also wanted to stop throwing money away on rent and to instead put their hard-earned dollars to better use—namely, home ownership. And they knew that a townhouse purchase would be a very wise investment for their future since the property's value would appreciate over time, creating home equity for them that could eventually become a major source of retirement funds.

Or, as Henry slyly pointed out to his fiancée, "We might even need the townhouse as an asset to borrow against when I turn thirty-five and you plan my big blowout bash with the Vegas dancing girls."

"Oh right, how could I forget about the dancing girls?" mocked Jill.

They also voiced their preference for a multi-level floor plan, rather than the single-floor design found in the majority of condos.

"We can even make those flights of stairs part of our workout," said Jill with a smile.

"Who says 'we'?" smirked Henry.

An affordable, centrally located townhouse seemed to be the perfect solution, since it offered them a comfortable middle ground between a too-demanding, or isolating, home in the 'burbs, and a claustrophobic, or utilitarian, condominium. And since that decision worked for them, well, it worked for me too.

FREEHOLD, HYBRID, CO-OP—WHAT'S BEST?

I proceeded to point out the different options available to them.

"Freehold townhouses, sometimes referred to as row houses, are a series of units that are attached to each other horizontally by a series of common walls, in which the wall that separates your unit from the adjacent unit is referred to as a 'party wall.' A freehold townhouse sits on its own piece of land, so your exclusive property purchase includes the building itself, as well as ownership of that individual plot of land, as well as the air above the building, which is great if you should ever decide to build up by adding another storey. And similar to the owner of a single-family house, the owner of a freehold townhouse pays no monthly maintenance fees and has the freedom to paint their exterior as they wish, landscape as they see fit or to hang up outdoor decorations at their discretion. But, unfortunately, it also means that you'll have to cut your own grass!"

Henry nodded uncomfortably.

"So as you both can see, a freehold townhouse purchase is unlike the purchase of a condo unit in which you don't own any actual land, you cannot build up, you must pay monthly maintenance fees, and you must adhere strictly to the rules, regulations and restrictions set forth by the condo's governing board."

"Gotcha," said Henry.

"But, because life apparently isn't complicated enough already, there is also a condominium-townhouse option."

"Which is what exactly?" asked Jill.

"Real estate titles to condominium-townhouses, condos and co-ops are often described as hybrid forms of ownership because they include a mixture of elements that are owned by the individual, while other elements are owned by the group. In effect a hybrid is a cross between being a homeowner and a tenant, just as with a condo, because each of those individual townhouse units is privately owned, but the land surrounding it is not. So all of that land, along with the other shared areas, becomes collectively known as the common elements. Those condominium-townhouse owners must pay their monthly maintenance fees to a homeowners' association for the upkeep of the shared areas and amenities and the appropriate insurance, just as in an actual condo complex. Are you still with me?"

"So far, so good," answered Jill.

"Great, because there's more," I laughed. While I was on a roll, I went one step further to also explain a co-op purchase to Jill and Henry, in case they opted for that. "If property is sold via a cooperative agreement, then title to all associated real estate is held by a designated corporation. In that case, the buyer who purchases stock in that co-op corporation is then considered to be a shareholder only because that individual is not the actual owner of any real property. Each individual shareholder holds a lease to their individual unit that runs for the life of that co-op's corporation, and the costs to maintain that building are divided among those shareholders. Also, any new potential buyers usually have to be approved by the co-op's administrative board."

"Thank you so much for clearing that up for us," Henry said, smiling. But I wasn't sure if he was just pulling my leg!

After viewing a sampling of affordable properties within their preferred geographic area, Jill and Henry eventually settled on a reasonably priced townhouse community that featured hundreds of similar triplex buildings. Each unit was constructed in the traditionally narrow, multi-floor style that made for an appealing overall conformity. Fortunately, the developers of that particular community, which resembled a small subdivision, had provided a selection of different "personal" styles within the townhouses themselves. Thus my clients were able to view a variety of interior layouts, and found that several of them suited their tastes. Each unit also included a small front yard, as well as a small back patio area that would require next to no exterior maintenance responsibilities.

"Sweetie, I don't think we could have designed these units any better if we'd been in charge!" Jill said, laughing.

"You could be right," Henry agreed. "Now let's go check out the pool."

After viewing the amenities—a large outdoor pool, a small shaded park area, a seasonal barbecue pit and a playground for children—my clients were very satisfied indeed.

TOO MUCH OF A GOOD THING

Perhaps a little too satisfied, in fact! They found themselves in an interesting situation without an easy answer since they had viewed two very different units—and liked them both equally. The very next day, I scheduled second viewings for each of those units.

Now, similar to some other townhouse structures in which the end units tend to be built a little larger, the end unit that my clients liked also offered a larger floor plan with additional square footage, thanks to a third bedroom. And because it shared only one common wall, there were additional windows that allowed for much more sunlight. That end unit also offered them more privacy and easier access to the parking lot—but it came with a higher price tag too.

"I know I like the extra bedroom and the extra privacy aspect, but when I reconsider, I'm not so sure that I like the extra cost," Henry said cautiously.

"I agree about the cost. But sweetie, won't we need that extra privacy for our nude sunbathing?" Jill teased.

"Oh right, how silly of me to forget the nude sunbathing aspect," deadpanned Henry.

"Just getting you back for that crack about the Vegas dancers," Jill replied, then gave him an affectionate peck on the cheek.

With the less expensive and smaller middle unit that my clients were also considering, the lower cost was in their favour, but they would have neighbours on either side of them, which presented the possibility of unwanted noise from both sides. That was a big consideration for Jill and Henry.

"Is there anything that can be done about that?" Jill wanted to know.

"Yes, simply ask your home inspector to check the level of sound insulation that's inside the common walls," I replied.

"Will that be a big deal?" asked Jill.

"Not at all. Basically he'll just choose a random spot that's discreetly out of the way and drill a hole in the wall to check what type of sound batting has been used. If he finds a greenish taupe insulation, rather than the standard pink, you can be fairly certain that the sound absorption level is excellent. That greenish insulation is one of the superior-quality products available to builders these days that provide very effective acoustical dampening properties. As well, most of those same products also possess excellent fire resistance properties that can withstand intense heat and delay the spread of flames."

"But what happens if …?" Jill's question trailed off.

"Since your offer to purchase will be contingent upon the acceptance of your home inspector's report, should his findings indicate anything about sound that makes you uncomfortable, you'll be able to walk away if you choose to."

"Does that also go for the musty smell in the basement?" Henry asked. He did have a point because there was a very slight mildew odour in the basement that would require checking into by their home inspector to establish its cause.

THE NON-NEGOTIABLE COSTS OF BUYING

Along with the actual purchase price of a property, there are a number of additional expenses that a homebuyer must also be aware of, and able to afford, so it's important to be realistic when calculating a budget. For instance, the closing costs are the homebuyer's responsibility and they usually include home inspection fee, appraisal fee, title search fee, lawyer's fees, paying the balance of your down payment, moving day expenses, financing fees, land transfer tax, and all other applicable taxes. There will also be "adjustments" made to the property taxes, since the taxes are pro-rated (calculated using a cost-per-day figure) and the seller will usually have paid for more or less than their share, and that has to be factored in. Unfortunately, we all know that there is no way to avoid paying taxes! (For a complete checklist of closing costs, see the Appendix of this book.)

In contrast to those one-time-only closing costs, there are also the "carrying costs" of any property. These are the ongoing, routine expenses incurred for the continuous operating and upkeep of a property, such as the monthly mortgage payment, various taxes, insurance, utilities, maintenance, etc. For Jill and Henry, who were looking at a community that was structured as a condominium townhouse, their share of the total common area's expenses would correspond to their "interest" (as a percentage of the whole) in those common elements. The owner of the end unit (with that third bedroom) would therefore own a larger percentage of those common elements and as a result would have to pay out a higher monthly maintenance fee than homeowners who had only two bedrooms in their units. The basic utilities (such as electricity, gas, water and cable television) were excluded from that townhouse's monthly maintenance fee, and because that end unit only shared one common wall, its fuel bills for heating and air conditioning would be higher than those in the middle unit.

. Individually, none of those separate amounts would be crippling to our young buyers, but to an accountant like Henry it's all about the bottom line. So, keeping in mind those additional expenses—as well as the expenses that would kick in very soon for Henry and Jill's upcoming wedding, as well as the fact that they were definitely looking to get a good deal—the number crunching began in earnest. Henry and Jill ultimately decided to compromise their desire for that end unit and make an offer on the centrally located unit instead.

Before they did so, however, I provided them with a lot of information about recent sales in that complex, and as much information as I could glean about the seller's situation and motivations. Homebuyers and their realtors need to work together to gather all the pertinent information that will allow them to make a realistic, savvy offer. Here's my top 10 list of questions you should ask your realtor.

THE 10 MOST IMPORTANT QUESTIONS TO ASK YOUR REALTOR BEFORE MAKING AN OFFER—AND WHY YOU SHOULD ASK THEM

1. **How long has the property been on the market?**

    Why: The length of time a property has been on the market may indicate the seller's willingness to negotiate.

2. **Have there been any price reductions during the listing period?**

    Why: The amount of any price reduction, as it relates to the overall purchase price, may indicate the seller's desire to attract an offer.

3. **Have there been any other offers on the property?**

    Why: It will be helpful to know what offers may have been turned down and for what reason.

4. **What is the motivation of the seller?**

   Why: Motivation is a key element in any negotiation. As an example, if the seller has already purchased a new property, your ability to close quickly may be an attractive element of the negotiations.

5. **What personal items ("chattels") are included in the sale?**

   Why: Anything the seller is willing to leave behind that you won't need to buy when you move in has real value. Consider asking for those items in your offer.

6. **What is the price range of properties that have sold recently in the area?**

   Why: This information is important since it will indicate the top and bottom of the specific market.

7. **What is the average time on market for properties in this area?**

   Why: Short market times may indicate a seller's market—that is, more buyers than sellers. If this is the case, you may face competition from other buyers.

8. **What is the list-to-sale price ratio in this area?**

   Why: This information will indicate other sellers' willingness to negotiate and by how much.

9. **What is the average sales price per square foot on recently sold properties?**

   Why: This approach to establish value works best where there are similar homes, lot sizes and improvements.

10. **What other known factors about the property or neighbourhood could affect value?**

    Why: There could be changes to the neighbourhood that will affect the economic outlook—and the future value of homes in the area. Review the Seller's Disclosure Statement very carefully with your realtor.

Jill and Henry arrived at an offer price they were comfortable with, and after they had signed all the paperwork I relayed their offer to the seller's agent. As so often happens, though, the seller signed back their initial offer as unacceptable and named a new figure. That's just par for the course when negotiations are taking place!

Henry and Jill talked about "meeting in the middle" with regard to the price. I added to their discussion by informing them that trying to meet in the middle is a slippery concept since we're not dealing with an Oreo cookie, so technically there is no middle. "Once the seller has changed his price," I told them, "the middle price would also change in comparison. Therefore a middle is almost impossible to rationalize. Besides, the market itself will determine the value of every property."

Following my advice that they put a brief time frame around their offer, they stipulated that their revised offer had to be signed back within a five-hour time period. Jill was supportive of this, not only because she liked instant gratification, but also because she understood the value of not getting wrapped up in an endless negotiating process about an elusive middle. She was able to convince Henry that offering a slightly higher price was necessary because even though she wanted a good deal too, she didn't want Henry to become Uncle Anal about trying to get it.

Well, that slightly higher offer proved to be the icing on the cake indeed, because it was immediately accepted by the seller. And that caused Jill and Henry to jump for joy when I told them the good news.

"I like the smell of success," Henry said, "but what I don't like is the smell of mildew."

And neither do I, so let's deal with that smelly issue now and get it over with.

ANOTHER ISSUE FOR YOUR TRUSTY HOME INSPECTOR

A qualified home inspector will always check a basement for signs of water damage caused by cracks (even very tiny ones) in the building's

foundation or its walls. If any leaks are found or if there is an accumulation of water due to faulty drainage, those problems would be
noted. Most inspectors will also be on the lookout for other potential
problems such as mould and mildew, since those types of fungus are
often caused by leaky pipes or flooded basements or buildings with
structural issues such as cracks in their walls. (Some inspectors don't
do this as part of a routine inspection, but they may do a mould inspection for an additional fee.)

Fortunately, in Jill and Henry's case, the mildew damage in their
townhouse had been confined to one small area and could therefore
be easily removed. And with a properly upgraded ventilation system
installed as a preventive measure, that moisture would dry out in the
affected area and keep any condensation from returning.

Another type of fungus associated with moisture is black mould
and it is commonly found in construction materials. It rots wood and
drywall and it should be removed immediately since it could be a
possible health hazard. The presence of fungus like that could also
lower your property's value, so it needs to be dealt with.

■ ADVICE FOR PROPERTY VIRGINS

Buyer Beware: The Grow-op Syndrome

Most mould grows for simple enough reasons, such as moisture somehow making its way into the house, whether through the exterior walls,
the basement floor, the roof, windows—or a combination of these. But
another cause for mould and mildew is a "grow-op" house that was
used to grow marijuana. The intensive heat and humidity used to grow
marijuana can cause an entire house—walls, ceilings, duct work, roof
vents—to become contaminated with mould. In that situation, extensive
cleaning and repairs will be required, since high-powered fans likely won't
be enough.

Aside from mould problems, a few other tip-offs to indicate that a property has been used as a grow-op are obvious evidence of tampering with the hydro meter, inexplicable garage or basement renovations and the obvious stench of the product still hanging around.

Fade out ... fade in. With their moving day just around the corner, Jill and Henry returned to their newly purchased property for one last look. The final walk-through was their last chance to do a personal inspection of the property before they actually took possession of it.

MORE THAN A CASUAL STROLL: THE FINAL WALK-THROUGH

All potential homebuyers should be aware that in order for that final walk-through to take place, it must have been specified in your original purchase agreement as a condition of the sale! With your realtor present, you'll do the walk-through just a day or two prior to the final closing date because you want to make sure the seller doesn't have additional time afterwards to make any changes or cause any damage before you actually move in. During that walk-through you are looking to verify that everything is exactly the same as when you originally viewed the property and agreed to buy it—with the exception, of course, of the seller's personal possessions (known as "chattels"). Clothing, furniture, televisions, major appliances, etc. may have been removed by the time of the walk-through, but if that's the case you'll want to make darn sure that none of the "real property" included in your purchase agreement has been either removed or exchanged with a cheaper substitute. You may have included items such as overhead lighting, broadloom carpeting, drapes, cabinet hardware, window-screens and major appliances.

Hold on a quick minute: why do major appliances appear in both of those descriptions? Could there be some confusion as to which household items belong in each category? Yes, unfortunately there will be instances in which the seller sees white and the homebuyer sees black. In order to avoid any overlapping grey area, you must not make any assumptions! Instead, make a thorough, itemized list that clearly establishes what can be removed and what must remain behind, and include the list with your offer to purchase. When it comes to major appliances, such as stove, fridge, washer and dryer, they cannot be considered chattels unless they're indicated as such on that itemized list. And here's a word of caution: it might even be beneficial to ask your realtor to obtain the serial numbers of those major appliances, just for the record. This gives you a way of checking to see that what you're receiving is the real deal. I know, it sounds slightly preposterous to be so careful. But the word "untrustworthy" is in the dictionary for a good reason!

In some cases, personal property may become affixed to real property and then it is called a "fixture." For instance, when you go to a lumberyard and buy wood, that's personal property. But if you take that wood and proceed to construct a built-in bookcase that is attached to the wall of your living room, you now have a fixture. And when you buy or sell a home, fixtures are automatically included as part of its real property. If the seller wants to remove certain fixtures from the property when they move out (without causing any residual damage to be left behind), those items must be listed as chattels within the purchase agreement. The seller may want to remove a window air conditioner, for instance, which could be easily unscrewed and transported, whereas the satellite dish and storage shed would probably stay.

As I've already indicated, some sellers can be deliberately dishonest, while others might only tend to be a little sneaky, while others might just turn out to be downright sentimental. I know this may sound hard to believe, but I know of an instance where a seller nearly demolished her property's landscaping just moments before vacating! On her moving day, at the eleventh hour, that perfectly sweet and harmless elderly woman didn't have the heart to say goodbye to the beautiful flowering shrubs in the front garden. So she impulsively just dug them all up and took them with her, presumably to re-plant in her new property's front garden instead! Who knew that somebody could become that attached to a bush!

During that final walk-through, if you do notice a few marks on the walls or floors, your experienced realtor will probably advise you not to make a mountain out of a molehill. After all, that's what cleaning products are for. But, on the other hand, if you notice any signs of actual damage, such as a hole in the wall, then you certainly have a legitimate complaint. The best way to address that or any other serious problem is to have your realtor write up a formal complaint and then present that report to the listing agent as a demand for a satisfactory solution. Bear in mind that the seller has the option to challenge that report, but since your realtor will be able to verify your findings and concerns, he or she can hopefully apply the necessary pressure to have the problem quickly remedied. In a worst-case scenario you may also have to contact your lawyer, so be prepared to be able to prove your assertions: it's a really good idea to bring a notebook and a camera along for the walk-through, as long as it is within your rights to photograph the home.

Jill and Henry's urban townhouse purchase (which, by the way, did contain more than adequate soundproofing within its party walls!) proved to be a very timely investment for them, since current trends show that townhouses are making a very big comeback. Their home equity in that unit indicates a healthy sign of appreciating, which will be a bonus for them when it comes to re-sale value. And a little future economic potential is nothing to sneeze at.

And thanks to the endless mortgage options that are now available to first-time homebuyers, Henry was also able to negotiate a very low, fixed-interest mortgage rate. Their payments would be consistent every month for the term of their loan, and how convenient is that?

According to Henry the accountant, the mortgage terms he negotiated were tailor-made for them.

And speaking of Henry, was he an original or what? I still chuckle to myself when I remember the day I stopped by to deliver their new house keys to them.

"You know, Sandra, throughout this entire transaction my eyes were really opened thanks to your knowledge, your skills and your patience," Henry said. "I really want to thank you for being so professional."

"Awwwww, that's so nice, thank you, Henry!" I said.

"Especially since we gave off such hostile vibes when we first met you," Jill squeaked.

"Hostile vibes? I have no idea what you're talking about, honey. Was I out of the room when you did that?" Henry said with a straight face.

I couldn't help but laugh.

"Do you see what I have to put up with?" Jill said, shaking her head. "And to think that in less than a year I'm going to marry this trouble-maker!"

"Not if I marry you first," said Henry, with a cocky smile and a very familiar look in his eye. Then he leaned over and planted a big wet one on Jill's blushing cheek.

"Okay then, I'll let that be my cue to split," I volunteered.

"You know where to find us," Jill said, as we all hugged each other tightly.

A few moments later, as I drove away, Henry frantically waved as he shouted, "Don't be a stranger; come on by anytime. You can even bring your tax forms!"

As I laughed, I wondered if he meant it. Or was he just pulling my leg again?

Upon reflection, I think the greatest satisfaction I gained from dealing with Jill and Henry was in knowing that I was instrumental in changing their initially distrustful and negative view of realtors into a more pleasant and positive one—especially since we all know it's sometimes very difficult to change a first impression. Now, to their credit, both Jill and Henry were always polite and respectful to me personally, but even so, their "never again" attitude toward realtors at the outset did seem just shy of a full-fledged grudge, so I'm glad they were able to overcome it.

For some of you, the discipline involved in facing a specific situation and being able to assertively say "never again" might be a snap. For others, that process might prove to be pure agony. Or perhaps the decision you would tend to make depends on the individual circumstances involved. That seems to be the pattern I've noticed with myself. I find that my ability to stick to a "never again" decision is much stronger within a business context where I can rely on my professional expertise as my client's fiduciary, where I must act for that client and function in that client's best interest. That role helps me establish a bit of distance, and within such a situation I'm able to remain loyal to my client's cause while also being detached.

Within a personal context, however, I sometimes can't even keep my own best interests at heart, and therefore I tend to be far more yielding. Let's face it, how am I supposed to say "never again" to the simplicity of a high-quality imported olive oil drizzled over thick slices of fresh buffalo mozzarella, juicy tomato slices and sweetly fragrant basil leaves? I would have to be crazy to even consider it! And what about freshly picked hot peppers, or meatballs made from a mixture of pork, veal and beef, or fresh garlic cloves, or homemade chicken soup—the list is endless.

As for the pasta, don't get me started! It is well known to all Italians that one style of noodle is for certain sauces and not for others. Hence we can be like dedicated wine connoisseurs when it comes to pasta because we each have our favourite types of noodles, so I'm warning you now: don't try to mess with my pasta! A select few of my favourite pasta dishes are a salty Putanesca sauce on penne noodles, or tortellini Alfredo in a thick cream sauce—or what about a tasty tomato and fresh basil sauce over homemade agnolotti stuffed with ricotta? Talk about a slice of heaven! I also like my agnolotti stuffed with butternut squash and topped with a simple but authentic herb and oil dressing. Or a spicy meat sauce ladled generously over rigatoni or tortellini or ravioli. Lastly, I really enjoy eating gnocchi, but could it possibly be any more labour-intensive to prepare! Where did my poor loving *nonna* ever find the time to prepare it from scratch so expertly for our Sunday night dinner for 30 every week? Talk about patience.

As you can plainly see, my life is in a quandary at times because although I want to be disciplined and exhibit the determination required by controlling my impulses, I'm not always successful. I happen to enjoy inviting Mamma Bravo, and occasionally Sara Lee, to my dinner table. Unfortunately, after I do, I end up having to pay the consequences by becoming a slave to my treadmill the next morning. When it comes to exercise, who needs it? The grunting, the groaning, the lifting, the sweating—followed by the weighing in, which usually causes even more groaning. To me, exercise is really nothing more than an exercise in frustration. Hey now, that's something I could definitely give up and not miss at all because when it comes to working out, I always want to say "Fuhgedaboudit!" Which, of course, is the Italian way to say "never again!"

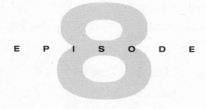

EPISODE 8

"You Like It? I Own It"

In which Sandra and Mr. Daniels shine a light on the shady dealings of mortgage fraudsters

When I answered my cellphone, my ear was nearly blown off by my friend Rosa's high-pitched shriek. "I've got some gossip fresh off the girlvine!" she said, then followed up that blaring headline with the news that our girlfriend Nicole's husband, Paul, had just won a million dollars in a lottery! Holy jackpot, Batman! Now, I am not personally a dedicated player of the weekly lotteries, but let's face it, becoming an instant millionaire is nothing to sneeze at, so it didn't take long for me to get caught up in Rosa's excitement over Paul's good fortune. In no time flat, it seemed both Rosa and I had begun plotting exactly how we were going to help Nicole spend some of Paul's just-won "do-re-mi" on ourselves. What are friends for but to lend a helping hand, right? And with a huge shoe sale on at the mall, I personally couldn't think of a better time to make my own hands available for the lending!

After that initial silliness wore off, Rosa gave me the lowdown on Paul's frantic call home to Nicole earlier that morning to tell her all the exciting details about his choice of lucky numbers. Even though it all seemed so simple, neither Rosa nor I could get over the fact that a few random family birthdates, mixed together with some blind luck, had played such a fortuitous role in Paul's life that morning. What a surprise. And since it honestly couldn't have happened to a nicer guy, it looked good on him too. I looked forward to congratulating him in person.

When I signed off a few minutes later, I figured that Rosa was probably on her way to lunch, that Paul was probably on his way to the bank, and that I was definitely going to make a left turn up ahead so I could dash into the convenience store on the corner to pick up a few lottery tickets! Why not? I had nothing to lose.

Well, the universe works in strange and mysterious ways to be sure. I immediately sensed that something was up when I heard back from Rosa later that night, her tone of voice subdued. I couldn't help but wonder how that day's earlier torrent of excitement had evaporated so quickly, and I cautiously asked, "Is everything all right?"

"I'm afraid not," Rosa said. "It looks like we'll have to leave those Jimmy Choos on the shelf a little while longer because even though it seemed like Paul had become an instant millionaire, it really wasn't that easy."

"Why not? What happened?"

"Well, Nicole told me that when Paul arrived at the lottery office to claim his million smackers in prize money, he was informed that there were *four other winners* with the exact same numbers! Can you believe that?"

"Wow, talk about a coincidence."

"No kidding. So instead of the cool mill that he'd been expecting, his share was only $200,000."

"Only 200K? Rosa, you say that like it's a bad thing," I scolded.

"Yeah, I guess you're right. I sort of did, but I didn't mean to." She sounded rather guilty now.

"You're reminding me of my Aunt Grace and her sour grapes attitude whenever it comes to someone else's good fortune. But you know what I say? Good luck and God bless to all the winners."

"I know, I know … You win some and you lose some, I guess. But I don't think Paul expected to do both at the same time!"

"It certainly was an unpredictable circumstance," I admitted.

"Can you just imagine my reaction if I'd been in his shoes?"

No doubt about it, disappointment can be a real bitch. Whether an individual experiences a major, life-altering disappointment or a more intimate, personal one—well, a close encounter with disappointment is never welcome.

And since one of the major highlights of many people's lives is becoming a homeowner for the first time, that moment when they purchase a property to call their own, it stands to reason that a low point for that same homeowner would be any unforeseen circumstance that would compel them to forfeit that same cherished property. When such a case occurs, whether due to an unfortunate bankruptcy, an unpleasant divorce, or the untimely death of a loved one, "disappointment" would be spelled out in capital letters a few storeys high.

MEET MR. DANIELS

Putting life's ups and downs aside for a moment, imagine how the average person would respond to an unforeseen eviction notice arriving completely out of the blue. This notice would inform them that they are no longer the legal owner of the cherished home they had purchased years before and for which they had diligently been making the monthly mortgage payments ever since. Do you think maybe a response such as total and complete apoplectic shock would cover it? That was precisely the response of my elderly neighbour when he received an eviction notice in his mailbox.

Mr. Daniels was a veteran of the Second World War whose wife of more than 40 years had passed away just a few years prior to the incident I want to tell you about. Although that sad occurrence left him a little on the reclusive side, he was always polite and friendly whenever I or another one of the neighbours encountered him at one of our block's Neighbourhood Watch meetings. Mr. Daniels faithfully attended those meetings, even though he preferred to sit in the back and keep mostly to himself. So it was quite a surprise when he approached me one night, after the meeting had ended, to seek my advice regarding his eviction notice problem.

I assumed correctly that he had singled me out because his inquiries were real estate related and he knew that I was a realtor. But even though I wanted to help out that sweet old widower as much as I could, I knew instantly that he needed to contact a reputable real estate lawyer. His problem was mortgage fraud and that is no joke.

EVERY HOMEOWNER'S WORST NIGHTMARE

Mortgage fraud, along with its closely related counterparts title fraud and value fraud, is a criminal act that is fast becoming an issue of grave concern to the public, as well as to the real estate industry itself, because of how rapidly it is proliferating. The damage that such cases cause can be horrifying indeed because there are many different ways and methods by which shrewd con artists, forgery experts and identity thieves can perpetrate that type of fraud and pull the rug out from under an unsuspecting homeowner. When those slick operators are convincing in their manipulative ways and successful in their duplicitous transactions, the innocent homeowner will not only lose his or her rug, but their entire property as well.

A recent case of mortgage fraud occurred when a tenant claimed ownership of the property that he was renting. He then attempted to sell that property right out from under its rightful owner by falsifying a power of attorney document with a forged signature. The tenant had boldly claimed to be a relative of the property's rightful owner, which made his actions very risky—and it was that misstep that turned out to be the greedy conman's undoing. Fortunately for the homeowner, his dishonest tenant was unsuccessful at his attempted crime.

In a different case, two crooks working in tandem backed up each other's untruthful claims by having one false contact pose as the rightful owner, who in turn would supply incorrect information to benefit the fraudulent transaction that was about to take place. Again, their combined actions were highly risky—and luckily they were also shut down midway through their scheme.

In yet another case, a couple of fraudsters legitimately acquired a property at market value and then, through a series of sales and re-sales in cooperation with other conmen working with them, were able to artificially increase the property's value. They attempted to deceive a financial lender by securing a mortgage based on that alarmingly inflated price. And did they get away with it? Fortunately not: they came close—but no cigar!

Last, but not least, another high-profile case involved the legitimate purchase of a property from an innocent seller who agreed to allow the buyer to assign the contract. That buyer then retained a lawyer to carry out the transaction. Almost immediately, that new owner "assigned" the contract to a second buyer—who was most likely complicit in this scheme—at an inflated price. That second buyer then took his contract to an alternative lender to arrange mortgage financing based on that inflated amount. Obviously, that alternative lender was kept totally in the dark regarding the original legitimate purchase contract. With the help of the lawyer, who was by that time acting on behalf of all the participants involved, documents were prepared that allowed the property to be transferred directly from the innocent seller to the second buyer, but at its original lower purchase price. However, the alternative lender had been duped into advancing the excessive amount necessary to cover the inflated amount that was agreed to with the second buyer! So, can you say surplus funds? And whose pocket do you think those funds went into? Unfortunately, in that case the scheme was "mission accomplished" rather than "mission uncovered."

Now with respect to my neighbour Mr. Daniels, the fraudsters essentially stole his mortgage-free property "on paper," via identity theft. While Mr. Daniels was out of town visiting his son's family, Imposter Number One fraudulently filled out a number of official documents that transferred Mr. Daniels' home to Imposter Number Two. That second imposter then successfully obtained a sizeable loan from a lending institution which would then register its mortgage against that property.

But before that fraudulent transaction was rubber-stamped, the chosen mortgage company needed to verify the property's worth by the usual means: they arranged to have an appraisal done. But those sneaky imposters had planned for such an event, because when the appraiser attempted to complete his assessment there was nobody at home. Since Mr. Daniels was actually out of town at the time, he was not able to pull the plug on the imposters' scheme by exposing them at that crucial point. The appraiser instead opted to do a "drive-by" of the property, in which he viewed the exterior of Mr. Daniels' house and its surrounding property, then took into account the location of the neighbourhood and what some comparable homes had recently sold for. Since the appraiser had already been informed of the listed square footage of the home's interior, and there were no undesirable factors like a smelly abattoir or an unsightly hydro station or a public garbage dump located next to the property, he was confidently able to make a written assessment of the market value of Mr. Daniels' property.

That was just one more step in a chain of events that spelled disaster for Mr. Daniels. The lending institution was satisfied with the appraisal, and since real estate transactions are usually time sensitive rather than open ended, and since the property was mortgage-free, and since the imposters had not over-valued it on their loan application and had in fact requested a mortgage for roughly half of the appraiser's assessed value—all things considered, it was reasonable that the lending institution was willing to assume the risk and grant the loan. Unbeknownst to that reputable lender, they unfortunately granted their loan to Imposter Number One and Imposter Number Two!

In effect Mr. Daniels and the lending institution had both been scammed. On paper Mr. Daniels didn't own his home, and the lender was left holding an invalid mortgage. In practice, what they had wasn't even worth the paper it was written on!

A similar case involved an appraiser ringing the doorbell of a particular property, only to have the door answered by a very unassuming, professional-looking man who seemed very at home in his surroundings—but who was actually the fraudster himself. That cool customer was friendly and accommodating, while exhibiting that he was knowledgeable about the property and that he clearly had full access to it—he could do that, of course, because he was the tenant. He allowed the appraiser to efficiently do his job. And since the fraudster had covered his tracks so well, why would the appraiser have been suspicious? After all, it's certainly not customary to ask a total stranger for photo identification, or to inquire why they aren't wearing a nametag, is it? Especially if that person is in "their own home"!

Mortgage fraud takes place when a whole bunch of things get tossed into the same pot: forged signatures, the registration of false documents, a legal loophole, a great deal of organization and great care to avoid suspicion, a bit of luck, some lax verification methods, some devious intent, a little sophistication, some unethical practices, a heightened sense of urgency, and an awful lot of nerve. How can such a nightmare be stopped from happening?

Lawyers frequently advise their clients to purchase land title insurance to help protect themselves should land title discrepancies arise. For a one-time cost of a few hundred dollars, title insurance inexpensively safeguards the new homeowner against any loss caused by "hazards and defects" that already exist in its title, as well as against the potential threat of fraud and forgery. Title insurance also protects the lending institution against any mistakes made during the actual title search process when a licensed and bonded title searcher will make a detailed check at the Land Registry Office to ascertain that there are no liens against the title, or that the property isn't being leased, and that the seller is in fact the lawful owner of that property before its title gets conveyed. That process will also reveal if there are any restrictive covenants or rights of way that might negatively affect the use or value of the property.

However if an error was to be made it could result in the buyer making mortgage payments on a home they don't actually own. Ouch! It is up to the lawyer to do some real digging to uncover any potential problems so that when the time comes for the new homeowner to gain possession of their property, the lawyer certifies that the property has a "clear and marketable" title.

Be forewarned that although title insurance is a hedge against some very serious offences, it is not a guaranteed cure-all for every offence. Like all other forms of insurance, there will be exceptions where compensation from title insurance will not apply. All first-time homebuyers and their lawyers should be certain to read the fine print.

WHAT THE LEGAL MUMBO-JUMBO REALLY MEANS

Let's take a quick timeout to avoid any confusion regarding specific terms that you may encounter when dealing with the legal aspects of buying a house.

A *lien* is a legal claim by a creditor that "encumbers" the title, affecting real property until an outstanding debt is fully paid. It essentially means that a homeowner owes money to someone, and that someone is making a claim against the house until they get paid.

Oftentimes a building contractor will institute such a proceeding if his company is owed a substantial sum of money by a homeowner, thus preventing the homeowner from being able to show "clear" title—and therefore preventing the homeowner from selling the house. In some cases, if the homeowner has not kept up payments on municipal taxes, a tax lien could be placed against the home. The lien will be lifted if and when the homeowner pays up—but if enough time passes without the taxes being paid, the house could be sold at a tax sale.

A *conveyance* is the lawful transfer of the real estate title from the seller to the new owner. This transfer is the legal assurance that the new owner holds the deed to the property.

An *encroachment* is a situation that occurs when a building, fence or driveway extends past the actual boundaries of one owner's property and onto the property of a neighbour. Oftentimes the new homebuyer's lawyer will request a property survey to establish if an encroachment exists, or to determine the seriousness of an actual encroachment.

A similar sounding term is *easement*, which is a legal provision in which one property owner grants permission for another person to cross onto, or use, that owner's property for a specific purpose. An encroachment, as described above, could be registered by the two neighbouring parties as an easement, which would mean that both parties agree to how the land is being used. Another example of an easement might be a service corridor in which a municipal easement allows access to the phone company or hydro company for servicing purposes. A property survey that clearly defines the boundaries of a property would indicate if an easement was present since that type of "right of way"—like other rights of way—is assigned to the property and cannot be removed at the seller's discretion. Instead it is passed from buyer to buyer of that particular property and can only be removed when all affected parties agree to its removal.

A *right of way* is yet another legal arrangement that can be made between two or more parties. It is a formal recognition that one party must have access (right of way) to a particular piece of land or section of a property, and that no other party can stop this access. Rights of way may be established over someone else's property if there is a particular need for the access, or if access has historically been allowed.

Not all property purchases require a property survey to be done, but your lending company could insist on one for its records, as well as for its own protection and peace of mind, before granting final approval of your financing. When that isn't the case, title insurance would probably suffice as a satisfactory alternative for your lending company.

■ ADVICE FOR PROPERTY VIRGINS
You Just Think You Live on River Street...

Here's an interesting bit of information about the "correct" address of your property. Let's say you were buying a house with a street address of 6970 River Street. This is not your property's legal address; it's only a convenient designation used for mail delivery.

The property's legal address is actually a description such as "Lot 22, map 50, of the Hoover subdivision, recorded in book 35 of the city of Glendale." Your lawyer will conduct a title search of this legal address before completing your transaction. Don't be totally confused when your Agreement of Purchase and Sale refers to a specific property with the terminology "commonly known as" 6970 River Street.

And because legal addresses tend to be fairly convoluted, be certain to have your lawyer check and double-check all legally binding documents to ascertain that an error of dyslexia hasn't listed the property incorrectly.

EVEN IF MORTGAGE FRAUD IS UNLIKELY, YOU NEED A REAL ESTATE LAWYER!

While a competent lawyer is clearly your ally in avoiding a case of mortgage fraud, don't for a minute think that a real estate lawyer should only be consulted to avoid that specific situation. That just isn't the case at all.

Hiring a professional, trustworthy real estate lawyer is of the utmost importance—not to mention being required by law in Canada when purchasing property—and I suggest that all potential homebuyers should take this step very early on in the home-buying process. This is especially true for first-timers, since the entire process is a brand-new procedure for them. I mean, just consider the copious number of essential documents alone! For example, finalizing a condominium's status certificate involves an awful lot of paperwork—and usually some mild confusion—so it is always better to be safe than sorry.

A lawyer will protect his or her clients by guiding them away from any potential risks prior to signing an Agreement of Purchase and Sale. If a potential buyer is told by the seller or the seller's agent that there is no risk, and if that buyer accepts their assurances on blind trust, then that buyer is assuming a risk. But why should they do so when they could just run all that information past their lawyer for approval instead? Again, it is better to be safe than sorry.

A trustworthy lawyer will act diligently on your behalf not only because they have professional integrity, but also because they are protecting themselves from liability. If that lawyer, or law firm, anticipates even the slightest risk of being sued, they will make every attempt to protect their clients and fulfill their duties to them in every conceivable way instead of facing a lawsuit.

In my years of experience I can honestly say that most of the lawyers I've dealt with are very congenial and professional, so in the vast majority of transactions with them everything goes as smooth as cream cheese. Mind you, the odd one will want me to think they're doing all the work and assuming all the liability throughout the transaction, but I usually just go with the flow on that score. When all is going according to plan with a purchase, I don't usually need to have much direct discussion with the lawyer. If I do have to make a call to a client's lawyer in the midst of a deal—to discuss how they would prefer an unusual clause to be written in the contract, for instance—the lawyer is usually grateful that I am trying to understand their point of view. The alternative would be that I'd just go ahead and word it my own way, without their input, and then they would have to deal with any problems that should arise. Most lawyers realize that cooperation limits aggravation.

Now, as we all know, haste makes waste. A busy real estate season could be a breeding ground for mortgage fraud, as well as other real estate scams. When a greater number of transactions occur, a few of them might get hustled through the system in a haphazard fashion. But because mortgage fraud is increasing, realtors are being educated and encouraged to keep a sharp eye out to recognize it, to report it and to thus hopefully help to stop it.

As a first-timer it is necessary that you seek advice from an accredited, licensed realtor who is an expert within the geographical area where you plan to go house shopping. Ask that realtor prudent questions and pay close attention to their expert advice on all matters.

THAT OLD OUNCE OF PREVENTION

If you're already a homeowner—or you're soon to become one—what can you do? Well, to begin with, keep a sharp eye on your own credit reports and bank statements for any unfamiliar charges or inconsistencies. Immediately alert a credit card company to any statement discrepancies regarding purchases that you did not authorize. Speak up immediately and ask questions of the proper authorities regarding an unrequested credit inquiry—this will be obvious if you get periodic credit reports on yourself. Watch out for unexpected mail that arrives at your home but is addressed to an unknown individual. Take notice if any regularly received bills do not arrive when they are expected to. Make note of any suspicious phone calls inquiring about real estate matters that pertain to your home. And exercise extreme caution by making sure you know whom you are dealing with when it comes to giving out your personal information; unfortunately, far too many people have become far too cavalier in that regard, and will naïvely answer questions of a highly sensitive or personal nature over the phone. How can you even be sure that the unknown voice on the other end of the line is really who they say they are? Or if that unknown voice is actually representing the company they say they are? Your personal information pertaining to birth certificates, passports, bank accounts, credit card numbers and their expiry dates, social insurance numbers, etc., should essentially be off-limits unless you know precisely with whom you are dealing.

■ ADVICE FOR PROPERTY VIRGINS

THE 11TH COMMANDMENT: SHRED THY GARBAGE

Although this might sound kind of silly, be careful with your garbage! Many people tend to dispose of old tax returns, bills and credit card receipts without properly destroying them first, and that laziness could come back to haunt them. Shred those documents that contain your signature instead of just putting them in the recycling box or the garbage, where they can easily be lifted and used by a person who is far more devious than you.

Another growing problem is the willingness of individuals to indiscriminately supply sensitive financial data and other personal information to strangers via the Internet. The increased use of the Internet and its lack of security have created many more opportunities for mortgage fraud, as well as identity theft, to take place. It's best never to reply to emails requesting that type of information.

Online consumers must also learn to be more accountable for their actions. I'm certainly not bashing e-commerce, but be careful to protect yourself, and your passwords, so that a stranger cannot pass himself off as you. Keep in mind that photo identification, and even a signature in most cases, is not required over the Internet, so false impersonation could be fairly easy for some clever, experienced fraudsters to commit. I have a friend who doesn't want to give up his online purchasing habits, so instead he unfailingly changes his three major credit cards every year just to confound any possible identity thieves. A bit extreme perhaps, but it works for him!

Similarly, what I've found works for me is a self-imposed rule to use only one of my credit cards for all online transactions. That way it's easier for me to stay familiar with the number of transactions I complete and their dollar amounts—I'll definitely notice if something unusual comes up on my bill. And because I purposely keep a low credit ceiling on that particular card, I can kill two birds with one stone: I literally can't give in to the temptation to make a lot of frivolous purchases, and I make it impossible for a criminal to scam my bank account for a major amount of moolah!

Fade out ... fade in. The good news is that some provincial laws are currently under review to protect homebuyers from mortgage fraud, and some pre-existing laws have already been revised to offer a speedier compensation process to victimized homeowners like Mr. Daniels. Those new amendments ensure that a victimized owner gets their rightful land title restored and that in turn the fraudsters have their documents declared invalid—and in a perfect world, the criminals are charged and convicted. Ownership of that particular property therefore cannot be lost as the result of a fraudulent sale, a counterfeit power of attorney (in which the borrower is not the legal property owner but is relying on a false power of attorney in order to borrow funds), or any other means of falsifying a mortgage registration. That new law also puts the onus of responsibility on the banks and other lenders to exercise the proper due diligence when registering mortgages, because they will no longer be eligible to make a claim for recovery of funds if they are negligent in that regard. With a more in-depth investigation of borrowers taking place by lenders, and perhaps even the eventual elimination of Internet mortgage arrangements, a significant decline in mortgage fraud will hopefully soon take place.

Unfortunately, many mortgage fraud perpetrators go unpunished since they are able to disappear quickly after their scam is completed and because they wisely use bogus identification throughout their crimes. With lending companies exercising greater caution, they will need to insist on a proper in-person appraisal (not a drive-by), which would involve both verbally contacting and meeting face to face with the lawful property owner—and not accepting any excuses to the contrary. Another recommendation is that the appraiser verifies the identity of the property owner via photo identification, and matches their signature with a previous legal document. By implementing these more rigorous processes, an unsuspecting owner would be given the opportunity to uncover an attempted fraud before it actually happens.

And when it comes to the rules governing the registration of a power of attorney, it is hoped that new regulations would ensure that a power of attorney could only be used if a lawyer certifies that all procedures and formalities were properly followed. The person granting the power of attorney would therefore be the only person who is actually allowed to sign that important document. In other words, no third parties allowed, thank you! Because it's such an important step to designate someone as your power of attorney, you should exercise extreme caution if you ever need to do it, and consult with your lawyer to institute appropriate limitations with regard to your personal assets.

After many, many months filled with lawyer's meetings and court dates, my innocent neighbour Mr. Daniels was finally able to tear up that nasty power of sale or foreclosure notice. Although Mr. Daniels never actually had to forfeit his property at any time—despite the fact that the defrauded company that held the illegally obtained mortgage made a grab for it—he had been temporarily forbidden to use it as collateral. Fortunately, that never became an issue for him, even though he faced extremely high legal bills. Throughout his strenuous ordeal, the support of his family had been a great comfort to him, but even so his health had suffered very noticeably.

But after regaining his health, one evening the most amazing transformation took place at one of our neighbourhood meetings. That quiet, elderly man temporarily came out of his shell to speak to the assembled crowd about his anxiety-inducing ordeal. He informed us of the ways and means to protect ourselves and our property—and believe me when I say that you could have heard a pin drop that night!

I learned that night that mortgage fraud—besides being a great disappointment and a total pain in the neck—can also turn out to be a very humbling experience. It's up to each individual to find a productive solution and to fight the good fight when they encounter disappointment face to face. When we are successful at turning the tables on disappointment and not letting it ruin our day, our week, our life, we're off to the races instead with a positive attitude and a smile on our faces.

Oh, but if you're really off to the races, then here's a hot tip: play the third horse in the sixth race. Why? Because those are my favourite numbers, of course! Otherwise, please limit your bets to just two bucks, because that way it's not as disappointing for you when your numbers don't win!

E P I S O D E

A Time To Sell

In which Katie and Bill look beyond "fluffing" and start seeing the flesh and bones of what's for sale, and in which Sandra shows readers how to sell that house when the time comes

Have you ever heard a friend complain about their job? Now that's a rhetorical question, isn't it? Of course you have and so have I. In fact, years ago it was probably me who was doing the complaining! While I was still in high school, my very first part-time job at the local mall was in retail where I worked at an upscale clothing store. But since I was the newbie on the scene I also got stuck doing all the boring chores, like cleaning the staff washroom, vacuuming the store's large main floor, cleaning the glass on all the display cases, helping to dress the mannequins, and so on. Then, when I wasn't relegated to those chores, my manager had instructed me to watch and listen to the experienced sales ladies. "One day," she said, "you'll be able to deal with our customers in the correct manner."

So, while making sure the store was clean and tidy, I also eavesdropped whenever I had the chance. Those chores weren't backbreaking work and I certainly respected the know-how of the older employees.

What I liked most was the weekly paycheque I received because it gave me a sense of freedom. My parents told me I could spend my small earnings on whatever I wanted to, so how cool was that? Their permission allowed me to go crazy—buying the latest trendy fashions, the highest platform shoes, some funky costume jewellery, and of course every new hair product I could find. Naturally I also had to experiment with every new hairstyle. I remember the hideous perm that made me look like a toy poodle, as well as my unfortunate experience with bangs, and I can assure you that an "asymmetrical cut" is not for everyone! Live and learn, right?

I ended up keeping that job for a year and a half, during which time I had plenty of opportunity to watch, listen and learn. I soaked up as much information as I possibly could about the selling techniques being used by the more experienced sales staff, and eventually I did learn how to deal successfully with the customers. In fact, even though I was the low woman on the totem pole, I had one very sweet customer tell me, "Sandra, honey, you're my favourite. You know I really only shop here because of you."

Well, that comment certainly boosted my self-esteem! As a result of my growing confidence, I was happy to change my personal schedule whenever my manager called at the last minute to ask, "Would you mind coming in an hour early tomorrow, Sandra? We could certainly use your help."

Don't get me wrong, there were still those days of drudgery when I thought I was truly living in retail hell. But on the other, more productive days, I could honestly admit to myself that I loved my job. I actually continued to work in the retail sector in one capacity or another for the next 16 years.

I now look back fondly on those years that I spent selling retail goods to the public as a valuable learning experience. I would even suggest to others that a really sound basis for becoming an accomplished realtor is to first spend some serious time working in the retail trenches. You will succeed in some sales transactions and you will fail in others. And guess what? It's not the end of the world when you fail. Over time you will be able to distinguish the "serious buyer" types from the "just looking" types and you'll learn that both types of customers are equally important. Especially when you can leave both types of customer impressed with your product knowledge and your engaging manner. The customer who was "just looking" in the morning might return in the afternoon to become a first-time buyer, thanks to your initial presentation of the product, your keen knowledge, your efficient demeanour and your persuasive attitude. And today's first-time customer could become tomorrow's return customer. When that happens, you can bet that return customer will want to be served by "that same young lady who helped me yesterday. Is she available?"

In retail, every situation teaches you to make the most of the moment so that every customer leaves with a completely satisfied, positive impression of their buying experience. Each of those satisfied customers will hopefully take the time to refer you to their friends—that is, other prospective buyers who will enjoy the same positive buying experience with you. And on it goes. With enough return customers singing your praises, you will quickly build up your own regular clientele, based largely on your expert service skills.

In the same way, so much of a realtor's business depends on the referral system. A high percentage of my sales come via one satisfied client referring my contact information to a friend or relative. Needless to say, I am truly flattered when my phone rings and I hear a total stranger making complimentary remarks about my skills as a realtor. Since those types of calls can brighten up a dull day in an awful hurry, I say, "Bring 'em on!" So a wise word to any budding realtors out there: don't ever underestimate the value of good old-fashioned word-of-mouth advertising. It's highly effective—and it's free!

The other essential lesson I learned during my years spent in retail was that product presentation is of key importance. Nobody is tempted to look at an item—whether it's an article of clothing, a piece of food, an arrangement of office furniture or even a used car—if it isn't displayed in an appealing manner. We all would like the clothing to look flattering and fashionable, the food to look tasty and fresh, the office furniture to look comfortable and functional, and the used car to look totally brand new. I know, I know—no such luck with that last example! But the used car should at least appear safe and affordable because nobody's going to seriously consider buying it if it looks like a rusty piece of junk in need of extensive repairs. The same attention to presentation must be paid when a house goes on the market for re-sale. Just how important is it? Well, some clients of mine *have refused to even get out of my vehicle* to go inside the house that I wanted to show them. They thought the house looked too pitiful from the outside. In each case I did my best to cajole those buyers with that old cliché: "Don't judge a book by its cover." But that didn't always convince them. And unfortunately too many other similar instances have happened as well, simply because the relevant house didn't have any "curb appeal."

Now, having said all that, I'm going to tell you about a pair of first-time homebuyers who demonstrate the flipside of the first-impression coin. They put too much stock in the appearance of the houses they looked at, and had to learn to look past the staging and "fluffing."

MEET KATIE AND BILL

Katie and Bill had definite ideas of what they were looking for in a new home. Being direct and responsible people, they had mutually agreed on a list of what they needed and a list of what they wanted. Oh, and they had most definitely agreed on a list of what they did not want, so there was very little room left to manoeuvre.

No problem. I had a particular house in mind to show them that had actually been up for sale the year before; however, the seller had been forced to withdraw it from the market after only two days because of a sudden family illness. Luckily, before that happened I had

had the opportunity to become familiar with it and now that it was back on the market, I was convinced that it would be really great for Katie and Bill. I had a feeling they would like it.

Whoa! What an understatement. Their reaction went through the roof because that home met their expectations to a "T." Every single feature on their very specific criteria list was present and accounted for. As I looked around the house with Katie and Bill—and the seller's agent—Katie gushed to her husband, "This is the perfect house, honey, because we can move right in."

"I've got to agree with you. It does seem too good to be true," Bill enthusiastically concurred.

Unfortunately, they didn't stop there! The remarks kept right on coming.

"Sandra, we love it. Yep, we really love it."

As their realtor I was thrilled that I'd chosen such an ideal house for them to consider—but they'd both forgotten my suggestion to play their reaction cards close to their chest. All those compliments were within earshot of the seller's agent! With their enthusiasm, Katie and Bill were unintentionally eroding my bargaining strength, my ability to strategically position their offer when it came time to negotiate a purchase on their behalf. Oops! But hang onto your hat because there were other dark clouds gathering on the horizon and I didn't like the looks of them at all!

Sure enough, it happened: I was informed that the seller had received an offer from another interested buyer. Katie and Bill were now in competition. When that occurs, it's always best for the potential homebuyer to keep their terms and conditions to a minimum, since too many specifics might seem objectionable to the seller. With more than one offer on the table, the seller is in the enviable position of being able to set their own terms, and they will want to entertain the cleanest offer. The price being offered becomes the major focus—hence the term "bidding war."

And so, with two determined buyers pitted against each other, the competition escalated and my clients became caught up in the moment. They really, really wanted to have that house, and that desire was making them lose their self-control and sense of perspective!

I warned them to remain sensible and calm, and most importantly to stay focused on relevant matters—such as the mortgage limit they'd been approved for, and how much they could really afford. Because although it might not cost an arm and a leg to bid impulsively for a collectible item on eBay, a home is a different matter. It would probably be the biggest investment of their lives and I didn't want them to look ridiculous—or to make themselves so strapped for cash that they would only be able to afford canned beans and day-old bread at dinner for the next couple of years! Although the original asking price was comfortably within their pre-approved mortgage limit, in the heated competition the price was quickly slipping beyond their reach. And because I strongly suspected that their admirable determination was really just a case of outright stubbornness, I suggested that they be patient. When faced with competition, most people hate to lose, but if they can step away from the competition they can regain their feeling of control and look more objectively at what they're doing. I like my clients to feel that they're in the driver's seat at all times, but sometimes, when the bidding war gets really frenzied, I will try to snap them out of la-la land and save them from overpaying in a big way. Some will listen; some won't. With Katie and Bill, I reminded them that they had only just begun looking and there were plenty of other houses to see. I suggested that there was no need to make a costly decision under such pressure.

Why was that only a "suggestion" on my part? Well, as you've probably seen by now, one of the situations I face as a realtor is the delicate balancing act of counselling my clients on a variety of important matters while never becoming pushy at any time. Every decision ultimately rests with my clients. I'm also aware that even as adults we can remain sensitive to our parents' or teachers' critical comments from years ago: "You'd better listen to me or else," or "Mark my words because I know what's right for you." Believe me, I know that a nagging know-it-all is not what my clients need.

Eventually, after some consideration, Katie and Bill took a deep breath, agreed with my sound reasoning and ultimately were gracious in their defeat. But I still sensed they weren't very happy campers when they "lost."

WHAT IF THERE ARE—GULP— MULTIPLE OFFERS?

With the real estate market being so hot in many parts of the country, it's no longer a rare thing to find yourself bidding against other eager buyers. So what's a first-time homebuyer to do?

My first piece of advice is that you should always submit your best offer from the start. You'll base your offer, as always, on recent comparable sales. You don't know what the other bidders will have in their offer, and you don't want to get knocked out of the running because you were playing it cool and conservative. I was once involved in a negotiation in which one hundred measly dollars separated the top offer from the second offer—and unfortunately, much to my clients' dismay, theirs was that second offer! I always recommend that a client's strongest, cleanest offer is required, because the seller may not be willing to sign back. And in the same vein, I feel that an uneven number like $306,600 is preferable to a flat $305,000 because you just never know what could give your offer the edge.

This is not a normal negotiation, so don't make the mistake of saying, "This is just our starting bid" because that bid may get you kicked out of the game before you can say "on your marks"! The seller may look at your offer and think that it is just too far from where he wants it to be and may tell you to go home. You may not get a second chance, and let's hope you don't: you want the seller to just accept your offer so you can celebrate by cracking open the champers.

I also believe that it's rarely a good idea to give a seller a long time to sit on your offer, especially when multiple offers are on the table. Until that deadline is up, you, as the potential buyer, are left on the hook waiting for the offer to be countered or rejected—and who needs that kind of anxiety for an extended period of time? Even a rejection is preferable to waiting around for a response, since that way you can plan your next course of action instead of being held up by a seller's whims. However, each situation is different and, in the case where many people on the selling side need to be consulted, such as in an estate sale, you may have to give them the time. Your realtor will be able to advise accordingly.

In a multiple-bid situation, the seller really holds all the marbles, and one way to make your offer stand above the others is to offer everything exactly as the seller has asked for it, including the exact closing date noted on the listing. Quite often the seller has already purchased another property and has a firm closing date, so a buyer is best to determine the date and motivation and move heaven and earth to make it work for them. It can be the difference between winning on offer day and looking for another home to buy.

■ ADVICE FOR PROPERTY VIRGINS
TAKING CHARGE IN A BIDDING WAR

Don't be afraid of multiple offers. You still have some control. There are a few things that can happen if you get into competition. The seller can accept your offer and you will have bought a house. Or the seller can accept someone else's offer and you need to keep looking. Or the seller can work with your offer, and sign it back to you with a counter-offer that you can accept or decline, and perhaps even counter-offer back to them. There is another scenario that I despise, but unfortunately it happens: the seller has a number of offers on the table, and decides to send them all back for improvement. Personally, I think they should just choose the best one and accept it or work with it. In the case where you are sent back to improve, you have control and choices. The seller is actually at risk of losing all the offers, and I've seen it happen.

Here are some of your choices if your offer is signed back to you and a higher figure is requested. You can simply walk away from the deal, as you are not obligated to increase your money or change any terms of the agreement. You can resubmit your offer as is, or you can make some improvements to the offer by way of increasing the money or removing a condition or changing any term on the contract that the seller wasn't happy about. Just remember, although emotions run high and it's not the most fun scenario for buyers, you should keep your head about you, and understand that you are always in control.

BACK TO THE DRAWING BOARD—AGAIN, AND AGAIN . . .

Now I would like to backtrack a moment to tell you that I've had similar situations to Katie and Bill's with other first-time homebuyers who also revealed—loudly!—their true feelings as they were viewing a home. That error also happened after I had repeatedly warned those clients that buying a house must remain a logical purchase and not a purely emotional one. Talk about selective hearing! Don't get me wrong, you have to love your new home, but I stress to all my clients the importance of remaining objective, of trying to be as detached as possible when viewing it. That way they can react to the home's basic value and not to its perceived value, and make a judgement based on its real characteristics and not the "dream home" appeal that impressed them. You don't want your emotions to cloud the issue—or to tip off the opposing realtor. When an enthusiastic couple like Katie and Bill mistakenly viewed their house subjectively, they were investing a great deal of additional perceived value into the property and that became an important factor in their decision-making process. And in doing so in front of the other realtor, they had put practically all the power directly into the seller's hands—and neutralized my own power—when it came time to submit and negotiate their offer. In fact, I've heard of situations in which the prospective buyer was so over-the-top in his enthusiasm that the sellers and their agent felt quite confident about sticking to their original asking price. In spite of the lower offer that came in from that buyer, the sellers held their ground—and got the full asking price.

Okay, so Katie and Bill learned from their first big mistake and assured me they would be much more rational as they continued their search. They understood that it was important for them to tell me what they were thinking, especially if there was a problem because that way we could work together to solve it. However, no other home they looked at over the next three-week period met their expectations. During that time I noticed that a little bit of steam had been let out of their sails. They seemed despondent. So we regrouped to redefine their main criteria and my suspicions were right: they weren't happy campers and a big part of their current dissatisfaction was residual disappointment from having "lost" that very first house, which they had loved so much. But thanks to our candid meeting, Katie and Bill arrived at a decision to be more flexible, and to put their desire for a move-in-ready home on the back burner. In its place was a willingness to look at homes that would need a few small repairs after all. Fine—go grab your sneakers because we're off and running again.

As planned, the next few houses they viewed all required some cosmetic work. After seeing them, however, Katie and Bill seemed a little disappointed. They noticed every small flaw and every untidy garden at each of those properties. All they could see ahead for themselves was work, work, work! Even though I had previewed the properties and found them acceptably within the couple's newly established criteria, both Katie and Bill felt that each one of those homes was a potential ball and chain. So it was back to the drawing board once again.

Unfortunately, I've found that same reaction to be quite common among first-time homebuyers, simply because they are first-timers. Generally, people who have previously owned a home have a greater acceptance of what is possible with a minor renovation because they have probably already completed a few on their own home, and enjoyed the results. But since Katie and Bill hadn't previously owned, they couldn't fully appreciate the fact that a property isn't just a house and yard, it's an investment, and it's worth improving it over time so that it meets your needs exactly. But, right or wrong, their current negative reactions were what they were, and it was my responsibility to keep those reactions filed away as a reference point when I took them to view the next prospect.

I chose a home at the opposite end of the spectrum. It had been staged within an inch of its life, with every precisely perfect room looking like it could literally have been "onstage" at your local theatre. As my clients viewed the house, I instinctively felt that Katie was a goner for what she saw and I was right. The moment we were alone outside she squealed, "Oh my God, I love it! Oh my God, it is so gorgeous!"

"You're absolutely right, it is gorgeous. But I can't believe you fell for it! That house has indeed been the shiniest apple in the bunch so far, but Katie it's still just an apple!" I replied.

"I'm not sure I follow," Bill said.

"Here it is in a nutshell. I know this particular property shows well and I'm not totally surprised by Katie's reaction to it. But I also know that this perfectly staged property is severely overpriced and I wanted to make you both aware of that fact as a point of comparison."

Then I quickly ran down a list of highly visible improvements that I had spotted, and that I was sure had been made simply to boost the seller's asking price. "The kitchen's granite countertops are all shiny and new, but the cupboards haven't been touched—and they're old and need to be replaced. The stainless steel appliances are obviously top of the line, but the sellers are planning to take those with them when they leave. And that newly tiled entranceway won't look quite so fabulous once winter rolls around, since that particular tile is very porous and requires a great deal of maintenance."

My clients briefly mulled over matters between themselves and then decided to play it cool. The final verdict of the evening was issued when Bill told me, "Sandra, we'd like to sleep on it." So when I dropped them off a short while later, I knew the wheels were still turning, and I wasn't surprised when Katie called me early the next morning and requested that we all go back again for a second viewing later that afternoon.

Because I insisted that they should slow down and spend more time during that second time around, I had the opportunity to point out some other tempting visual traps that they had fallen for. "Look really hard at just the bones and not at the fluffing. Let's begin by ignoring this picture-perfect living room furniture because it's obviously been rented simply to impress, and instead let's concentrate on the living room's actual size and layout. After you've purchased the house, and this furniture is back in its proper showroom, that's what you are actually buying." I repeated that same advice—to look beyond the decorator's attention-grabbing flourishes—for the dining room, the bedrooms, the bathrooms and the basement as well.

Because Katie and Bill had been more observant during that second viewing and had paid more attention to the property's features that wouldn't change—its location, lot size, exposure, interior floor plan and the small back yard —Bill asked, "Well, honey, who wants the bones when they don't have any meat on them?"

"Yeah, I don't want to buy this house and not get the eye candy too."

Bill nodded, shrugged and walked away. Once Bill was out of ear-shot, Katie confessed that she knew the price of the house would have cramped their lifestyle. "It would have been totally useless trying to convince my husband to give up some of life's little pleasures like din-ing out regularly, his sporting activities, our entertainment events and hobbies, to say nothing of the yearly vacation—all for the sake of a lavishly decorated home interior instead. Because believe me, once he's plunked down in front of his wide-screen plasma TV, he'd be the last person in the world to care about the colour of the sofa or the shape of the coffee table in front of him!"

"I hear you loud and clear on that one," I responded.

We both laughed while admitting that neither of us could under-stand what it was with men and their TV sets anyway—especially the obsessive attachment they all have to that darn remote control!

So it was finally coming full circle for them. Thanks to their many viewing experiences, that couple's eyes had been opened to possibility. Forget the unreasonable bidding or the fluffing or the fear of having to do a little work. Especially the fear of work! When I gently reminded them of what they had told me weeks earlier about their willingness to consider a home that still required some minor repairs, they both smiled and nodded. And when I confessed to them that my current plan was to take a step backward by showing them homes that were similar to the group they had seen earlier (but had initially been discouraged with), they were open and receptive. And that was great news because I felt that this time around, with their new eyes, they would recognize inherent potential within imperfect surroundings, and not be so quick to hit the reject button. I was confident that their combined frame of reference had been expanded and that together they had acquired suf-ficient knowledge to make a wise purchase decision. When I gently reminded them once again not to invest too much of their imagination into any of the upcoming properties before it was actually theirs, they clearly understood the reasons why.

I also reminded them that their attitude during the negotiations was of great importance, and that they must be prepared to walk away from any specific property if they couldn't get their significant terms and conditions met. I stressed the importance of teamwork, and that as their realtor I wanted to put the emphasis on getting them the best home, at the best price possible, along with the most favourable terms— and that I was not interested in getting them just any old property!

In a positive turn of events, out of the next four homes Katie and Bill viewed, two were being seriously considered. We returned to each of them a day later for a second viewing. I had purposely scheduled those return visits within an hour of each other, knowing that the most important pros and cons of each home would remain fresh in Katie's and Bill's minds when quickly compared back to back. Let me stress that neither property was in perfect condition, and that the homes' basic layouts contrasted in significant ways. In both cases I made a quick list of recommendations for the most necessary cosmetic touch-ups— and that really tickled Bill who especially appreciated that my top 10 ideas for adding some lustre to either home didn't require any money at all! That's right, my suggestions would improve the appearance, and the functionality, of specific areas within either of those homes without costing a dime! (Those suggestions are usually specific to the home in question, but they might range from removing wallpaper and taking down heavy drapery to let light in, to lifting up carpet to reveal hardwood floors and cutting back overgrown bushes or perennials to reveal a beautiful ornate fence. And, in almost every case with these slightly down-at-the-heels houses, one piece of advice is appropriate: clean, clean, clean!)

The next few ideas I offered would also be very beneficial upgrades and could collectively be completed inside either home for the nominal sum of about $1,000. And since Katie's opinion was no longer swayed by the fancy bedspreads, or the gorgeous set of matching leather chairs that she had spotted at a previous viewing, she could look past the current furnishings in each home and imagine her own decorating ideas taking shape. After all, decorating is essentially adding those unique touches to a space to personalize it and make it your own, and from the way she spoke, it seemed she had no shortage of ideas that she wanted to try out. She really laughed at herself when, at one of the homes, she opened up a closet door and an avalanche of junk came tumbling down from a shelf. When Bill came running to see what had caused the noise and commotion, Katie's only remark was "If all this junk could fit in there, then I'll definitely have enough storage space for mine!"

Now you won't believe this, but out of the two homes they were considering, they actually placed an offer on, and then bought, the house that would require the most work on their part! I'm not kidding! They had completely changed their earlier negative "ball and chain" outlook to one of acceptance and inevitability when it came to purchasing their home. They made their decision by comparing the re-sale potential of the two properties they were considering. As a concerned realtor, I always point out the advantages or disadvantages that a property has when it comes to re-sale potential. Since the property Katie and Bill purchased was located in an up-and-coming neighbourhood that was gaining fast acceptance as the trendy place to live, it seemed destined to appreciate in value faster than the other property. And although they hadn't even moved in yet, Katie and Bill's plan was to re-sell that "starter" home five years down the road, and hopefully upgrade to their "dream home" at that time.

Now that's not to say that the house itself wasn't in good shape, because it was: the plumbing system and the electrical system were in very good working order, the foundation was solid, the roof was in extremely good condition, the main appliances were fine, the surrounding yard was excellent. All in all, who could ask for more? But the house definitely presented some challenges as well, largely because the previous owners had attempted a renovation that was by no means successful! Since that job had been poorly done, the end result actually interrupted the flow of the home's interior, with a wall that seemed to jut out from nowhere and stall traffic. Katie and Bill would definitely require some professional help to correct that problem. Oh, and what about that floor over there? Have you ever seen a dark hardwood floor flush against white ceramic tiles? Well, it's not very pretty, I can assure you. There was a long list of other minor repairs needed as well, but as Bill said, "Challenges are there to be conquered!"

SELLING YOUR HOME—FAST AND PROFITABLY

There are, as everyone knows, at least two sides to every story. We've seen some houses from the buyer's point of view—now let's turn to the seller's point of view. What does it take to make that all-important favourable first impression on the buyer? And when you, as a first-time homebuyer, are ready to move upwards and onwards to another house, how do you make your house appear in the best light possible?

Exteriors: Your chance to grab the buyer's attention

As you could tell from my stories of buyers who were reluctant to even get out of my car, the exterior appearance of any home and its surrounding property is a crucial factor in successfully selling it for the asking price. You must remember that potential buyers are not going to walk up your driveway wearing blinkers! That is, of course, if they decide to walk up your driveway at all, since the first view they get will likely be from the safety of their car. The snapshot the buyer gets of your home's exterior is what realtors refer to as "curb appeal." I know that sounds like some fancy selling term, but it's actually a realistic one, since you just never know who's going to drive by and check out your property—and will that driver keep on driving while shaking her head in disappointment, or will she like what she sees and immediately contact her realtor? Like this:

"Hi Sandra, my husband and I just drove past that listing you gave us. It's a really nice-looking house," a client told me recently.

"I'm so glad you liked it," I responded. "Would you like me to arrange a viewing for you?"

"Yes, please; the sooner the better because we're definitely interested in taking a closer look."

"No problem, I'll get right on it."

As simple as that, the wheels can be set in motion. A properly prepared seller might soon be receiving a purchase offer! Just remember that you've only got one chance to make a first impression, so as a seller you must consider an attractive, well-kept exterior as a major contributing factor to your marketing strategy. The exterior should be the magnet that initially captures the buyer's eye. Once their interest has been piqued, those potential buyers will be eager to walk through the front door, and ready to be equally impressed by your home's interior. Highlight your property's best features, and don't leave anything to chance.

Getting the right kind of attention for your property requires the right kind of planning. Think budget-conscious improvements, since your ultimate aim is to increase the property's appeal by maximizing its overall value, while still leaving a profit in your pocket. Begin by making any smaller renovations and repairs that aren't costly: repair that cracked plaster, fix those leaky faucets, replace any broken windows or screens, tighten up loose doorknobs and handles, remove the rust from outdoor ironwork, and scrape away the peeling paint from all surfaces before you apply a fresh new coat in an appropriate colour.

But keep in mind not to get carried away by allowing those few small, smart renovations to turn into major, expensive remodelling projects. Be sure to plan strategically before you decide to undertake any possible larger renovations, because you're moving after all. Do you really need to complete a major, costly renovation when you won't even be around to enjoy it? For example, you don't want to drastically alter your home's existing floor plan just to match one that you were so impressed with on a TV renovation show, because the time and money you sink into such a venture may not actually increase the value of your home significantly enough for you to see a return on your investment. And if those renovations also require you to pay for building contractors, building permits and specialized tradesmen, then you should seriously rethink your position.

Don't make any changes that will limit the number of potential buyers for your home. For example, I would caution most people against increasing the size of the master bedroom by eliminating a smaller bedroom, and not to remodel that third bedroom into a large walk-in closet either. Why not? Well, as I said to one of my clients many years ago, "Did you just hear that loud noise? Guess what it was? It was your property value crashing! Because remodelling a three-bedroom house into a two-bedroom house does not give great odds in your favour when it comes to re-sale in most areas."

Instead, keep it simple and keep it necessary. Do not attempt to reinvent the wheel because you might be surprised to find out that not every upgrade will be seen as valuable to every potential buyer. Often a seller will spend money on a special feature, such as a sunken hot tub, for example, convinced that it will enhance the market value of their home. Now I'd be the first to admit that a sunken hot tub, and the brand-new deck and minor landscaping that usually go along with it, will surely enhance the *appeal* of your back yard. But the value? That money may not have been wisely spent in the long run, because the sunken hot tub will almost certainly have a negative impact on the young couple with two small children who are considering purchasing your home. They will likely see it as a potential safety hazard instead of an inviting luxury.

Spend your money on features that will become a stronger asset overall, and appeal to the majority of buyers. You'll be more likely to get a higher return on your investment. Even though we live in a materialistic world, don't be tempted to over-improve just for the sake of improvement. (To compare the average cost recovery on re-sale for various renos, see the Appendix of this book.)

A tidy, well-landscaped property can have a major impact on a buyer. An inexpensive but concise upgrade on your landscaping over-all will increase the property's value, so if it's necessary to do any new planting, choose some attractive plants that will catch the eye but not break the bank. Almost invariably I will tell a seller, "You will have to trim those trees, hedges and bushes in front of the house so that more of the windows can be revealed. That simple procedure will have a positive effect on your home's interior as well because additional light will flow in." I also encourage the seller to spruce up the lawn by keep-ing it green and keeping it cut. You want your yard to have a low-maintenance appeal, so its well-kept appearance should look effortless. And please do some weeding! Remember that flowerbeds are for flowers, so put the kids to work if necessary to help you clear out any dead plants or old roots, to rake up the leaves and to pull out those darn weeds!

The front walkway and the driveway must also get some attention. Be sure to clean them both thoroughly. Repair or replace any dam-aged concrete or asphalt and perhaps consider resealing the driveway so that it is one even colour.

The front entranceway must be inviting, so go ahead and repaint the front door and its surrounding area if necessary, clean the mail-box and by all means remember to put out a brand-new welcome mat. Sometimes the smallest touches can make the biggest difference. Be sure to think visual first impression, because that's what the potential buyers will be thinking—whether they know it or not!

Don't forget to give the same amount of attention and detail to your back yard as you did to the front. Keep the kids' toys, bikes, sports equipment, wading pools, etc., tucked away as much as possible. Make sure that your deck or patio looks like a fun, friendly environment. Clean the patio stones or re-stain the deck, wash down the patio or deck furniture, cover up the barbecue and roll away the hose.

The same approach goes for your pets too: clean them up, and clean up after them! Oh, and since we're discussing animals, don't forget to eliminate any pesky rodents if necessary because when I take a first-time homebuyer to view a house that advertises "country charm," I'm thinking shuttered windows, a large veranda and maybe even an apple tree in the front yard—not a menagerie of wildlife. Trust me, there is absolutely nothing charming about an infestation of four-legged vermin, thank you!

Now it's time to roll up your sleeves and tackle the garage. If you've been using the garage for any other purpose—such as an elaborate personal home gym, or a woodworking shop perhaps—immediately restore it to its original function. Otherwise, grab your mop and pail and clean the garage out thoroughly because the buyer will want to look in there. If it doesn't look to them like their vehicle(s) will fit because there's too much of your "crap" there, that could cost you a sale. If necessary, temporarily store your tools, seasonal decorations, and that broken TV set you never got around to fixing, at a friend's or relative's place so that your garage looks tidy and spacious. However, if it is a matter of practicality that you must keep items stored in the garage, then make sure that they are packed and piled away as neatly as possible, and preferably confined to one corner.

A word to the wise: you might want to clean the garage and the basement in tandem. Otherwise you could be tempted, as I was during one of my own moves, to clear stuff out of the garage by putting it into the basement. But then what do you suppose happens when it comes time to clean out the basement? Since you also want that area to look tidy and spacious, does everything just go directly back to where it came from? Gee, I guess that's why it's called a garage sale, huh? It will probably be a good idea for you to hold one of your own at some point. You can also donate or, as a last resort, throw some stuff away. Whatever—just get rid of it!

Interiors: The proof is in the pudding

Well, congratulations on all your hard work so far. But realize that in many cases your re-sale property will have to compete with a newly built model home, so a commanding exterior is great, but now it's time to concentrate on the interior. And that is a horse of a different colour to be sure.

Besides granting the potential buyer a pleasant visual impression, it is vitally important that the interior should look comfortable and functional as well. It may be necessary to "stage" or "fluff" it to achieve that effect. I'm not trying to be dramatic, especially since your family has probably been comfortably living there in its current state, but you have to remember that your home has now become a product for sale and that each potential buyer wants to envision himself living within that same environment. They want to start calling it *their* home instead of yours.

So, not to sound insulting, but you'll have to begin by eliminating your own personality from the rooms, along with the memories you created during the years that you lived there. To do that you'll have to remove as many physical traces of yourselves as possible: the family pictures, the bowling trophies, the fridge magnets, and all the other items of sentimental but wholly personal value. You must de-personalize so as to maximize interest and increase appeal for a much wider range of potential buyers. So remove that impressive collection of antique plates from the wall and pack them all away. I mean, since you'll be moving soon anyhow, why not get a head start? The more knickknacks, dust collectors and just general clutter that you get rid of, the more space you create. And you definitely want to create space, because ideally your goal is to have an overall minimalist look so that the size and functionality of each room is accentuated.

Your money will be well spent on fresh paint. Though it won't cost much to paint a few rooms, the effect will be stunning. I remind my clients, "Neutral colours will make the rooms appear brighter and larger, so selecting the popular magazine colours like taupe, sand, custard or beige will refresh your rooms without overpowering them. And don't forget to paint the trim too, so that your rooms have a professionally finished look instead of a slapdash one. You will definitely need to steer away from the funky individualism of deep plum walls with icy mint ceiling trim. Remember that I'm Italian, so whenever I see dark purple topped with green, I immediately think eggplant!" (Just so you know, having the image of a vegetable jump to mind apparently isn't so unusual for me. My stepson tells me that I reference food items when I begin making comparisons to almost anything else! You already know that I like to cook, and that I like to eat, so what can I tell you? Guilty as charged!)

I also recommend that sellers resist the urge to hang patterned wallpaper. Instead, be aware of the overall neutrality of the interior and the connecting flow of its rooms, because you want prospective buyers to feel a certain ambience within your home. You want them to get a comfortable vibe from the first moment they step through the front door. And because each buyer will want to move from one room to another in a leisurely, unrestricted way, make sure the passageways and traffic paths are uninterrupted. If you need to move (or remove) any large, overstuffed furniture pieces or hanging plants to accentuate the flow, do so without hesitation. Evaluate your rooms objectively and highlight their best features to keep that flow of traffic moving right along. If you keep these principles in mind, the potential buyers won't be forced to run an obstacle course down a hallway—nor will they be stuck with the labour-intensive task of removing wallpaper that's not to their taste!

The three main rooms that a first-time homebuyer will be most concerned about, regarding their size, layout and appearance, are the living room, kitchen and master bedroom. A few simple cosmetic improvements that are relatively inexpensive can make a big difference as to how these rooms are perceived. I will often inform a seller, "When you decide to upgrade in either the kitchen or the bathroom, simply replacing countertops, light fixtures or cabinet hardware can have a very dramatic and beneficial effect. Once again, stick with neutral colour tones and attractive doorknobs. Lose the impulse to decorate with garish, shiny gold hardware." Then, of course, you must clean the walls, floors, cabinets and windows thoroughly. Clear away the small appliances, bottles and other miscellaneous gadgets that cause unnecessary countertop clutter. Finally, organize your cupboards and closets efficiently (removing some items and storing them if necessary) so that your storage areas do not looked stuffed to overflowing.

■ ADVICE FOR PROPERTY VIRGINS
WHAT'S THAT ...? EEWWW!!

There have been, unfortunately, occasions when I have had to very tactfully mention the following real estate maxim: "Your house won't sell if it smells!" Be sure to get rid of any unpleasant odours, such as the smell of a cat's litter box, cigarette smoke hanging in the air, mildew under the sink—or the lingering odour of the cabbage that was cooked the night before. By the same token, be careful not to go overboard in the other direction. I remember one instance in which some potential buyers attended a viewing of a house that smelled overly sweet. They were very suspicious that the seller had maxed out on the room freshener as a way to cover up some real problems!

Fade in ... fade out. I was pleasantly surprised to receive a call from Katie, less than a year after she and Bill had purchased their house, inviting me to their housewarming party. And that wasn't the only pleasant surprise! When I walked in the front door, I honestly could not believe the visual transformation I saw before me. Bill had very wisely hired an experienced contractor who was willing to do the major building work and complete the largest repairs. The contractor had also agreed to supervise Bill, on a part-time basis, as he went about completing the additional work, which made it possible for Bill to look after the smaller jobs himself. That approach saved the couple a lot of money because they were willing to spend their time and energy instead. It also allowed Bill to work at his own pace. Old cupboards were torn out and replaced with new cabinetry, old windows in the two bedrooms were upgraded, a skylight was installed in the bathroom, a beautiful new floor was laid, and the ceilings and walls were freshly painted in more compatible colours. Everything looked great! Unlike the previous owner, Bill obviously cared enough to do his work well.

When I complimented him on a job well done, he joked proudly, "I figured that I had to do it well or go home, and since my wife reminded me that I already was home—well, I had no other option!" He looked over at Katie, who laughed before dragging me away to show off her handiwork with the finer details. Closets had been cleaned out and painted, broadloom had been eliminated and replaced with area rugs, new light fixtures had been installed in the bedrooms and hallways, the bathroom had been subtly upgraded with new hardware and trim, and her own personally made pillows had become the perfect accents in each bedroom.

Perhaps those individual improvements don't sound like much, but added together they had made a dramatic improvement. Together Katie and Bill had realized that some creativity, some sweat and some good old-fashioned elbow grease were indeed a small price to pay for the home they were so proud of.

Katie had even splurged on a cleaning woman to come by earlier that day to put the final polish on everything, because as she said, "The party's purpose is to show off the star attraction!" That smart decision of hers had also left her the time to do some cooking. And I was glad, because the food was nothing to sneeze at!

"You never told me you were such a good cook," I said while reaching for another yummy appetizer.

She shrugged and smiled appreciatively. Then I gently teased her that with the money she and Bill had managed to save by not losing their minds and overspending on that very first property they had loved so much, it was no wonder she'd been able to whip up such a delicious spread of snacks, salads and desserts. She laughed as she remembered that same event and then winked as she said conspiratorially, "When I think about how close we came to getting stuck with eating nothing but canned beans and day-old bread!"

What I've Been Trying To Say

In which Sandra tells her own real estate story, and in which the reader gets the last word on how to buy right—the first time or the fifth

"Sandra, I'm ready for my dessert now," my stepson said, pushing his dinner plate away from him.

"Well, I'm not so sure, don't you think your rapini and those potatoes deserve a little more attention?" I asked, as I gently replaced his plate in its original spot.

"But ..." He frowned.

"Two more big bites of each vegetable and we'll call it a deal," his father told him.

"Okay," he smiled. "And then I get dessert, right?"

"Yes, Edward, then you get dessert," I said, and smiled back at him. I chuckled to myself as I thought, still a little boy but already such a charmer—just like his father!

In record time, he had finished his second helping of ice cream before asking to be excused from the table.

Later that same evening, after Edward and his father had finished working together on his homework assignments, he gave me a big sloppy kiss as I tucked him into bed.

"Goodnight, Sandra. Don't forget to leave the hall light on, okay?"

"I'm not sure if I heard a ..."

"Please!"

"Of course I will, since you asked so politely," I replied, as I winked at him and pinched his big toe. "Now sleep tight."

Well, what can I tell you? I had met a new guy who turned my crank, but apparently he didn't fly solo. To have that guy appear in my life when I least expected it, and for him to be the single parent of a rambunctious three-year-old—well, can you say rapid adjustment to my single-gal lifestyle? As my relationship with that special guy deepened, so did the realization that I was looking at a package deal in which my future would include a full-time stepson. Me, a parent, who knew? I never became pregnant while I was married (which in hindsight was a blessing in disguise), and then I suffered through a few unfaithful boyfriends who were clearly unsuited to the demands of fatherhood. So as time passed I'd reluctantly become resigned to the fact that being a working mom wasn't going to be an issue for me to contend with.

But then I met Gary and his son, Edward, so as a result let's just say that my earlier beliefs about where my life was headed were now being put to the test. And it was apparent to me that I would have to hang on pretty tightly to keep things from spinning out of control! I meant spinning in a literal sense, because along with less-than-perfect household management skills, I had also felt a lifelong hatred for doing laundry, and now laundry was unavoidable. I was realizing what unbelievably busy schedules young kids have these days, with so many different sports and activities, and how unbelievably dirty they get while doing them. Yikes! I was soon stuck with laundry up the wazoo, and that darn chore seemed to be never-ending. I was spending so much time in the basement doing it that it felt like I was having a ménage à trois with my washer and dryer!

But I really didn't mind, especially since Edward was a fairly un-spoiled "typical boy" who loved to horse around with his father, who loved to play with his toys, who was growing like a weed—and who had a very big appetite. An appetite that I must admit includes a lot of pizza and ice cream, mind you, but he does love my homemade pasta dishes and he's working on those tricky vegetables!

MEET MY FAMILY— GARY AND EDWARD

My commitment to Gary and to Edward is total. And that loyalty was certainly evident when I was considering making my own recent prop-erty purchase. Its prime location within a very specific, well-established neighbourhood that I had a personal attachment to was one of my original reasons for contemplating that particular home in the first place. The house's finished basement along with its large back-yard pool and beautiful flagstone patio were features that strongly appealed to me since I love to entertain as frequently as possible. The basement even had a walkout to the pool and patio area—so what was I waiting for? Let me get the water boiling, start the sauce simmering and make sure the wine and the beers are chilled.

But wait. Let's hold on a minute here because we also had to satisfy Edward's needs. In fact, many parents usually move in the first place to satisfy their children's needs. And while kids themselves seldom object to a different house, they always object to the move, because that means leaving their school and their friends behind. Therefore, it is necessary to integrate them as quickly and as smoothly as possible into their new surroundings, and establish a new comfort zone for them. The house I was considering was near an extremely good public school, and rea-sonably close to an excellent secondary school, and clearly both those factors would benefit Edward considerably. When it came to finding new friends, well, we discovered that the neighbourhood was practi-cally crawling with kids of all ages so we both knew that a fun-loving extrovert like Edward would have no trouble fitting right in. Another advantage was the street itself, with its very low volume of local traffic. Edward and his new friends could play quite safely out on the road without too many annoying interruptions—I say "annoying" because have you ever noticed how much kids hate yelling *"car"* during their game of road hockey?

Now besides being so enamoured with that property's location, suffice to say that the home's floor plan was suitable to our collective needs and its selling price was within my pre-approved mortgage range. The house and its surrounding property were in excellent shape overall, so no major renovations or repairs would be required (but I'll get to the hideous interior decorating in a minute). I did have to bite the bullet regarding the fact that there is very little back yard to plant a garden. Okay, who am I kidding? There is no back yard at all! Why not? Because it is totally taken up by our very popular pool and its surrounding patio. Oh well, I just remind myself of what I tell my first-time homebuyers: compromise and flexibility are key. And so a few planters here and a few hanging pots there, all overflowing with a variety of colourful fresh flowers, seem to have done the trick. Even though I also had to contend with a very short closing date, I signed on the dotted line.

Sure, I'm a realtor by trade, but during a property purchase I am subject to the same set of conditions that would govern any other buyer's decision-making process. There isn't any favouritism thrown into the mix just because of my job title. That particular re-sale property showed the same for one and for all, whether its features were good, bad or indifferent. And when I purchased it, I actually got a little of each from columns one, two and three!

And that brings me back to the hideous interior decorating. Quite frankly, I don't even know where to start, except to say that after taking possession, we actually delayed moving in for a full month while broadloom was removed and hardwood floors in four rooms and the main hallway got installed, wallpaper from nearly every room was stripped, rooms were repainted, new appliances arrived, custom-made drapes and other window coverings were completed, etc., etc., etc. I thought the redecorating would never end, but thankfully it did. Just in time too, because we had only been moved in for about two weeks when the doorbell rang one evening and some neighbours from down the block introduced themselves to me. I was confident enough to invite them in because I could now offer them a place to sit!

EXPECTATIONS—AND THE DREADED WORD "COMPROMISE"

People often ask me to define the first-time homebuyer. They want to know what are average first-time buyers like these days? Are most of them looking for starter homes or are they looking to do so some serious nesting and raise their families for years? Are they young, singles, couples, do they have kids? My answer is always the same: the market is filled with first-time buyers, and each one's story is unique. There are people of all backgrounds and stages of life—single, married, divorced, divorced with kids, new immigrants, mid-twenties, thirties, forties and so on—making their first real estate purchase.

But if there's one trait that I've seen most often among the first-time homebuyers I've known, it's this: their expectations are not in line with what they can afford. Solving that real estate problem is a big part of my job. First-time buyers are most likely to be surprised and even disbelieving about the price of homes and what you get for the money—simply because they are inexperienced as homeowners. They tend to believe they can get a lot more than they really can and the first few days of their home search is a real learning experience for them. This is true in every market. And *compromise*—a word that almost everyone dreads—is the only answer.

Let me give you an example. I had a client who was an elderly widow. She was downsizing from a 4,000-square-foot house, and thought she would like to buy a condominium. The first property I showed her was, to my mind, a perfect match for her. At 1,600 square feet, it was quite large, and beautifully decorated. She thought it was far too small, and wanted to keep looking. After a month of looking at other condos in her price range, and finding that all of them had drawbacks of one kind or another, I suggested that we go back and look at that first one. She was puzzled. "Humour me," I said. So she said yes, we went back, and she bought it. Her expectations had changed. After looking at so many properties, she'd become more realistic about what she could afford, and she'd become more willing to compromise.

Almost every buyer has to come to terms with the hard reality of compromise. But here's the thing: only you can make the decisions on how and where you'll compromise. Maybe you want a particular location, so you have to sacrifice in terms of interior square footage. If you really want that main-floor family room, you might have to look in another area of the city. It's my job to show people that you don't want to be house poor by spending all your money on a mortgage, but you also have to be realistic about what your money can buy. Once you've accepted that, you can start making decisions about what you can—and can't—live without, and your realtor can help you find the home that's right for you.

BLUNDERS AND BLOOPERS OF THE FIRST-TIME HOMEBUYER

Most of the mistakes I've seen from first-time homebuyers are due to inexperience or shortsightedness. There are a lot of details to manage when you're buying a home, and some of them you might not even be aware of. That's why I always say that part of a realtor's job is to steer you away from pitfalls—especially the ones you don't know are there. Occasionally, though, a buyer will be warned by their realtor and will continue stubbornly on a particular course of action. Unless it's illegal, the realtor can't do a thing to stop them.

Here are some examples of common mistakes I've seen:

- Some buyers do not ask the right questions (what might be called "due diligence"), and therefore aren't aware that renovations have been completed without the proper building permits being issued. Later, it's common for those buyers to find there are major problems with the reno work.
- Some clients let their impulsive nature get out of control by rushing into an offer to purchase contract, but neglect to insert necessary terms and conditions that would be recommended safeguards—such as a home inspection. Never make an offer without some of those "escape clauses" written in.
- Many first-time buyers will forgo an experienced real estate lawyer (who charges accordingly for expertise and knowledge) in favour of a relative who isn't as well versed in the field. An experienced real estate lawyer can save you money and headaches in the long run.
- In the same vein, many buyers put too much stock in the advice of family and friends. Always communicate fully with your realtor, and take their professional and informed advice over water-cooler discussions.
- Some buyers insist on buying a condominium from a set of plans and then may be disappointed with the reality. Its small size may make it look like a hotel room, which will be a disappointment for the buyer, and may be a deterrent when it's re-sale time.
- It's easy to forget re-sale potential when choosing a home. Make sure the house fits your needs, and that you love it, but also be sure to make a wise choice. If the house has a permanent stigma, such as a dump or a noisy highway in the vicinity, be sure to take that into account when you think about the future. Don't get me wrong, literally hundreds of thousands of folks

live in just such a home and for them it's not a problem. It will only be an issue when the time comes to sell. Will it ever sell? Sure it will, but in a soft market you may wait a very long time for the right buyer to come along. The longer a home sits on the market, the harder it is to sell, and the value goes down. Try not to buy a house that will be hard to re-sell—such as the largest house on the street, or the most unusual—since that decision could come back to haunt you.

But rather than looking at the mistakes people are oh-so-likely to make, let's look at all of this in a more positive light. Here they are— drum-roll, please—my top 10 recommendations for how to do this home-buying thing *right*!

SANDRA'S TOP 10 RECOMMENDATIONS FOR FIRST-TIME HOMEBUYERS

1. **Get your expectations in line with your reality.** How much is it really going to cost to get the house you want? How much can you really afford? Let's look at the first question for now. A lot of first-time homebuyers come to the process with an unrealistic idea of what it will cost—and it's almost devastating to them when they realize how different the reality is. So rather than pull a number out of the sky because you're comfortable with it, start by finding out how much housing really costs these days. Do some preliminary scanning of the real estate advertisements, either in the newspapers or on www.mls.ca. Even though you'll be seeing only the asking prices rather than the actual sale prices, at least you'll know what ballpark you're playing in. Then talk to your realtor and ask them for recent sales figures for the area and the size of house you have in mind. They can give you the real facts—and you can begin to look at the real estate world without

those rose-coloured glasses that so many first-timers seem to own! The good news is this: the more realistic you are, the less likely you are to miss out on a really great house when it comes along.

2. **Number-crunch properly.** This is the second part of the point above, the "how much can you afford?" part. If you're not using realistic figures, you could underestimate your spending power and miss out on your dream home—or overextend yourself and find out what "house poor" really means. I've seen it, and trust me, it isn't pretty! So how do you number-crunch properly? Start by using the worksheets I've provided in the Appendix to determine the real cost of buying and your real financial picture. Talk to the mortgage experts—a mortgage broker can help you make sense of everything that goes into a mortgage, and will also be able to explain the ratios that are used to determine what you can afford. Track your expenses—and I mean all of them—for one month. I guarantee you will be floored when you discover how much you spend on things you take for granted: car insurance, birthday gifts, dry cleaning, coffee with friends, etc. Once you discover your real spending habits, you can buy a house that allows you to keep spending the way you like doing presently, or you can cut back on your spending in some areas in order to afford a bigger or better house. But again, be realistic about what you can do without! If you can no longer afford dinners out with friends, or the vacation that keeps you sane during the winter months, you'll come to resent your house. One big advantage that's now available to homebuyers is the 30-year mortgage. Because it's amortized over a longer time period than the standard 25-year mortgage, the monthly payment costs are much lower. Does it mean you really will take 30 years to pay it off? Not likely. As your earning power grows, you'll be able to make higher monthly payments, and in a short enough time you'll renegotiate that mortgage for

a shorter amortization.

3. **If you're buying with a partner, put your wish lists together and find out what really works for both of you.** If you haven't had this kind of conversation before you meet with your realtor, you're going to slow down the process. By talking about your basic wants and needs before you see the realtor, you and your partner will make the process easier on everyone involved. The worst thing you can do is assume that your partner thinks exactly the same way you do about what kind of house you should buy, and where, and how much it should cost. You've probably discovered other ways in which you don't see completely eye-to-eye—so why should the biggest financial investment of your lives be an exception?

4. **Use your realtor to the maximum.** Remember, you're the buyer: that means you're not paying anything for your realtor's services—the seller pays the whole commission. So why not take advantage of all that expertise and experience? In a big business deal like this, you really do need someone to represent you. You need someone in your corner. It's not like buying an item of clothing. Be sure to sign a Buyer Representation Agreement with your realtor in order to benefit fully. Once you do that your realtor is obligated to provide a higher level of service. When I bought outside of Canada, I insisted on using a realtor. Even though I'm a realty expert, I know that when I venture outside my own territory, I need to turn to other experts. There were a lot of local concerns and bylaws and other details that I would not have known. A realtor will have an objective, business-like approach to the deal you're trying to make. If you have an emotional buyer and an emotional seller trying to negotiate a deal, you get fireworks—you get people thrown out of houses in anger. The realtor is your buffer.

Some people would ask why they shouldn't just use a lawyer. In Canada, a lawyer is required to close a deal, but they're not able to give you the same kind of advice about the market that a realtor can. Sometimes lawyers can also add too much detail to a contract, one that can even ruin the deal. Yes, I've seen it happen! With the advice of a realtor, you can find out which risks to take and which not to take. And if you're feeling overwhelmed or really concerned about something in the process, ask your realtor what they suggest. Most of the time people are pleasantly surprised that these "problems" can be solved so easily, or that the issue has come up before!

5. **Take professional advice from your realtor instead of the advice of family, friends.** Of course it's okay to discuss your plans and concerns with friends and family members, but remember that very few of them will have the experience and the intimate knowledge of the local real estate market that your realtor does. As well, family and friends are biased sources of information: they want what's best for you and may give you advice that is naïvely simplistic—or, perhaps, there might be a negative one in the bunch who's just determined to tell you that your dreams are unrealistic. In either case, you should have whatever conversations with family and friends you want to, but take their advice with a grain of salt. Then bring your questions and concerns to your realtor for a different kind of discussion. Always remember, no matter who is giving you advice, it's your money, not theirs!

6. **Remember that your first home is not likely to be your last, nor are you likely to live there for decades.** What's that old saying—the only constant in life is change?

Or something about never standing in the same river twice? The point is that your life will change from where it is now, and that means there may come a time—maybe not too far in the future—when you'll want or need to move on from your first home. That's why, if you're in your twenties for instance, it's probably not important to think about buying a home that will be good for your retirement years. I met a young couple who were a little like that. They came to me and asked me to help them find a home, and it was abundantly clear right away that a major factor for them was the schools in the neighbourhood they were considering. They wanted to know the ranking of the grade schools as well as the high schools. When I asked them how old their children were, they said they didn't have any but were planning to have a family in a few years! Statistically speaking, chances are they will move at least once, and maybe twice, before they need to worry about schools. Buy a house that fits your needs today. As your earning and borrowing power goes up, you can move from starter home into your next "move-up" home.

7. **Look at the home, not the decor.** Focus on the things that can't be easily changed—such as the location of the house, or its basic size—instead of the dated decor or fixtures. So what if the living room walls are covered in smoked mirrors from 1976? The mirrors can come off. A much bigger problem might be the highway that's practically in the back yard and can be heard in every room of the house. Or the fact that the house is tiny and so is the lot—which might mean there's no chance you could ever get approval to add on. Look past the decor, and instead of focusing on the silly things that can easily be changed, look at the bones underneath. By the same token, don't be taken in by an elaborately staged home. There could easily be problems that you're not spotting because you're too busy oohing and ahhing over the leather club chairs. The kitchen may have stainless steel

appliances, but does it have enough cupboard space?

8. **Use your imagination!** A few cans of paint and a bottle of Pine-sol can go a long way to transforming a home. A bit of grime can actually be a blessing in disguise, since many buyers won't go near a house that shows badly. You might not face as much competition if you're willing to consider using some elbow grease when you get possession.

9. **Don't rely on the Internet as your source for house hunting.** A lot of people who find the MLS website think they've found Shangri-La—they don't need a realtor anymore! But there is so much that doesn't appear in those online listings, and what does appear is just the tip of the iceberg. For one thing, there are the listings that never even make it to the website because they sell so quickly. Good realtors are on top of new listings, and they may spot something that's perfect for you before it makes its way onto the open market. If you don't have a realtor, your chance of seeing a listing like that is precisely zero! You also should keep in mind that an online MLS listing will not tell you why the asking price has been set where it has; it will not tell you how long the house has been on the market; it will not tell you if there have been price reductions (or how many, or how significant); it will not tell you anything about the motivations of the seller. A realtor is likely to have all, or at least most, of that information. He or she can tell you why two seemingly identical houses will have a $50,000 difference in the asking prices. Get the real story—and get the inside information that gives you negotiating power—by having a realtor work with you.

10. **Get your financial ducks in a row *before* you go house-hunting.** You don't want to fall in love with a house and not be able to buy it. Buying a house is such an emotional roller

coaster anyway without having to deal with the disappointment of being turned down for financing just when you most want it. It's not fair to you, or the realtor, or the seller. Go back to my earlier points about how much real estate really costs, and what you can afford—then find a mortgage broker or lender who can pre-approve you for a mortgage ASAP! Once you've got that, your negotiating leverage increases by leaps and bounds because you can make a purchase offer with confidence. And remember that when you're finding the right mortgage, there are lots of "financial products" out there, and you need to find the right one for your situation. A mortgage is not just about the lowest interest rate.

If you can take in those top 10 tips—and really use them—you'll be way ahead of most other first-time buyers. I love working with first-time buyers because they look to me for guidance and I can bring so much to the table to make the home-buying experience easier for them. It's wonderful to see how far people can come in just a short time! But buying a home—whether it's your first time or your fifth—is always a learning experience.

And because I've become a stepmother in recent years, I can sure empathize with others who are going through a learning experience! Now I am not gunning to win the Mother-of-the-Year Award just yet, but I accept the daily ups and downs that my new role as a parent throws my way and I take pride in the fact that I haven't made any major screw-ups. Okay, wait—I just fibbed. There was the time I almost forgot to pick Edward up from the daycare centre and didn't even realize I'd made that error until I was busy peeling the potatoes for dinner. *Hello?* I quickly grabbed my cell and the car keys as I tore into action to get him. I mean, forgetting to pick up milk from the grocery store is one thing, but almost forgetting to pick up your stepson from his daycare is, let's face it, not a smooth move at all. And even though I knew that he was perfectly safe, as I raced through every amber light to retrieve him, well, do I need to confess that I was consumed with guilt? When I finally arrived, I can't tell you how happy I was to see Edward playing boisterously with another child, totally oblivious to the predicament. Hallelujah! I couldn't possibly begin to describe to you how relieved I was, even though his clothes were, as usual, filthy!

As for learning experiences and adjustments, I'll admit that during the first few months the three of us were living together I was uncomfortable with Edward in the house because it signified that my stepmother role was now permanent. It was also the first time in my entire life that I was around a child every hour of every day—and night. I suddenly found myself sleeping with one eye open and one ear on acute alert "just in case" Edward needed something. The stress to be a perfect mother was so exhausting that I secretly wished I could somehow become a combination of June Cleaver, Carol Brady and Wilma Flintstone!

Then we had to establish a set of rules and be able to enforce those rules when it became necessary, because Gary and I were determined that we wouldn't be emotionally exploited by, or held hostage to, the demands of a little boy. So when a power struggle arose one time—and you just knew it would—because Edward wanted to continue playing with a particular toy on a glass-topped table, even though it was causing some nasty scratches, I had to make it clear to him that "no" definitely meant "no." Being a disciplinarian can be tough, there's no doubt about it, but my acceptance threshold for his misbehaviour is the same as what I would expect from my similarly aged nephews.

Thankfully Gary and I make a good tag team, so we bolster each other and support one another during thorny situations with Edward when we might tend to question ourselves or feel a pang of guilt.

We remind ourselves that children also need to recognize their parents' feelings and identify with their parents' difficulties as well as their own, so that they can learn how to empathize.

Speaking for myself (and no doubt many other people too), the main difficulty and enemy that I face on a daily basis is time. I always seem to need more of it, as I attempt to manage my career, nurture my relationship with my partner, be a guiding influence, teacher and chauffeur to my stepchild, and also be the chief planner, daily cook and bottle washer! The stress of coping with all those unrealistic expectations can be enormous, but I'm grateful that babysitters and a weekly housecleaner are affordable. A competent office assistant is also a top priority for me, so that together we can tackle the staggering amount of paperwork that my job entails.

Believe me, even if I thought I could be a successful thief, the one and only item I would be tempted to steal—if it were possible—would be time! I would drive the biggest truck imaginable right up to the take-out window and then load that sucker up until it was full and even spilling over with as many minutes as possible because there just never seem to be enough hours in the day.

Even so, I'm happy to say that within the past few years I have taken the time to develop an area of interest that provides me with a happy alternative to becoming too stressed out by other obligations. Like many other realtors who want to give back to their communities and connect with people on something other than the business level, I've become involved in the world of charities. The Canadian Breast Cancer Research Alliance, the Children's Wish Foundation, the Humane Society, the Heart and Stroke Foundation, and Easter Seals—each one of those names represents a reputable and extremely worthy charitable organization to support. But the catalogue of possibilities is endless, since there are thousands of other worthy names that I could have listed as well. But with limited time and discretionary funds at our disposal, how does one decide which charity to support?

In my case, I helped to organize the Ladies' Lousy Golf Tournament, which raised more than $30,000 over a period of four years. If you read the name of that event closely, you would likely surmise that all the participants and organizers had a whale of a good time at not taking ourselves too seriously! And you would be right. Mind you, I'd still like to know whose idea it was to have designed the golf ball so darn small. I'd give you great odds that it was a guy!

I was also an active participant in the Coats for Kids program that was sponsored by my real estate company for two consecutive years. I helped to buy new coats, and to collect and clean gently used coats, which were then distributed by neighbourhood churches to benefit needy local children, and recently landed immigrant children.

And I especially enjoyed taking part in a Breakfast with Santa gift-wrapping event because, let's face it, Christmas is for kids. To see so many cute little faces lit up with such innocent joy really does put you into a holiday spirit. I secretly look forward to that exciting time of year with as much anticipation as the kids themselves do!

And lastly, due to family matters that are very close to my heart (pardon the pun), I have founded another fundraiser, called the Horse and Boogie FUNdraiser with proceeds going to Toronto General Hospital, specifically for Dr. R.J. Cusimano in the cardiac department and for Dr. J. Granton, for his work with pulmonary hypertension. Our aim is to raise funds to improve the quality of life for patients, to lobby government bodies, and to continue the education and research necessary to find a cure one day for that rare and often life-threatening lung disorder. Those in attendance enjoy a fun-filled night of laughter and dancing with the knowledge that they are also contributing to an important cause. The first event was successful in raising more than $38,000 in total.

But I'm not a saint, or a crusader, and since I have to draw the line somewhere, my present charitable efforts are not enormous. But I am hoping for improvement in that area and I've noticed that one day at a time seems to make an enormous difference—in other people's lives and in my own too. So wish me luck!

In the meantime, it's been a pleasure to be with you, my readers, on your journey toward home ownership. From my earliest days in real estate (and even before, if you recall that story about my love of Monopoly!), I've found so much satisfaction in the world of real estate. I know that if you take the time to educate yourself, find a great realtor to work with, and make realistic plans for yourself, you too can find the pleasure and pride of owning your own home. I wish you luck too!

What to Consider and Do When Buying a Property

1. Understand why real estate could be a good investment for you.
   - ❑ Do your research and ascertain the advantages and potential disadvantages of buying a property.
   - ❑ Make a list of the benefits of owning your own home.
   - ❑ Make a list of any potential disadvantages of owning your own home.

2. Know how the real estate market works. If you are ready to buy, there's no time like the present. If you're not ready to buy, even in a buyer's market, then you should wait.
   - ❑ Understand the cycles involved in the real estate market and how they work.
   - ❑ Understand what factors affect the real estate market and prices—supply, demand, and the state of the economy.

3. Educate yourself about real estate.
   - ❑ Take courses or seminars offered locally through school boards, colleges, institutes, or universities.
   - ❑ Read books on real estate and real estate investment.

- ❏ Familiarize yourself with the components of a mortgage, how mortgages work, and mortgage tables.
- ❏ Familiarize yourself with on-line mortgage calculators.
- ❏ Research the Internet for property search opportunities, e.g., www.mls.ca
- ❏ Use www.google.ca for research information.
- ❏ Subscribe to publications, including newspapers, magazines, or newsletters that cover real estate issues.
- ❏ Subscribe to free publications such as the *Survey of Canadian House Prices* and the various Canada Mortgage and Housing Corporation (CMHC) surveys and forecasts.
- ❏ Look out for free weekly real estate publications available in your community.

4. Analyze your present financial situation. Be honest with yourself. For one full month, try paying for everything in cash, debit or by credit card to help you track your spending. Everyone I know who has done this has been shocked at just how much they spend every month!
   - ❏ Work up your personal cost-of-living budget (income and expenses).
   - ❏ Calculate your personal net-worth statement (assets and liabilities).
   - ❏ Calculate your gross debt-service ratio (GDS).
   - ❏ Calculate your total debt-service ratio (TDS).
   - ❏ Determine the maximum amount of mortgage that you could be eligible for.
   - ❏ Determine the maximum amount of mortgage that you would feel comfortable with.
   - ❏ Utilize on-line mortgage calculators.

5. Establish your goals in buying a property.
   - ❏ Determine your personal and family needs and goals in the short, medium, and long term.
   - ❏ Determine what time and talent involvement that you expect or require from your family as you go through the buying process.

6. **Select your professional and business advisers. Do this carefully. You must carry out a thorough analysis of a property and have wise counsel from trusted advisors.**
   - ❏ Select your Realtor. He or she can help you choose the rest:
   - ❏ Lawyer
   - ❏ Financial planner
   - ❏ Building inspector
   - ❏ Insurance broker
   - ❏ Lender/mortgage broker
   - ❏ Ensure you carefully analyze and understand the buyer representation agreement with your Realtor.

7. **Determine the form of legal ownership of property.**
   - ❏ Joint tenancy: Where two or more persons have an undivided interest in the whole. At the death of one of the joint tenants, the entire tenancy remains with the others, and at length down to the last survivor.
   - ❏ Tenants in common: Where an undivided interest in a property passes to an heir or estate. In other words, unlike joint tenancy, the interest does not terminate upon the death of as tenant.
   - ❏ Freehold: Where you own the land and the building(s) situated on it.
   - ❏ Leasehold: Where you do not own the land but lease the rights to it.

8. **Locate your investment property.**
   - ❏ Review the amount of money you have available for purchase purposes.
   - ❏ Review the maximum amount you are willing to pay for the property.
   - ❏ Review your purchase criteria.
   - ❏ Select the geographic area or areas in which you want to buy.
   - ❏ Familiarize yourself with municipal zoning if you want to use your property for other than a principal residence or if you are concerned that commercial/ industrial sites can spring up nearby.
   - ❏ Obtain a municipal street map showing the geographic area in detail.

❏ Contact your Realtor and provide him with the guidelines of what you are looking for. Have him utilize the MLS to search for properties within your guidelines.

❏ Review all real estate newspapers in your area to become aware of available properties in your areas of interest, as not all listings are on MLS.

❏ Use the Internet as an effective research tool, but not as the ultimate tool.

9. **Understand the legal criteria.**

❏ Run the standard offer by your "counsel"—that is, your Mom and Dad, or your lawyer, at the beginning of your search. Don't wait until the point when you're about to put an offer on the table.

❏ Decide if you want to purchase through a limited liability company or in your personal name.

❏ Determine if you want to purchase the property with partners and, if so, make sure the partnership arrangement is clearly documented in writing in advance.

❏ Make sure that you insert appropriate conditions or "subject clauses" in the agreement of purchase and sale to protect your interests. For example, you may insert a condition in the offer that the terms in the agreement of purchase and sale have to meet the approval of the purchaser's lawyer. This will protect you and save time in the event of multiple offers.

10. **Negotiate the purchase.**

❏ Determine your best terms for an agreement and your bottom-line fallback position in advance.

❏ Make sure that you feel comfortable with the terms of the offer with regard to the overall package.

❏ Insert all the necessary conditions in the agreement for your protection. When appropriate, follow your Realtor's advice.

❑ Negotiate with your "head," not your "heart."

❑ Make sure that you have listed all items that are part of the purchase agreement and all documents that you want from the vendor.

❑ Never buy a property without viewing it thoroughly inside and out, and on more than one occasion, if possible, beforehand.

❑ Make sure that you are satisfied with the overall deal before removing the conditions in the agreement and thereby having a firm legal commitment.

❑ If you run into a problem ask your Realtor for solutions.

11. **Take necessary steps before and after closing the purchase.**

❑ Make sure you have selected a lawyer who is experienced in the type of real estate purchase you are making. Never attempt to close your own real estate transaction.

❑ Ask your lawyer in advance what the anticipated fees and disbursement costs will be for the property transfer and mortgage.

❑ Calculate realistically all your closing costs. Refer to Checklist 3.

❑ Do an itemized list of all the documents or items you want to receive from the vendor at the time of closing. All these matters should be reflected in the agreement of purchase and sale, so that there is no misunderstanding.

❑ Visit your property before the day of closing. Make sure that it is in the same condition as when you last inspected it.

What You Need to Know about a Mortgage

Taking out a mortgage is a serious commitment. For a period of 20 or 25 years or longer, you will be making monthly payments to a lender until the mortgage loan is paid off and the property becomes yours. So here is a list of questions and other items you must take into consideration. Be honest in your replies.

A. ASK YOURSELF THESE QUESTIONS

1. Is your income secure?

2. Will your income increase or decrease in the future?

3. Are you planning on increasing the size of your family (e.g., children, relatives) and therefore your living expenses?

4. Will you be able to put aside a financial buffer for unexpected expenses or emergencies?

5. Are you planning to purchase the property with someone else?

6. If the answer is yes to the above question, will you be able to depend on your partner's financial contribution without interruption?

7. If you are relying on an income from renting out all
   or part of your purchase, have you determined:
   ‣ If city zoning and use bylaws permit it? ....
   ‣ If the condominium corporation bylaws permit it? ....
   ‣ If the mortgage company policies permit it? ....

8. Have you thoroughly compared mortgage rates and
   features so that you know what type of mortgage and
   mortgage company you want? ....

9. Have you determined the amount of mortgage that
   you would be eligible for? ....

10. Have you a pre-approved mortgage? ....

11. Have you determined all the expenses you will incur
    relating to the purchase transaction?
    (See "Closing Cost" Checklist.) ....

12. Have you completed your present and projected
    financial needs analysis (income and expenses)? ....

13. Have you completed the mortgage application form,
    including net-worth statement (assets and liabilities)? ....

B. ASK THE LENDER THESE QUESTIONS

Interest Rates

1. What is the current interest rate? ....

2. How frequently is the interest calculated?
   (semi-annually, monthly, etc.) ....

3. What is the effective interest rate on an annual basis? ....

4. How long will the lender guarantee a quoted interest rate? ....

5. Will the lender put the above guarantee in writing? ....

6. Will you receive a lower rate of interest if the rates fall
   before you finalize your mortgage? ....

7. Will the lender put the above reduction assurance in writing?

8. Will the lender show you the total amount of interest you will have to pay over the lifetime of the mortgage?

Amortization

1. What options do you have for amortization periods? (10, 15, years, etc.)

2. Will the lender provide you with an amortization schedule for your loan showing your monthly payments apportioned into principal and interest?

3. Have you calculated what your monthly payments will be based on each amortization rate?

4. Are you required to maintain the amortized monthly payment schedule if annual pre-payments are made, or will they be adjusted accordingly?

Term of the Mortgage

1. What different terms are available? (six months, one, two, three, five years, etc.)

2. What is the best term for your personal circumstances?

3. What are the different interest rates available relating to the different terms?

Payments

1. What is the amount of your monthly payments (based on amortization period)?

2. Are you permitted to increase the amount of your monthly payments if you want to without penalty?

3. Does the lender have a range of payment periods available, such as weekly, biweekly, monthly, etc.?

4. What is the best payment period in your personal circumstances?

Prepayment

5. What are your prepayment privileges?
   ‣ Completely open?
   ‣ Open with a fixed penalty or notice requirement?
   ‣ Limited open with no penalty or notice requirement?
   ‣ Limited open with fixed penalty or notice requirement?
   ‣ Completely closed?
   ‣ Some combination of the above?
6. What amount can be prepaid and what is the penalty or notice required, if applicable?
7. How long does the privilege apply in each of the above categories, if applicable?
8. When does the prepayment privilege commence? (six months, one year, anytime, etc.)
9. Is there a minimum amount that has to be prepaid?
10. What form does your prepayment privilege take—increase in payments or lump sum?
11. Is your prepayment privilege accumulative (e.g., make last year's lump sum prepayment next year)?

Taxes

1. How much are the property taxes?
2. Does the lender require a property tax payment monthly (based on projected annual tax), or is it optional?
3. Does the lender pay interest on the property tax account? If yes, what is the interest rate?

Mortgage Transaction Fees and Expenses

1. What is the appraisal fee? Is an appraisal necessary?
2. What is the survey fee? Is a survey necessary?
3. Will you be able to select a lawyer of your choice to do the mortgage work?

4. Does the lender charge a processing or administrative fee? ....

5. Does the lender arrange for a lawyer to do the mortgage documentation work at a flat fee, regardless of the amount of the mortgage? ....

6. Does the lender know what the out-of-pocket disbursements for the mortgage transaction will be? ....

7. Does the mortgage have a renewal administration fee? How much is it? ....

Mortgage Assumption Privileges

1. Can the mortgage be assumed if the property is sold? ....

2. Is the mortgage assumable with or without the lender's approval? ....

3. What are the assumption administrative fees, if any? ....

4. Will the lender release the vendor of all personal obligations under the terms of the mortgage if it is assumed? ....

Portability

1. Is the mortgage portable (e.g., can you transfer it to another property that you may buy?) ....

C H E C K L I S T

Closing Costs and Other Purchase Expenses

In addition to the actual purchase price of your investment, there are a number of other expenses to be paid on or prior to closing. Not all of these expenses will be applicable. Some provinces may have additional expenses.

Type of expense	When paid	Estimated amount
Deposits	At time of offer	
Mortgage application fee	At time of application	
Property appraisal	At time of mortgage application or on closing	
Property inspection	At inspection	
Balance of purchase price	On closing	
Legal fees re: property transfer	On closing	
Legal fees re: mortgage preparation	On closing	
Legal disbursements re: property transfer	On closing	
Legal disbursements re: mortgage preparation	On closing	
Mortgage broker commission	On closing	
Property survey	On closing	

Property tax holdback (by mortgage company)	On closing	....
Land transfer or deed tax (provincial, municipal)	On closing	....
Property purchase tax (provincial)	On closing	....
Property tax (local/municipal) adjustment	On closing	....
Goods and services tax (GST) (federal)	On closing	
New Home Warranty Program fee	On closing	....
Mortgage interest adjustment (by mortgage company)	On closing	....
Sales tax on chattels purchased from vendor (provincial)	On closing	....
Adjustments for fuel, taxes, etc.	On closing	....
Mortgage lender insurance premium (CMHC or GEM)	On closing. Can be added to mortgage pay't	
Condominium maintenance fee adjustment	On closing	....
Building insurance	On closing	....
Life insurance premium on amount of outstanding mortgage	On closing	....
Moving expenses	At time of move	....
Utility connection charges	At time of move	....
Redecorating and refurbishing costs	Shortly after purchase	....
Immediate repair and maintenance costs	Shortly after purchase	....
House and garden improvements	Shortly after purchase	....

Other expenses (list):

....

....

....

TOTAL CASH REQUIRED $ ....

Property Checklist

This assessment checklist has most of the essential features to look for in a house, condominium, or townhouse. Note that not all the categories listed below are necessarily applicable in your individual case. Terminology in some instances can vary from province to province. Use this checklist to indicate your rating of the listed factor as: excellent, good, poor, available, not available, not applicable, further information required, etc.

A. GENERAL INFORMATION

✎ Location of property ....

✎ Condition of neighbourhood ....

✎ Zoning of surrounding areas ....

✎ Prospect for future increase in value ....

✎ Prospect for future change of zoning ....

✎ Proximity of

› Schools ....

› Churches ....

› Shopping ....

› Recreation ....

- ‣ Entertainment
- ‣ Parks
- ‣ Children's playgrounds
- ‣ Public transportation
- ‣ Highways
- ‣ Hospital
- ‣ Police department
- ‣ Fire department
- ‣ Ambulance
- ✍ Traffic density
- ✍ Garbage removal
- ✍ Sewage system
- ✍ Quality of water
- ✍ Taxes:
  - ‣ Provincial
  - ‣ Municipal
- ✍ Maintenance fees/assessments (if condominium)
- ✍ Easements
- ✍ Quietness of
  - ‣ Neighbourhood
  - ‣ Condo complex
  - ‣ Individual condominium unit
  - ‣ House
- ✍ Percentage of units that are owner-occupied (if condominium)
- ✍ If next to commercial centre, is access to residential section well controlled?
- ✍ Is adjacent commercial development being planned?
- ✍ Size of development related to your needs (small, medium, large)
- ✍ Does project seem to be compatible with your lifestyle?

✍ Style of development (adult-oriented, children, retirees, etc.) ....

✍ Age of development ....

B. EXTERIOR FACTORS

✍ Privacy ....

✍ Roadway (public street, private street, safety for children) ....

✍ Sidewalks (adequacy of drainage) ....

✍ Driveway (public, private, semi-private) ....

✍ Garage:

› Reserved space (one or two cars) ....

› Automatic garage doors ....

› Security ....

› Adequate visitor parking ....

✍ Construction material (brick, wood, stone) ....

✍ Siding (aluminum, other) ....

✍ Condition of paint ....

✍ Roof:

› Type of material ....

› Age ....

› Condition ....

✍ Balcony or patios:

› Location (view, etc.) ....

› Privacy ....

› Size ....

› Open or enclosed ....

✍ Landscaping:

› Trees ....

› Shrubbery, flowers ....

› Lawns ....

› Automatic sprinklers ....

✍ Condition and upkeep of exterior ....

C. INTERIOR FACTORS

✍ Intercom system

✍ Medical alert system Fire safety system (fire alarms, smoke detectors, sprinklers)

✍ Burglar alarm system

✍ General safety:
  ‣ TV surveillance
  ‣ Controlled access

✍ Pre-wired for television and telephone cable

✍ Lobby:
  ‣ Cleanliness
  ‣ Decor
  ‣ Security guard

✍ Public corridors:
  ‣ Material used
  ‣ Condition
  ‣ Plaster (free of cracks, stains)
  ‣ Decor

✍ Stairs:
  ‣ General accessibility
  ‣ Number of stairwells
  ‣ Elevators
  ‣ Wheelchair accessibility

✍ Storage facilities:
  ‣ Location
  ‣ Size

✍ Insulation: (The R factor is the measure of heating and cooling efficiency; the higher the R factor, the more efficient)
  ‣ R rating in walls (minimum of R-19; depends on geographic location)

- ‣ R rating in ceiling (minimum of R-30; depends on geographic location) ....
- ‣ Heat pumps ....
- ‣ Windows (insulated, storm, screen) ....
- ‣ Temperature controls: ....
- ‣ Individually controlled ....
- ‣ Convenient location ....

✍ Plumbing:
- ‣ Functions well ....
- ‣ Convenient fixtures ....
- ‣ Quietness of plumbing ....

✍ Suitable water pressure ....

✍ Heating and air conditioning (gas, electric, hot water, oil) ....

✍ Utility costs:
- ‣ Gas ....
- ‣ Electric ....
- ‣ Other ....

✍ Laundry facilities ....

✍ Soundproofing features ....

D. MANAGEMENT

✍ Condominium management company ....

✍ Owner-managed ....

✍ Resident manager ....

✍ Management personnel:
- ‣ Front desk ....
- ‣ Maintenance ....
- ‣ Gardener ....
- ‣ Trash removal ....
- ‣ Snow removal ....
- ‣ Security (number of guards, hours, location, patrol) ....

E. CONDOMINIUM CORPORATION

- ✎ Experience of directors of corporation ....
- ✎ Average age of other owners ....

F. RECREATION FACILITIES (IF CONDOMINIUM)

- ✎ Clubhouse ....
- ✎ Club membership fees (included, not included) ....
- ✎ Sports:
  - ‣ Courts (tennis, squash, racquetball, handball, basketball) ....
  - ‣ Games room (ping-pong, billiards) ....
  - ‣ Exercise room ....
  - ‣ Bicycle path/jogging track ....
  - ‣ Organized sports and activities ....
- ✎ Children's playground:
  - ‣ Location (accessibility) ....
  - ‣ Noise factor ....
  - ‣ Organized sports and activities (supervised) ....
- ✎ Swimming pool:
  - ‣ Location (outdoor, indoor) ....
  - ‣ Children's pool ....
  - ‣ Noise factor ....
- ✎ Visitors' accommodation ....

G. LIFESTYLE FACTORS

- ✎ Location in complex ....
- ✎ Size of unit ....
- ✎ Is the floor plan and layout suitable? ....
- ✎ Will your furnishings fit in? ....
- ✎ Is the unit exposed to the sunlight? ....
- ✎ Does the unit have a scenic view? ....
- ✎ Is the unit in a quiet location (away from garbage unit, elevator noise, playgrounds, etc.)? ....

✍ Accessibility (stairs, elevators, fire exits) ....

✍ Closets:

   ▸ Number ....

   ▸ Location ....

✍ Carpet:

   ▸ Colour ....

   ▸ Quality/texture ....

✍ Hardwood floors ....

✍ Living room:

   ▸ Size/shape ....

   ▸ Windows/view ....

   ▸ Sunlight (morning, afternoon) ....

   ▸ Fireplace ....

   ▸ Privacy (from outside, from rest of condo) ....

✍ Dining room:

   ▸ Size ....

   ▸ Accessibility to kitchen ....

   ▸ Windows/view ....

✍ Den or family room:

   ▸ Size/shape ....

   ▸ Windows/view (morning or afternoon sunlight) ....

   ▸ Fireplace ....

   ▸ Privacy (from outside, from rest of condo) ....

✍ Laundry room:

   ▸ Work space available ....

   ▸ Washer and dryer ....

   ▸ Size/capacity ....

   ▸ Warranty coverage ....

✍ Kitchen:

   ▸ Size ....

   ▸ Eating facility (table, nook, no seating) ....

   ▸ Floors (linoleum, tile, wood) ....

- ‣ Exhaust system ....
- ‣ Countertop built in ....
- ‣ Countertop material ....
- ‣ Work space ....
- ‣ Kitchen cabinets (number, accessibility) ....
- ‣ Cabinet material ....
- ‣ Sink (size, single, double) ....
- ‣ Sink material ....
- ‣ Built-in cutting boards ....
- ‣ Oven (single, double, self-cleaning) ....
- ‣ Gas or electric oven ....
- ‣ Age of oven ....
- ‣ Microwave (size) ....
- ‣ Age of microwave ....
- ‣ Refrigerator/freezer (size/capacity) ....
- ‣ Refrigerator (frost-free, ice maker, single/double door) ....
- ‣ Age of refrigerator ....
- ‣ Dishwasher (age) ....
- ‣ Trash compactor/garbage disposal ....
- ‣ Pantry or storage area ....
- ‣ Is there warranty coverage on all appliances? ....

✎ **Number of bedrooms** ....

- ‣ Master bedroom:
  - · Size/shape ....
  - · Privacy (from outside, from rest of condo) ....
  - · Closets/storage space ....
  - · Fireplace ....
  - · Floor and wall covering ....
- ‣ Master bathroom (en suite):
  - · Size ....
  - · Bathtub ....
  - · Whirlpool tub/jacuzzi ....

- Shower
- Steam room
- Vanity
- Sink (single, double, integrated sink bowls)
- Medicine cabinet

🖎 Number of bathrooms

🖎 Complete or two-piece?

🖎 Overall condition of condo, or house

🖎 Overall appearance and decor of condo, or house

H. LEGAL AND FINANCIAL MATTERS

🖎 Project documents (e.g., disclosure/declaration)
received and read (if new condominium)

🖎 Bylaws received and read (if condominium)

🖎 Rules and regulations received and read
(if condominium or apartment)

🖎 Financial statements received and read
(if condominium or revenue-generating property)

🖎 Condo council minutes, and annual general
meeting and special general meeting minutes
over past two years received and read
(if condominium or revenue-generating property)

🖎 No litigation or pending litigation

🖎 No outstanding or pending special assessments

🖎 No pending repairs, or leaky condo problems

🖎 Other documents (list):

▸

▸

▸

▸

🖎 All above documentation (as applicable) reviewed by
your lawyer and legal advice on investment obtained

✍ Financial statements reviewed by your accountant
and tax advice on investment obtained ....

✍ All assessments, maintenance fees, and taxes detailed ....

✍ Condominium corporation insurance coverage adequate ....

✍ Restrictions acceptable (e.g., pets, renting of unit,
number of people living in suite, children, etc.)
for rental property ....

✍ All verbal promises or representations of sales
representative or vendor's agent that you are relying
on written into the offer to purchase ....

✍ Other

▸ ....

▸ ....

▸ ....

▸ ....

Your Personal Cost-of-Living Budget (Monthly)

I. INCOME (AVERAGE MONTHLY INCOME, ACTUAL OR ESTIMATED)

Salary, bonuses, and commissions $ _____

Dividends $ _____

Interest income $ _____

Pension income $ _____

Alimony / child support $ _____

Other: $ _____

   $ _____

TOTAL MONTHLY INCOME $ _____ (A)

II. EXPENSES

Regular Monthly Payments:

Rent or mortgage payments $ _____

Property taxes pro-rated monthly $ _____

Automobile(s):

Purchase payments $ _____

Lease $ _____

Fuel $ _____

Insurance $ _____

Maintenance	$ ....
Car washes	$ ....
Snow tires	$ ....
Credit card payments:	
Card #1	$ ....
Card #2	$ ....
Card #3	$ ....
Card #4	$ ....
Personal loan	$ ....
Line of credit	$ ....
Student loan	$ ....
Medical plan	$ ....
Instalment payments—deferred	$ ....
Life insurance premiums	$ ....
House insurance premium	$ ....
Other premiums (auto, extended medical, etc.)	$ ....
RRSP deductions	$ ....
Pension fund (employer)	$ ....
Contributions to savings account	$ ....
Miscellaneous	$ ....
Other:	$ ....
	$ ....
TOTAL REGULAR MONTHLY PAYMENTS	$ .... (B)

Household Operating Expenses:

Utilities	$ ....
Gas	$ ....
Hydro	$ ....
Water	$ ....
TV/Cable	$ ....
Internet	$ ....
Telephone	$ ....

Home	$
Cell	$
Other household expenses (repairs, mainten., etc.)	$
Other:	$
	$
TOTAL HOUSEHOLD OPERATING EXPENSES	$ _____ **(C)**

Food Expenses:

At home	$
Away from home	$
TOTAL FOOD EXPENSES	$ _____ **(D)**

Personal Expenses:

Clothing	$
New purchases	$
Dry cleaning	$
Drugs	$
Transportation (other than auto)	$
Autoshare	$
Public transit	$
Taxi	$
Medical/dental	$
Daycare	$
Education (self)	$
Education (children)	$
Dues	$
Gifts	$
Donations	$
Travel	$
Recreation	$
Sports	$
Movies	$

Entertainment $ ....

Restaurants / bars $ ....

Health club $ ....

Poker nights / casino (be honest!) $ ....

Newspapers, magazines, books $ ....

Spending money, allowances $ ....

Other: $ ....

                                        $ ....

TOTAL PERSONAL EXPENSES $ .... (E)

Tax Expenses:

Federal and provincial income taxes $ ....

Other: $ ....

TOTAL TAX EXPENSES $ .... (F)

III. SUMMARY OF EXPENSES

Regular monthly payments (B) $ ....

Household operating expenses (C) $ ....

Food expenses (D) $ ....

Personal expenses (E) $ ....

Tax expenses (F) $ ....

TOTAL MONTHLY EXPENSES   ....

                                        $ .... (G)

TOTAL MONTHLY DISPOSABLE INCOME AVAILABLE (A – G) $ ....

(subtract total monthly expenses from total monthly income)

W O R K S H E E T

Calculating Your Gross Debt-Service (GDS) Ratio

Your GDS ratio is calculated by adding the total of your monthly mortgage principal, interest, and taxes (PIT) together and dividing that figure by your monthly income. Guidelines have been set that generally allow a maximum of 27% to 30% (or more, depending on the financial institution), of your gross income to be used for the mortgage PIT:

$$\frac{\text{Monthly principal} + \text{Interest} + \text{Taxes (PIT)}}{\text{Monthly income}}$$

Gross (pre-tax) *monthly* income of purchaser(s) $ ....

Other forms of income (e.g., annual) averaged to monthly $ ....

TOTAL MONTHLY INCOME $ ....

Estimate monthly property tax on home (net after
any provincial homeowner's grant is taken into
consideration, if applicable) $ ....

   1. To estimate the *maximum* monthly mortgage
       payment, plus property taxes and condo
       maintenance fees, that you could carry
       (monthly PIT), calculate 30% of the total
       monthly income: 30% of $ .... equals $ ....

2. To estimate the maximum monthly mortgage payment, not including taxes (PI), that you could carry, subtract the monthly tax amount from the monthly PIT:

Monthly PIT $ _____

Less: Monthly property tax $ _____

MAXIMUM MONTHLY MORTGAGE PAYMENT $ _____

(not including taxes) = Monthly PI

Use the chart below to determine the maximum mortgage (not including taxes) for which you qualify under your GDS ratio guidelines. Simply look up your maximum monthly mortgage payment under the current interest rate. Maximum mortgage available under GDS ratio guidelines: $ _____

MONTHLY MORTGAGE PAYMENTS FOR PRINCIPAL PLUS INTEREST

The table gives the monthly payments for principal and interest* (not including taxes) for each $1,000 of the amount of the mortgage.

Interest rate %	5 years $	10 years $	15 years $	20 years $	25 years $
3.50	$18.19	$9.88	$7.14	$5.79	$5.00
4.00	$18.41	$10.11	$7.39	$6.05	$5.27
4.50	$18.63	$10.35	$7.63	$6.31	$5.54
5.00	$18.85	$10.59	$7.89	$6.58	$5.82
5.50	$19.08	$10.83	$8.14	$6.85	$6.11
6.00	$19.30	$11.07	$8.40	$7.13	$6.40
6.50	$19.53	$11.32	$8.67	$7.41	$6.70
7.00	$19.76	$11.56	$8.94	$7.70	$7.01
7.50	$19.99	$11.82	$9.21	$7.79	$7.32
8.00	$20.22	$12.07	$9.49	$8.29	$7.64

*Interest being compounded semi-annually.

Note: The GDS calculation is not a pre-approval. You must consult with a lender to see what percentage that lender uses to calculate the GDS ratio. The percentage varies from lender to lender, and changes over time.

Calculating Your Total Debt-Service (TDS) Ratio

Most lenders require that an applicant meet a TDS ratio, in addition to looking at the GDS ratio. The TDS ratio is generally a maximum of 35% to 40% or more of gross income—actual rules may vary between financial institutions. The TDS ratio is calculated in much the same way as the GDS ratio, but takes into consideration all other debts and loans you may have.

$$\text{TDS ratio} = \frac{\text{Monthly principal} + \text{Interest} + \text{Taxes (PIT)} + \text{Other monthly payments}}{\text{Monthly income}}$$

Gross (pre-tax) monthly income of purchaser(s)	$ ....
Other forms of income (e.g., annual) averaged to monthly	$ ....
TOTAL MONTHLY INCOME	$ ....

Other monthly payments:

Credit cards	$ ....
Other mortgages	$ ....
Car loan	$ ....
Other loans	$ ....
Alimony/child support	$ ....
Charge accounts	$ ....

Other debts (list):

....

....

....

TOTAL OTHER MONTHLY PAYMENTS $ ....

To calculate your TDS ratio, take 40% of $ .... (total monthly

income) = $ .... available for monthly principal + interest +

taxes + other payments (PIT + Other).

To estimate the maximum monthly mortgage payment you could carry
within your allowable TDS ratio:

Monthly PIT + Other $ ....

Less: Other monthly payments $ ....

SUBTOTAL $ ....

Less: Estimated property taxes $ ....

MAXIMUM MONTHLY MORTGAGE PAYMENT $ ....

Use the monthly mortgage payment chart in worksheet #2 to determine
the maximum mortgage for which you qualify under the TDS ratio
guidelines. Simply look up your maximum monthly mortgage payment
under the current interest rate.

Maximum mortgage available under TDS ratio guidelines $ ....

C H A R T

Recovery on
Renovation Costs

Renovation project	Recovery on resale
Adding a full bath	96% to 200%
Adding a fireplace	94%
Remodelling kitchen (minor)	79% to 150%
Remodelling kitchen (major)	70% to 200%
Remodelling bathroom	69% to 150%
Adding a skylight	68%
Adding new siding	67%
Adding insulation	65%
Adding a room	62% to 150%
Re-roofing	61%
Adding a wood deck	60%
Adding a greenhouse	56%
Replacing windows, doors	55%
Adding a swimming pool	39%

Glossary

Acceleration clause: A clause written into a mortgage agreement to allow the lender to accelerate or call the entire principal balance of the mortgage, plus accrued interest, when the borrower is delinquent with payments.

Adjusted cost base (ACB): The value of real property established for tax purposes. It is the original cost plus any allowable capital improvements, certain acquisition costs and any mortgage interest costs, less any depreciation.

Agreement of purchase and sale: A written agreement between the owner and a purchaser for the purchase of real estate for a predetermined price and terms.

Amenities: Generally, those parts of the condominium or apartment building that are intended to beautify the premises and that are for the enjoyment of occupants rather than for utility.

Amortization period: The actual number of years it will take to repay a mortgage loan in full. This can be well in excess of the loan's term. For example, mortgages often have five-year terms but 25-year amortization periods.

Amortization: The reduction of a loan through periodic payments in which interest is charged only on the unpaid balance.

Analysis of property: The systematic method of determining the performance of investment real estate using a property analysis form.

Appraised value: An estimate of the fair market value of the property, usually performed by an appraiser.

Arrears: Arrears are the overdue payments owing on either a mortgage or a lease; it also refers to the state of being late in fulfilling the obligations of the mortgage or lease agreement.

Assessment fee: A monthly fee that condominium owners must pay, usually including management fees, costs of common property upkeep, heating costs, garbage-removal costs, the owner's contribution to the contingency reserve fund, and so on. In the case of time-shares, the fee is normally levied annually. Also referred to as the maintenance fee.

Assign: The act of transferring ownership of or responsibility for a property to a purchaser or tenant; usually a step that occurs prior to the original owner or tenant completing the purchase or lease term. The assignee assumes the right to purchase a property, or becomes the subtenant of the original tenant.

Assumption agreement: A legal document signed by a home buyer that requires the buyer to assume responsibility for the obligations of a mortgage made by a former owner.

Balance sheet: A financial statement that indicates the financial status of a condominium corporation or apartment building, or other revenue property, at a specific point in time by listing its assets and liabilities.

Blended payments: Equal payments consisting of both a principal and an interest component, paid each month during the term of the mortgage. The principal portion increases each month, while the interest portion decreases, but the total monthly payment does not change.

Budget: An annual estimate of a condominium corporation or apartment building's expenses and the revenues needed to balance those expenses. There are operating budgets and capital budgets. (See also *Capital budget.*)

Canada Mortgage and Housing Corporation (CMHC): The federal Crown corporation that administers the National Housing Act. CMHC services include providing housing information and assistance, financing, and insuring home-purchase loans for lenders.

Canadian Real Estate Association (CREA): An association of members of the real estate industry, principally real estate agents and brokers.

Capital budget: An estimate of costs to cover replacements and improvements, and the corresponding revenues needed to balance them, usually for a 12-month period. Different from an operating budget.

Capital gain: Profit on the sale of an asset that is subject to taxation.

Capital improvements. Major improvements made to a property that are written off over several years rather than expensed off in the year in which they are made.

Charge: A document registered against a property, stating that someone has or believes he or she has a claim on the property.

Closing costs: The expenses over and above the purchase price of buying and selling real estate.

Closing date: The date on which the sale of a property becomes final and the new owner takes possession.

Closing: The actual completion of the transaction acknowledging satisfaction of all legal and financial obligations between buyer and seller, and acknowledging the deed or transfer of title and disbursement of funds to appropriate parties.

Collateral mortgage: A loan backed up by a promissory note and the security of a mortgage on a property. The money borrowed may be used for the purchase of a property or for another purpose, such as home renovations or a vacation.

Common area maintenance fee: The charge to owners to maintain the common areas, normally due on a monthly basis.

Common area: The area in a condominium project that is shared by all of the condominium owners, such as elevators, hallways, and parking lots.

Condominium corporation: The condominium association of unit owners incorporated under some provincial condominium legislation, automatically at the time of registration of the project. It is called a strata corporation in British Columbia. Under each of the provincial statutes, it will differ from an ordinary corporation in many respects. The condominium corporation, unlike a private business corporation, usually does not enjoy limited liability, and any judgement against the corporation for the payment of money is usually a judgement against each owner. The objects of the corporation are to manage the property and any assets of the corporation, and its duties include effecting compliance by the owners with the requirements of the Act, the declaration, the bylaws, and the rules.

Condominium council: The governing body of the condominium corporation, elected at the annual general meeting of the corporation.

Condominium: A housing unit to which the owner has title and of which the owner also owns a share in the common area (such as elevators, hallways, swimming pool and land).

Conventional mortgage: A mortgage loan that does not exceed 75 percent of the appraised value or of the purchase price of the property, whichever is the less. Mortgages that exceed this limit generally must be insured by mortgage insurance, such as that provided by CMHC and GEM.

Conversion: The changing of a structure from some other use, such as a rental apartment to a condominium apartment.

Conveyancing: The transfer of property, or title to property, from one party to another.

Credit bureau: An agency that maintains credit files, such as Equifax and others.

Credit check: A report typically run to review the credit history of an individual to assist in determining whether or not the individual is worthy of receiving credit.

Credit rating: The score – usually expressed as a number – calculated using information in an individual's credit file. The credit rating is typically used to determine credit worthiness. The better the score, the more worthy of credit an individual is.

Debt service: Cost of paying interest for use of mortgage money.

Deed: This document conveys the title of the property to the purchaser. Different terminology may be used in different provincial jurisdictions.

Depreciation: The amount by which a property owner writes off the value of a real estate investment over the life of the investment. Depreciation is not applicable to the value of land.

Down payment: An initial amount of money (in the form of cash) put forward by the purchaser. Usually it represents the difference between the purchase price and the amount of the mortgage loan.

Equity return: The percentage ratio between an owner's equity in a property and the total of cash flow plus mortgage principal reduction.

Equity: The difference between the price for which a property could be sold and the total debts registered against it.

Escrow: The holding of a deed or contract by a third party until fulfillment of certain stipulated conditions between the contracting parties.

Estate: The title or interest one has in property such as real estate and personal property that can, if desired, be passed on to survivors at the time of one's death.

Fair market value: The value established on real property that is determined to be one that a buyer is willing to pay and for which a seller is willing to sell.

Fee simple: A manner of owning land, in one's own name and free of any conditions, limitations, or restrictions.

Financial statements: Documents that show the financial status of the condominium corporation, apartment building, or other revenue property at a given point in time. Generally includes income and expense statement and balance sheet.

Floating-rate mortgage: Another term for variable-rate mortgage.

Foreclosure: A legal procedure whereby the lender obtains ownership of, or the right to sell, the property following default by the borrower.

Freehold: The outright ownership of land, or land and buildings; differs from *leasehold*.

GE Mortgage Insurance Canada (GEM): A private company providing mortgage insurance in Canada.

GEM: The initials for GE Mortgage Insurance Canada. See **GE Mortgage Insurance Canada.**

Guarantor: A party that guarantees to pay the debts of an individual in the event the individual is unable to pay the debts.

Guarantor's letter: A legal document by which the guarantor agrees to assume the debt of another party.

High-ratio mortgage: A conventional mortgage loan that exceeds 75 percent of the appraised value or purchase price of the property. Such a mortgage must be insured.

Highrise: Any multi-unit residential building of six or more storeys.

Income, gross: Income or cash flow before expenses.

Income, net: Income or cash flow after expenses (but generally before income tax).

Interest averaging: The method of determining the overall average interest rate being paid when more than one mortgage is involved.

Interim financing: The temporary financing by a lender during the construction of real property for resale, or while awaiting other funds.

Judgement: The official outcome of a lawsuit or other legal proceeding. The judgement may be financial or otherwise.

Legal description: Identification of a property that is recognized by law, that identifies that property from all others.

Lessee: The tenant in rental space.

Lessor: The owner of the rental space.

Letter of intent: Used in place of a formal written contract with a deposit. The prospective purchaser informs the seller, in writing, that he or she is willing to enter into a formal purchase contract upon certain terms and conditions if they are acceptable to the seller.

Leverage: The use of financing or other people's money to control large pieces of real property with a small amount of invested capital.

Limited partnership: An investment group in which one partner serves as the general partner and the others as limited partners. The general partner bears all of the financial responsibility and management of the investment. The limited partners are obligated only to the extent of their original investment plus possible personal guarantees.

Listings, exclusive agency: A signed agreement by a seller in which he or she agrees to co-operate with one broker. All other brokers must go through the listing broker.

Listings, multiple: (See also *Multiple Listing Service*.) A system of agency/sub-agency relationships. If Broker A lists the property for sale, "A" is the vendor's agent. If Broker B sees the MLS listing and offers it for sale, "B" is the vendor's sub-agent.

Listings, open: A listing given to one or more brokers, none of whom have any exclusive rights or control over the sale, by other brokers or the owner of the property.

Marginal tax rate: That point in income at which any additional income will be taxed at a higher tax rate.

MLS: See *Multiple Listing Service*.

Mortgage wraparound: Sometimes called an all-inclusive mortgage. A mortgage that includes any existing mortgages on the property. The buyer makes one large payment on the wraparound and the seller continues making the existing mortgage payments out of that payment.

Mortgage, balloon: A mortgage amortized over a number of years, but that requires the entire principal balance to be paid at a certain time, short of the full amortization period.

Mortgage, constant: The interest rate charged on a mortgage consisting of both the rate being charged by the lender and the rate that represents the amount of principal reduction each period.

Mortgage, deferred payment: A mortgage allowing for payments to be made on a deferred or delayed basis. Usually used where present income is not sufficient to make the payments.

Mortgage, discounted: The selling of a mortgage to another party at a discount or an amount less than the face value of the mortgage.

Mortgage, first: A mortgage placed on a property in first position.

Mortgage, fixed: This is a conventional mortgage, with payments of interest and principal. Fixed terms with a fixed rate can vary from six months to 10 years or more.

Mortgage, insurance: Insurance provided by the lender as an option for the borrower. It would pay out the balance outstanding on the mortgage, in the event of the borrower's death.

Mortgage, interest only: Payments are made only of interest; the payment does not reduce the principal of the debt.

Mortgage, points: The interest rate charged by the lender.

Mortgage, second: A mortgage placed on a property in second position to an already existing first mortgage.

Mortgage, variable: A mortgage with an interest rate that fluctuates with the Bank of Canada interest rate. The mortgagee just pays the interest, with optional pay-down on the principal. Different from a fixed-rate mortgage (see *Mortgage, fixed*).

Mortgage: The document that pledges real property as collateral for an indebtedness.

Mortgagee: The lender.

Mortgagor: The borrower.

Multiple Listing Service (MLS): A service licensed to member real estate boards by the Canadian Real Estate Association. Used to compile and disseminate information by publication and computer concerning a given property to a large number of agents and brokers.

National Housing Act (NHA) Loan: A mortgage loan that is insured by Canada Mortgage and Housing Corp. to certain maximums.

Offer to purchase: The document that sets forth all the terms and conditions under which a purchaser offers to purchase property. This offer, when accepted by the seller, becomes a binding agreement of purchase and sale once all conditions have been removed.

Operating budget: An estimate of costs to operate a building or condominium complex and corresponding revenues needed to balance them, usually for a 12-month period. Different from a capital budget.

Operating costs: Those expenses required to operate an investment property, generally excluding mortgage payments.

Option agreement: A contract, with consideration, given to a purchaser of a property, giving him or her the right to purchase at a future date. If the individual chooses not to purchase, the deposit is forfeited to the seller.

Personal property: Property in an investment property, such as carpeting, draperies and refrigerators, that can be depreciated over a shorter useful life than the structure itself.

PI: Principal and interest due on a mortgage.

PIT: Principal, interest, and taxes due on a mortgage.

Prepayment penalty: A penalty charge written into many mortgages that must be paid if the mortgage is paid off ahead of schedule.

Principal: The amount the purchaser actually borrowed, or the portion of it still owing on the original loan.

Property manager: A manager or management company hired to run an investment property for the owner.

Purchase-and-sale agreement: See *Agreement of purchase and sale.*

Tax shelter: The tax write-off possible through the depreciation benefits available on investment real estate ownership.

Title insurance: This insurance covers the purchaser or vendor in case of any defects in the property or title, that existed at the time of sale but which were not known until after completion of the sale.

Title: Generally, the evidence of right that a person has to the possession of property.

Trust account: The separate account in which a lawyer or real estate broker holds funds until the real estate closing takes place or other legal disbursement is made.

Trust funds: Funds held in trust, either as a deposit for the purchase of real property or to pay taxes and insurance.

Unit: Normally refers to the rental suite or that part of a condominium owned and occupied or rented by the owner.

Useful life: The term during which an asset is expected to have useful value.

Utilities: Any one of the array of services that allow a property to function, and which typically deliver a basic social good, such as heat, water and electricity, or phone and television service. The landlord may provide access to utilities for a fee, or the tenant may be responsible for arranging a connection to the utilities.

Value, assessed: The property value as determined by local, regional, or provincial assessment authority.

Vendor take-back: A procedure wherein the seller (vendor) of a property provides some or all of the mortgage financing in order to sell the property. Also referred to as vendor financing.

Vendor: A person selling a piece of property.

Zoning: Rules for land use established by local governments.